30,00

DATE DUE

THE SHIFT

MENACHEM KLEIN

THE SHIFT

Israel-Palestine from Border
Struggle to Ethnic Conflict

Columbia University Press
New York

Columbia University Press
Publishers Since 1893
New York   Chichester, West Sussex
Copyright © Menachem Klein, 2010

Library of Congress Cataloging-in-Publication Data

Klein, Menachem.
 The shift : Israel-Palestine from border struggle to
ethnic conflict / Menachem Klein.
     p. cm.
 Includes bibliographical references and index.
 ISBN 978-0-231-70196-9 (alk. paper)
 1. Arab-Israeli conflict—1993– 2. Israel—Politics and
government—1993– 3. Palestinian Arabs—Politics and
government—1993– 4. Palestinian National Authority.
 5. Land settlement—Government policy—Israel.
 6. Land settlement—West Bank. I. Title.

 DS119.76.K518 2010
 956.9405'4—dc22

                        2010029992

∞

Columbia University Press books are printed on permanent and durable
acid-free paper. This book is printed on paper with recycled content.
Printed in India by Imprint Digital

c 10 9 8 7 6 5 4 3 2 1

References to Internet Web sites (URLs) were accurate at the time of
writing. Neither the author nor Columbia University Press is responsible for URLs that may have expired or changed since the manuscript
was prepared.

CONTENTS

CONTENTS

ACKNOWLEDGMENTS

This book developed out of my short article 'One State in the Holy Land: Dream or Nightmare?'[1] Since its publication I have extended my research, collecting and analyzing more data. My article 'Settlements and Security'[2] is also based on this work. A significant part of the research for this book was supported by the International Peace Research Institute Oslo [PRIO]. I wish to thank PRIO director Kristian Berg Harpviken and his fellows for their substantive support and fruitful discussions. The book was written in Jerusalem and finished during my first weeks as Fernand Braudel Senior Fellow at the Department of History and Civilization of the European University Institute, Florence, Italy. I thank the EUI staff and researchers for welcoming me warmly at their beautiful campus. The peaceful olive groves on the hills of San Domenico and the Renaissance treasures of Florence should serve as a model for Israelis and Palestinians determined to find better ways of living than those discussed in this book. The contribution of my devoted and highly professional editor Haim Watzman can be felt in every word. Of course the errors are all mine.

ABBREVIATIONS

ACRI   Association for Civil Rights in Israel
AP   Associated Press
FMEP   Foundation for Middle East Peace
ICG   International Crisis Group
OCHA   United Nations, Office for the Coordination of
        Humanitarian Affairs

INTRODUCTION

In their article on Obama and the Middle East,[1] Hussein Agha and Robert Malley raise a number of questions about the possibility of implementing a two-state solution for the Israeli–Palestinian conflict. In the current climate, they ask, would the people on both sides welcome such a solution? Would they view it as legitimate or illegitimate? If the latter, what would a two-state solution actually accomplish? They rightly focus on the fact that the discourse on ending the Israeli–Palestinian conflict is almost entirely on the details of the two-state agreement: where the future borders should run, how and where to divide Jerusalem, and on technical arrangements for resettling and compensating the Palestinian refugees. The common assumption is that an equilibrium of interests can be established in a two-state solution; '[i]t's just been seen as a matter of trying harder,' they write. Yet when Palestinian President Mahmoud Abbas and Israeli Prime Minister Ehud Olmert failed to reach an agreement following the Annapolis conference of 2007, they inevitably cast doubt on and led observers to doubt whether, as the authors say, 'more of the same can produce something different.'

Agha and Malley identify two problems with the two-state solution: first, that it is, at least at this point, perceived as serving external and foreign interests, principally those of the United States; and second, that it is poorly packaged and promoted. The peace camps on both sides have not been able to sell it to their peoples. Agha and Malley call for new language and new marketing strategies; they express their hope that President Obama be able to initiate such a change.[2]

Are language and marketing really the two major obstacles to achieving a two-state solution? Methodologically, Agha and Malley have a problem. Their approach barely extends beyond the narrow sphere of politics. They ask good questions, but seek answers only in the field of political rhetoric. My purpose here is to examine political actions. To do so, it is first necessary to recognize the uncomfortable realities on the ground and understand their political ramifications.

In contrast with many other writers who have addressed the conflict, I shall start with the facts as they are on the ground rather than as they ought to be. My goal is not to prescribe treatment for a critically ill peace process[3] or to analyze Israeli and Palestinian public opinion polls relating to hypothetical compromises. Instead, I will describe and evaluate where things now stand. Public opinion polls track the facts on the ground—they do not create them. Similarly, my research is not based solely on the legal status of the Palestinians—that is, on the distinction between those under Israeli occupation and those who are Israeli citizens. Of course, I do not ignore their legal status, but I understand it as a manifestation of their position within the Israeli control system, with which it is only partly congruent.

In depicting the Israeli regime, I cast familiar facts and data in a new light rarely seen in policy debates. Published separately and seldom integrated, these facts and data, when taken together, offer a comprehensive picture and a new framework for understanding the current nature of the intractable Israeli–Palestinian conflict, its history, and even, to a certain extent, its future.

This study focuses on Israeli actions, since Israel is the powerful actor in its asymmetric conflict with the Palestinians. In keeping with this, I shall examine the impact of the Israeli measures on the Palestinian regime in the West Bank, on the victory of Hamas in the Palestinian Authority (PA) elections of 2006, and on the role played by the United States under Presidents George W. Bush and Barak Obama.

Seventeen years after the signing, in Oslo, of the declaration of principles that laid the ground for the establishment of the Palestinian Authority and for negotiations to resolve the conflict; fifteen years after the assassination of Yitzhak Rabin, which buried the hopes that the Oslo agreements had raised; and ten years after the failure of Camp David 2 talks and the outbreak of the Second Intifada, the time has come to sum up what has changed.

This work considers the decade that began, in 2000, with the collapse of the Israeli–Palestinian final status talks and the outbreak of the Second Intifada. During this period, Israel expanded its settlements in the West Bank and Gaza Strip and conducted security operations that changed the nature of the Israeli–Palestinian conflict. To a great extent, this was facilitated by regime changes in Israel, the US and the PA. Israel has been ruled throughout this period by governments that, while declaring their willingness to reach a negotiated peace, have not succeeded in bridging their differences with the Palestinians. For all their rhetoric about the need to end Israel's occupation of the territories, the operations on the ground pursued by Prime Ministers Ariel Sharon and Ehud Olmert belied their stated goal. The same contradiction between declaration and action can be seen with the current Prime Minister, Binyamin Netanyahu. While he has publicly accepted a two-state solution as a goal, he has in fact pursued policies that make the likelihood for such an accommodation even more remote.

President Bill Clinton's failure to solve the Israeli–Palestinian conflict prompted his successor, Bush, to pursue a policy of conflict management, while disengaging from any attempt to mediate a comprehensive peace between Israel and its neighbors. Following the terrorist attacks of September 2001, the Bush administration closely cooperated with Israel in its war against terror. They put Arafat under siege; the US allowed Israel to dismember Arafat's Palestinian Authority, creating enclaves subject to de facto Israeli control; and when Arafat died in 2004 they both supported the election of a weak and accommodating successor, Mahmoud Abbas, whose leadership qualifications were questioned by his own people, indeed by his own Fatah party. When, in 2009, President Obama reasserted the goal of reaching a comprehensive peace in the Middle East in the form of a two-state solution, he found himself facing a new reality on the ground. It was impossible to pick up where the parties had left off in 2001, as if nothing had happened in between.

I argue here that the quantity of Israeli operations created a qualitative change. Israeli settlement expansion and security operations since 2000 have stripped political negotiations of nearly any value and have returned the Israeli–Palestinian conflict to its original status—it is once again primarily an ethnic, rather than a territorial, conflict. Indeed, the Abbas regime in the West Bank has tried to maintain the framework of the Oslo period—that is, to keep the struggle a border conflict. Yet Israeli military superiority and the failure of any third party to intervene have returned the conflict to its ethnic origins, albeit in a different form. This new creation is the focus of my book.

Thus, the Israelis and Palestinians find themselves trapped between what is unachievable today—the two-state solution—and what can never be achieved—a unitary non-ethnic democracy based on the principle of 'one man, one vote'.

Given the seemingly insurmountable difficulties of arriving at a two-state solution, and assuming the irreversibility of the

Israeli settlement enterprise in the occupied West Bank, many observers reason that a peace process based on the two-state model, as envisioned implicitly by the Oslo accords and explicitly by the Road Map,[4] has come to a dead end. The only just solution to the Israeli–Palestinian conflict, they maintain, is a single democratic state in which Jews and Palestinians live side by side as citizens with equal rights and equal obligations.

I maintain, in contrast, that a single state—although hardly the democratic one its advocates dream of—is the current problematic reality rather than a viable solution. Of course, one-state advocates also see the current state of affairs as fraught with danger, but they believe that it can be transformed into an egalitarian democracy on the Western model. But this, as I will argue below, is an illusion.

The main part of this study examines the structure of Israeli rule over the Palestinians, and the costs and benefits incurred by the Jewish state as a result of this policy. It suggests that the costs of delaying the decolonization of the territories Israel captured in 1967—the West Bank and Gaza Strip—will become unsustainable if Israel seeks to remain both Jewish and democratic. In this light, the two-state model appears to be the only feasible solution, even if the road to it is now longer and the price higher than it was during the years of the Oslo accords.

While the Israeli control system in the West Bank and Gaza Strip is commonly called an 'occupation,' a few writers seek more precision by using other terms. Jeff Halper shows how different Israeli policies join together to create a 'matrix of control.'[5] Ghazi Falah prefers to write of 'enclavization,' which weakens the Palestinians economically, politically and socially in order to neutralize the population's will to resist;[6] Leila Farsakh calls the territorial fragmentation of the Occupied Palestinian Territories 'Bantustanization,' enumerating the similarities with the policy of that name pursued by South Africa's apartheid regime;[7] Sari Hanafi labels the Israeli system as 'spacio-cidal,' pursuing a bio-politics of geographical exclusion and racism.[8] Lisa Taraki prefers 'enclavization' and 'dismemberment' to signify the devastating impact of Israel's policy on the Palestinian communities in the territories occupied in 1967.[9]

This book goes beyond these approaches and argues, first, that due to its territorial expansion, and especially to the events of the last ten years, Israel has already assumed de facto control of the entire area stretching from the Jordan River to the Mediterranean. In particular, Israel has, since 2004, exerted effective control even of those territories that, under the Oslo agreements, were handed over to the exclusive control of the Palestinian Authority. While it does not rule these areas directly as it once did, it controls them by using the PA as a proxy. Hence the border that existed before the Israel–Arab war of 1967 (known as the Green Line) exists only in international law textbooks. Israel has been able to gain suzerainty without formally annexing most of the territories it gained in the 1967 war. The exception is East Jerusalem, which Israel unilaterally annexed de jure following the war, immediately setting out to change its urban fabric. Outside Jerusalem, it has annexed Palestinian areas de facto by expanding settlements and by building a Separation Barrier.

Secondly, I argue that the Israeli control system applies also to those Palestinians who are citizens of Israel and live within the state's formal boundaries. Usually, writers about the conflict address only the Palestinians of the West Bank and Gaza Strip or the refugees outside historical Palestine. In contrast, I intend to include in my discussion those living in Israel proper. Kimmerling and Migdal have already shown that, in the late '80s and early '90s, Israeli Palestinians shifted from concerning

themselves exclusively with local issues such as municipal budgets and building permits to taking positions on national issues.
They increasingly came to identify with the aspiration of the
Palestinians of the West Bank and Gaza Strip to establish a
state there at the same time that they pursued their own goal of
achieving equality and full civil rights within Israel.[10] However,
as this book shows, the shift in the Israeli–Palestinian conflict
in the first decade of the twenty-first century changed their status in the mind of the Jewish majority and their treatment by
several state agencies. Unlike the 1990s, when Israeli society
was more open then ever to liberal values, a decade later Israeli
Jews are less comfortable with including Israeli Palestinians as
part of their Israeli polity.

1

HISTORICAL AND THEORETICAL BACKGROUND

The New Millennium: A New Phase in the Old Conflict

Students of the conflict between the Jews and the Palestinians debate whether it has colonial origins. Gershon Shafir disagrees with Moshe Lisak who concludes that in early twentieth-century Palestine there were only 'several symptoms of colonial situation' that 'did not evolve into a full-scale colonial situation.' According to Shafir, 'at the outset, Zionism was a variety of Eastern European nationalism; that is, an ethnic movement in search of a state. But at the other end of the journey, I argue, it may fruitfully be seen as a late instance of European overseas colonialism. What, after all, should we call transplanting one group into land inhabited by another that was followed by the displacement of part of the latter group?'[1] With this statement Shafir extends to 1948 his earlier study on Zionism and models of colonialism, which ended with 1914.[2] However, for the period covered in this study there is no need to use Shafir's model. After 1948 Israel did not manage an operation of mass deportation of Palestinians. Its settlement project in the territory it occupied in 1967, as I shall show, did not create a demographic turnover in favor of Israel.

9

For this reason, scholars who study the post-1967 period tend to use either the apartheid or the ethnic model. According to the ethnic model, the Israeli–Palestinian conflict is an ethnic conflict rather then a purely territorial dispute. Ethnic nationalism claims a right to national self-determination, with the nation based on a common origin and 'tribal' affiliation of its members, a shared history, culture, language and, most often, a common or dominant religion. From this perspective, both Zionism—the Jewish national movement—and its Palestinian counterpart are ethno-national movements. This is evident in the constitutive texts of each. The Israeli Declaration of Independence of 14 May 1948 opens: 'The Land of Israel was the birthplace of the Jewish people. Here their spiritual, religious and political identity was shaped. Here they first attained to statehood, created cultural values of national and universal significance and gave to the world the eternal Book of Books.'[3] The PLO counters with its own vision: 'Palestine, the land of the three monotheistic faiths, is where the Palestinian Arab people was born, on which it grew, developed and excelled. Thus the Palestinian Arab people ensured for itself an everlasting union between itself, its land, and its history.'[4] Ethnic conflicts within a state or between states tend to be zero-sum games, therefore difficult to resolve. Where ethnic affiliation overrides citizenship and civil rights to define 'us' against 'them,' state cohesion is in danger. Ethno-national movements fight in part over intangible assets, which often leave little room for compromise.

The Israeli–Palestinian conflict was indeed ethnic, but between the years 1948–51 and 1967–74, Israel sought to solve this ethnic conflict by negotiating—in secret—with a third party, Jordan.[5] The collapse of the 1948–51 negotiations on nonbelligerency and border resolution has been widely debated among historians, who have sought to determine the reasons for the failure and to assign blame for it. Itamar Rabinovich believes that King Abdullah's political maneuverability within his government was weakened when he annexed the West Bank, with its Palestinian population, and that he lacked energy and dynamism at that time. Avi Shlaim, on the other hand, believes that Israel made excessive demands and is therefore culpable. Israel, Shalim maintains, preferred to wait for an opportunity to conquer Arab Jerusalem.[6]

After the 1967 war, Israel revived the 'Jordanian Option' by making it possible for Israel to propose that its eastern neighbor conclude a peace treaty, in exchange for which Israel would return to Jordan the populated area of the West Bank, excluding Jerusalem. Israel, however, was not prepared to share with Jordan sovereignty over Jerusalem, nor to withdraw from the Jordan Valley. In 1972, Israel rejected King Hussein's proposal to establish a federation of the East and the West Banks under his dynasty, instead of an independent Palestinian state as the PLO demanded. The broad gap between the positions of Israel and Jordan deflected their efforts from reaching an overall agreement into a number of limited understandings and ad hoc arrangements. Israel allowed Jordan to consolidate its hold on East Jerusalem Islamic religious institutions and on West Bank municipalities.[7] During the years 1974–87, the prospects for the Jordanian option gradually diminished. In 1974, an Arab summit recognized the Palestine Liberation Organization (PLO) as the sole legitimate representative of the Palestinian people; and when the Likud party came to power in 1977, Israel embarked on an expansion of its settlements enterprise in the heavily populated areas of the West Bank. Instead of bringing back Jordan, the Likud government offered the Palestinians autonomy—but only over their persons, not the land. At the same time, it endeavored to reduce PLO influence over the inhabitants of the West Bank and Gaza Strip.

But, despite these intensive Israeli efforts, the PLO in fact succeeded in establishing itself in the territories during the decade of 1977–87. Local institutions in the West Bank and Gaza Strip linked themselves to the PLO establishment and its leaders gained grass-roots support.[8] With the outbreak of the Palestinian uprising of 1987 (the First Intifada), Jordan severed its legal ties with the West Bank and Israel's ostensible Jordanian option became irrelevant. Israel was eventually impelled to negotiate with the PLO.

The Oslo agreement of 1993 set in motion a transformation of the Israeli–Palestinian conflict from an ethnic into a border struggle. The Palestinian side began its shift by accepting, in its Declaration of Independence, UN General Assembly Resolution 181 of 1947, which stipulated that Palestine would be partitioned into two states. In 1993, the PLO and Israel signed the first Oslo agreement, which established a border between them. The Oslo agreements changed the pattern of the conflict, although in a limited way. It had a potential to evolve into a comprehensive change. But it failed in part because the Israeli leadership miscalculated by expanding settlements in search of tactical gains. Armed attacks by radicals on both sides, who opposed the concessions the agreements mandated, helped turn the Israeli and Palestinian publics, who felt they were under attack from the other side, against accommodation. Following the collapse of the Oslo agreements in 2000–2002, Israel instituted, in response to a series of terrorist attacks inside its main cities and to other perceived threats, a patchwork of policies that have effectively produced a regime of Israeli control over a divided Palestinian territory. There is no evidence showing that this was premeditated by Israel. Rather, it was the cumulative consequence of its policies. The result is that the conflict has reverted to an ethnic one, although in a different form. This new mode is my subject here.

Israel and the Palestinians have sought a negotiated agreement that would separate them into two ethnic entities (the Oslo accords of 1993 and 1995, the Camp David summit of 2000,[9] and Annapolis talks of November 2007–October 2008). Israel has tried to achieve the same result through unilateral action. Such was the case when, seeking to protect its citizens from Palestinian terrorists, it embarked, at the initiative of Prime Minister Sharon, on construction of a Separation Barrier in the West Bank in 2003. The same goal lay behind Sharon's withdrawal from the Gaza Strip in 2005, accompanied by the evacuation of dozens of settlements there and in the north-west corner of the West Bank. However, such unilateral acts ran starkly counter to achieving a two-state solution through political dialogue with the Palestinian Authority. Sharon's successor, Ehud Olmert, sought to use Israel's unilateral moves as a springboard for new negotiations with the Palestinian Authority. Following the opening of these talks, in Annapolis, Maryland, Olmert made far-reaching territorial offers, but no agreement resulted (see below). Even during the Annapolis talks Israel expanded its settlements in the West Bank. Furthermore, the Barrier has proven to be not a border-in–the-making but rather just one more tool for containing and controlling the Palestinians of the West Bank. Rather than marking a clear border between the Israeli and Palestinian ethnic entities, the fence encloses the Palestinians and perpetuates the unitary regime that rules both Israel proper and the areas that were designated, in the negotiating process, to constitute the Palestinian ethnic state.

Control Systems, Ethnocracy and Apartheid

A number of scholars have debated whether the structure of the Israeli state itself contributes to the conflict. The discussion revolves around three dimensions of the Israeli state system: its geographical expansion, the people it includes, and the effect of time. Regarding geographical expansion, the question is whether the territories Israel occupied in 1967 are actually part of the state or external to the system and thus relatively easy to hand over to the Palestinians. Regarding the Israeli people, the division is between those who base their arguments on Israeli citizenship—that is, they point to the fact that Palestinians living in Israel are citizens of the state and legally entitled to full and equal rights—and those who maintain that Israel is first and foremost a Jewish ethnic state—meaning that Israel's Palestinian inhabitants are by definition second-class citizens. The time factor separates those who argue that the Israeli system evolves over time and in reaction to historical circumstances from those who maintain that it has, from its inception, been a colonial project, and will continue to be such in the future.[10]

In his pioneering study,[11] Jeff Halper coined the term 'matrix of control' to designate Israeli rule over the Occupied Territories. His matrix consists of three interlocking systems: the military administration of much of the West Bank and incessant army and air force incursions elsewhere; a skein of 'facts on the ground,' notably settlements in the West Bank, Gaza and East Jerusalem, but also bypass roads connecting the settlements to Israel proper; and administrative measures like house demolitions and deportations. As Halper notes in a subsequent article,[12] the occupation has grown immeasurably stronger and more entrenched since the publication of that previous study. However, Halper addresses only the Israeli control system over the Occupied Territories, whereas I suggest the inclusion of the Israeli Palestinians. Palestinians living inside Israel's post-1948 borders and those living in the areas occupied in 1967 are, in fact, ruled according to the same principles, even if they are implemented in different ways.

Ariella Azoulay and Adi Ophir[13] challenge those who apply the term 'occupation' only to the lands Israel captured in 1967. They argue that the Israeli occupation regime in these territories shapes the structure of the state within its 1948 borders as well. Ruling the territories is not an enterprise conducted by remote control, external to Israel's governing institutions. It is rather an inherent function of those institutions. In other words, in 1967, Israel did not expand its regime into the West Bank and Gaza Strip; on the contrary, the regime imposed in these territories diffused into Israel proper.

In this, Azoulay and Ophir contest the analysis of Neve Gordon, Halper, and many others who prefer to make a clear distinction between the state of Israel and its occupation project. Within the West Bank and Gaza Strip, whose borders are sealed off from the state within its pre-1967 boundaries, Israel uses surveillance and coercive measures to shape the everyday lives of the Palestinians. Israel dictates correct conduct in homes, schools, workshops, farms and cities via its institutions, regulations, spatial divisions, military practices and bureaucratic edicts. According to Gordon, the control system was configured shortly after the 1967 war. Since then, Israel has done no more than shift its emphasis from one mode of power to another.[14] I maintain that Israeli–Palestinian relations are more dynamic. Substantial changes took place in the 1990s and in the first decade of the twenty-first century. Among these is the virtual disappearance of the Green Line, the boundary that divided Israel's sovereign territory from the land it took in the 1967 war. The Green Line is no longer the effectual border inasmuch as it no longer marks the division between different forms of the implementation of the Israeli control system. Neither does the Barrier mark off the territory where one form of control gives way to another. The distinction, in fact, is no longer territorial.

15

Sammy Smooha defines Israel as the archetype of ethnic democracy:

This is democracy that contains the non-democratic institutionalization of dominance of one ethnic group. The founding rule of this regime is an inherent contradiction between two principles—civil and political rights for all and structural subordination of the minority to the majority. The 'democratic principle' provides equality between all citizens and members of society, while the 'ethnic principle' establishes explicit ethnic inequality, preference and dominance. The organization of the state on the basis of this structural incompatibility constantly generates ambiguities, contradictions, tensions and conflicts, but not necessarily ethnic and political instability. The state belongs to the majority, not to all of its citizens, and the majority uses the state as a means to advance its national interests and goals. The minority encounters the hard problem of potential disloyalty to the state because it can neither be fully equal in nor fully identified with the state. Yet the democratic framework is real, not a façade. The conferral of citizenship on the minority enables it to conduct an intense struggle for fulfilling its rights and for improving its situation without fearing repression on the part of the state and majority. The state imposes various controls and restrictions on the minority in order to prevent subversion, disorder and instability. As a result, the status quo is preserved, but over time the minority experiences a partial betterment of its status.[15]

According to Smooha, Israel is ruled by two contradictory elements: relations between the Jewish majority and Palestinian minority, and the provision of civil and political rights to every citizen regardless of ethnic origin. Hence, Israeli Palestinians are included in Smooha's model, while the West Bank and Gaza Strip Palestinians are excluded. I argue, however, that since 2000 it has become impossible not to include the Palestinians who live in the West Bank and Gaza Strip within the Israeli ruling system. From this perspective, Oren Yiftachel's model is more useful.

Oren Yiftachel calls the Israeli ruling system an ethnocracy. Accordingly, he sees the conflict with the Palestinians as an ethnic struggle over control of the entire region between the Jordan River and the Mediterranean Sea. 'Ethnocratic regimes,' by his definition, 'promote the expansion of the dominant group in contested territory and its domination of [the] power structure while maintaining a democratic façade.'[16] According to Yiftachel, an ethnocracy is hard to dismantle. It expands geographically, reproduces itself and, in the Israeli case, has recently developed into a system of creeping apartheid.

Yiftachel's comparison of Israel with South Africa is a cautious one. Others unhesitatingly define Israel as a racist state. According to a study published by the Middle East Project of the Human Science Research Council of South Africa,[17] apartheid is an aggravated form of a state-sanctioned discriminatory regime in which one ethnic group dominates and systematically oppresses others. The apartheid regime in South Africa stood on three pillars that, this study argues, are also the foundation of Israel's occupation of the Palestinian Territories: division of the population into distinct racial groups; state determination of which may live and move where; and a matrix of draconian security laws and policies aimed at suppressing all opposition to the regime. 'The comparison need not be exact,' argues the report's author, Julie Peteet. 'South Africa is not the benchmark against which all claims of apartheid must be measured; by the terms of the 1973 UN convention, apartheid is a crime wherever it occurs.'[18]

The International Convention on the Suppression and Punishment of the Crime of Apartheid, the document to which Peteet refers, was adopted by the UN General Assembly in November 1973. It defines apartheid as racial segregation and discrimination. Article 1 says that apartheid consists of 'inhuman acts resulting from the policies and practices of apartheid and similar policies and practices of racial segregation and discrimination.' Article 2 of the Convention defines the crime of apartheid, 'which shall include similar policies and practices of racial segregation and discrimination as practiced in southern Africa,' as covering 'inhuman acts committed for the purpose of establishing and maintaining domination by one racial group of persons over any other racial group of persons and systematically oppressing them.'[19]

The South African study contains two methodological problems. First, it broadens the definition of racial apartheid[20] to include ethnicity and discrimination against a subject community under a colonial regime. But the Israeli–Palestinian conflict can be understood better as an ethnic struggle. As I shall show, the Israeli ethnic system is fundamentally softer and more multi–layered than was South African apartheid.

Second, since it bases itself on international law, the South African study deals only with the Occupied Territories. The present book takes instead a bottom-up approach, by analyzing the situation on the ground. From this perspective, the division between the Occupied Palestinian Territory and Israel's internationally recognized sovereign area is not clear-cut, since Israel has annexed, de facto, large parts of the lands it captured in 1967. The legal status of Israeli Palestinians differs from that of their co-ethnics in the Occupied Palestinian Territories. Yet Palestinian communities are subject to the same ruling system. Any comparison with South Africa should not ignore this.

Kimmerling asserted as early as 1989 that the Occupied Territories are more a part of Israel than separated from it. He used the term 'control system' to describe this.[21] Smooha has noted, however, that few Israeli sociologists followed Kimmerling in studying the occupation as a system that Israel simultaneously manages and is affected by.[22] The present work aims to fill this gap by building on and updating Kimmerling's concept. What Kimmerling defined as a control system in the late 1980s underwent far-reaching changes in 2000–2002.

Smooha finds two contradictory trends in Israeli social science.[23] On one side are those who include the Israeli settlers in the West Bank and Gaza Strip as if they resided within Israel's borders, while excluding the Palestinians who live in these same areas. They justify this approach by pointing out that the former are subject to Israeli law, while the latter are under military occupation. On the other side are radical social scientists who argue that Israel in fact maintains a colonial regime over all of Palestine. I propose that neither of these characterizations is correct. Rather, I maintain, Israel operates a regime that includes and excludes the Palestinians under its rule via a graduated system of controls.

In addition to ethnicity, security concerns have been a formative influence on the Israeli regime, as Nadim Rouhana has observed.[24] Israel combines the imperatives of ethnicity and security to enforce an ethno-security regime in the entire area from Jordan to the Mediterranean. However, as I will show below, in Israel proper, ethnicity and security do not trump all. The state maintains civil rights and operates its security forces in a differential way. These limits on the power of ethnicity and security enable Israel to present itself as a democracy, and to sustain the system.

2

A COMPLETE ISRAELI VICTORY?

*The Palestinian Authority's Financial
and Operational Dependency*

As of this writing, in December 2009, Israel seems to have achieved a complete victory over the Palestinian national movement. Palestinians lack the capabilities to achieve independence and are unlikely to acquire them in the foreseeable future. During the years 2000–2001 Israel, with the help of the United States, crushed the Palestinian Authority. It ceased, effectively, to govern its own territory, and became for all intents and purposes the administrator of an Israeli protectorate.

Financially, the Authority is fully dependent on external funds. It pays wages directly to some 150,000 people, who provide a livelihood for about half a million individuals; while a similar number live off the charity of foreign organizations. The cost for maintaining services to the West Bank's population is about US $1 billion a year.[1] The donor countries decided, in November 2007, to allocate to the regime of Palestinian Authority President Mahmoud Abbas more than $7.4 billion over three years. However, in 2009 the Palestinian Authority received less then a quarter of the $1.45 billion promised for that year.[2] In 2009, Palestinian Prime Minister Salam Fayyad had no choice but to borrow $530 million from local banks in order to pay the salaries of PA employees, who with their families constitute one-quarter of the West Bank Palestinian population.[3] To the same end, in January 2010 the EU pledged €160 million to Fayyad's government.[4] According to a report by the Washington Institute for Near East Policy, the Ramallah-based PA government is already spending almost half of its budget on Gaza, in an effort to keep a political foothold there, while the revenues from Gaza economic activity go to the Hamas government there, not to the PA.[5]

In July 2009 the US transferred $200 million to Fayyad's government to ease the growing budget deficit. According to Fayyad, including this transfer, donor countries gave his government $606 million in support during that year, covering only about one-third of the estimated annual deficit of $1.45 billion.[6] Hence, in September 2009 the donor states pledged to give the Fayyad government $400 million to cover the 2009 deficit.[7]

The Israeli army (Israel Defense Forces, IDF) freely operates in the Palestinian Territories to secure Israelis, mainly settlers, while the donor countries pay to repair the damage caused by Israeli security measures, maintain basic social services, and prevent a Palestinian humanitarian catastrophe.[8] Following Israel's massive military operation against Hamas in the Gaza Strip in December 2008–January 2009, donor states contributed $5.4 billion for the reconstruction of Gaza Strip infrastructure, houses, institutions and services.[9] In addition, in July 2009 the World Bank announced plans to spend an additional $33.5 million on Palestinian infrastructure initiatives, including $21.5 million for six Gaza projects (the Electric Utility Management Project, the Emergency Services Support Project, the Gaza Emergency Water Project, the Emergency Municipal Services Rehabilitation Project, the Palestinian NGO Project and the Tertiary Education Project). The Gaza Strip funding, which will in part cover damages caused to these projects by Israel's military incursion, comes in addition to the $77.3 million pledged to these projects before the Israeli raid.[10] 'The Europeans are financing the occupation. And the Europeans are happy, because they feel like they are doing something, it cleanses their conscience. And the Israelis are happy because they're not paying for it,' says Sari Nusseibeh, the president of al-Quds University and former Palestinian Authority minister and negotiator.[11] Due to Israeli pressures and Palestinian mismanagement, the occupied territories display all the characteristics of state collapse, Yezid Sayigh asserts.[12]

Politically, Israel has, since the Annapolis conference of November 2007, sidetracked President Abbas into futile negotiations. He wanted to prevent the US from repeating the accusations it made against Palestinian leaders following the Camp David summit of 2000—that they consistently missed all opportunities to reach an accommodation with Israel. As a result, Abbas neither developed alternative strategies, such as a non-violent Intifada, nor means to exert pressure on Israel. He believed naively that by December 2008, President George W. Bush and Prime Minister Ehud Olmert would agree to conclude with him a framework agreement that would lay the groundwork for a comprehensive peace treaty, or approve the creation of a fully sovereign, territorially contiguous, and economically viable Palestinian state. Instead, the US and Israel adhered to a conflict management strategy under the aegis of the unimplemented Road Map to Israeli–Palestinian Peace of 2002. Under this policy, any declaration or agreement relating to the final resolution of the conflict was to be shelved until the Road Map's provisions were fulfilled.[13] Israel set the agenda of the talks, and its territorial proposals were similar to those it presented at Taba in 2001, the post-Camp David round of negotiations that ended without an agreement. In September

2008, after his resignation and before leaving office, Olmert offered Abbas

93.5 to 93.7 per cent of the Palestinian territories, along with a land swap of 5.8 per cent and a safe-passage corridor from Gaza to the West Bank that he says would make up the rest. The Holy Basin of Jerusalem would be under no sovereignty at all and administered by a consortium of Saudis, Jordanians, Israelis, Palestinians and Americans. Regarding refugees, Olmert says he rejected the right of return and instead offered, as a 'humanitarian gesture,' a small number of returnees, although 'smaller than the Palestinians wanted—a very, very limited number.'[14]

According to Abbas, 'Olmert showed me one map and I brought back one of ours. He showed me a new map and I brought back a map of ours. And so it went. We [the Palestinians] agreed that 1.9 per cent would be with you and Olmert demanded 6.5 per cent. It was a negotiation, we didn't complete it.' While Abbas's figures are almost the same as those of Olmert's, he sums up the negotiations in quite a different way. 'Olmert understood the way things stood. He also agreed to the approach that what was Arab would remain in Arab hands.... On the matter of the holy places, he proposed international monitors.'[15] Abbas presumed that Olmert's final proposal was open to further negotiations, but Lieutenant General Udi Dekel, Olmert's peace talks coordinator, maintains that the Prime Minister's offer was a package deal not open to modification.

In any case, the Israeli offer fell short of the Arab Peace Plan and the Palestinian consensus, which are: full Palestinian sovereignty over Arab Jerusalem; recognition of the right of Palestinian refugees to return to their former homes in what is now Israel, while reaching specific arrangements with Israel for implemention; and territorial exchange at a 1:1 ratio, after recognizing the pre-1967 border in principle.[16] Israel also formulated an eight-point document laying out its security requirements. These included supervision of Palestine's border crossings, use of Palestinian airspace, regulation of radio frequencies, and the construction of hilltop early-warning stations.[17] At the Camp David summit of 2000, where these demands were presented formally for the first time, the Palestinians rejected them on the grounds that they violated the principle of sovereignty. Olmert transferred his security document to the American administration, perhaps to help him overcome the Palestinian opposition.[18] Furthermore, Olmert's offer was problematic because he made it without consulting with his Foreign Minister, Tzipi Livni, who was then conducting a parallel negotiating track with Palestinian leader Ahmed Qurei (Abu Alaa),[19] or with his Defense Minister, Ehud Barak. Throughout the year of the Annapolis negotiations, the US acted as a caretaker rather than as an interventionist broker. Thus, during 2008–9 the sides were able to agree only on the principles governing their negotiating process. No substantive issues were resolved.[20]

In October 2009, under Israeli and American pressure,[21] Abbas instructed the Palestinian delegation to the UN Human Rights Council to drop its efforts to send the Security Council the report of the United Nations Fact-Finding Mission on the Gaza Conflict of December 2008–January 2009. The mission was led by Judge Richard Goldstone of South Africa, an internationally respected jurist, who was also a Jew and Zionist with strong ties in Israel. The Mission found strong evidence that both Israel and Hamas had committed war crimes and crimes against humanity. It recommended that its report be forwarded to the Security Council or the General Assembly, for consideration of whether to institute legal proceedings in the International Criminal Court at The Hague. According to Palestinian sources, Yuval Diskin, chief of the General Security Service (GSS, Israel's secret internal security agency, sometimes known by its Hebrew acronyms Shabak or Shin Bet) warned

Abbas that if he did not ask for a deferral of the vote on the report, Israel would turn the West Bank into a 'second Gaza.' Diskin threatened to rescind the loosening of restrictions on movement within the West Bank, and said that Israel would withdraw its consent for the operation of the Wataniya mobile phone company in the Palestinian Authority. The latter action would require the PA to pay out tens of millions of dollars in compensation to the company.[22]

Abbas's decision set off an outpouring of public anger against his leadership. The members of his cabinet were also highly critical. PA Economy Minister Bassem Khouri resigned in protest, as did Nabil Amro, the ambassador to Cairo. Minister of Social Affairs Majida al-Masri called Abbas's decision 'embarrassing,' while Yasser Abed Rabbo, secretary-general of the PLO Executive Committee, admitted that Abbas had erred. The PA cabinet resolved that the decision was unacceptable and urged that the report be sent to the Security Council. Under this heavy barrage of criticism, the PLO Executive Committee and the PA cabinet decided to establish a commission of inquiry to determine who was responsible for the decision.[23] The commission published its report in January 2010. It found that President Mahmoud Abbas gave the directive to change the Palestinian stance on the Goldstone report at the UN Human Rights Commission following a September meeting with US and Arab officials.[24] In the meantime, Abbas reversed himself and the PA delegation asked the Human Rights Council to readdress the Goldstone report. On 16 October the Council endorsed the report. It called on the UN General Assembly to take it up and for UN Secretary-General Ban Ki–moon to report back to the Human Rights Council on Israel's adherence.

Many of Abbas's loyalists have publicly criticized him for weak leadership, or demonstratively distanced themselves. They refer to his acquiescence in the policies of foreigners, despite the international sympathy that he enjoys.[25] A poll of voting intentions conducted in the West Bank and Gaza Strip by the Palestinian Center for Policy and Survey Research in March 2008 found that Fatah's lead over Hamas decreased significantly during the first part of 2008, from 18 per cent in January to 7 per cent. In August, Fatah's lead increased to 22 per cent. However, in December its advantage plummeted to 14 per cent, while in March and June 2009 Fatah lost much public support and led with 7–8 per cent (respectively) only. In December 2009 Fatah led Hamas by 16 per cent; almost the same as in August.

Figure 1: Fatah's Lead Over Hamas

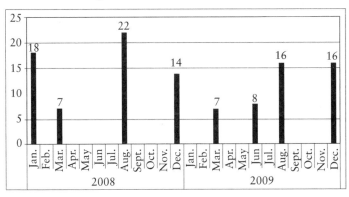

Source: The Palestinian Center for Policy and Survey Research.

Similarly, in March 2008, virtually identical numbers said they would vote for Fatah's leader, Abbas, and Ismail Haniyeh, the Hamas Prime Minister of the Gaza Strip (46 per cent and 47 per cent respectively); Abbas had led by 19 points earlier in December 2007, by 56 per cent to 37 per cent.[26] Abbas regained a lead of 14 per cent in August 2008, when 53 per cent supported him against 39 per cent to Haniyeh. However, in December the gap narrowed to 10 per cent: 48 per cent for Abbas, compared to 38 per cent to Haniyeh. In 2009 Haniyeh scored 47 per cent in the virtual voting in March, and 44 per cent in June. Abbas had 45 per cent in March and 49 in June. The voting intentions improved in favor of Abbas in December 2009. Then Abbas achieved 54 per cent compared with Haniyeh's 38 per cent. Only 40 per cent said in March 2009 then that they were satisfied with Abbas's performances. Here, too, Abbas improved his standing in December when 48 per cent said that they were satisfied with his performance.[27]

Figure 2: Abbas versus Haniyeh

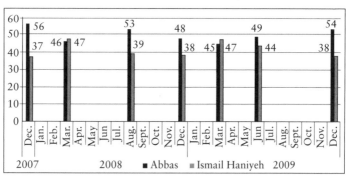

Source: The Palestinian Center for Policy and Survey Research.

Abbas's West Bank government has improved personal and family safety by reforming and strengthening its police forces. In 2007 the National Security brigade and civilian police forces, trained in Jordan by Lt. Gen. Keith Dayton of the US Army, were deployed in Jenin where they succeeded in re-establishing law and order. This success has encouraged the Palestinian Authority, Israel and the US, who trained these forces, to deploy a battalion each in the cities of Nablus, Qal-qilya and Hebron.[28] Consequently, the economy and commercial life improved in these places. But these gains could not have been achieved had Abbas not acceded to Israel's conditions. Those were, first, that Palestinian police and security personnel could operate only within geographical and operational limits unilaterally set by Israel. Protective vests, helmets and rubber bullets paid for by donor countries would remain in storage in Egypt and Jordan, awaiting Israeli import permission. In addition, Israel has not allowed the entry of fifty badly-needed Russian-made armored personnel carriers.[29] In 2009, the IDF vetoed Palestinian requests to receive explosives training and to set up an advanced military communication system.[30] 'We don't provide anything to the Palestinians unless it has been thoroughly coordinated with the state of Israel and they agree to it,' said Lt. Gen. Dayton. 'Sometimes this process drives me crazy—I had a lot more hair when I started—but nevertheless, we make it work.'[31]

The second condition was that the Palestinian forces also act against Hamas in accordance with guidelines established by Israel. Israel fears that any part of the West Bank from which it withdraws will fall into the hands of Hamas, an outcome Israel cannot tolerate. Until 2009, Israel did not trust the willingness and the capabilities of the Palestinian forces to prevent terrorism. Following Hamas's brutal takeover of the Gaza Strip in June 2007, Palestinian Authority forces loyal to Abbas closed down hundreds of Hamas's charitable organizations, and the Palestinian Authority replaced 150 Hamas-affiliated mosque imams with Fatah loyalists. Then they arrested about 2,000 Hamas operatives of whom some 800 were still incarcerated in September 2009. In May and June 2009 Abbas police killed, in Qalqilyah, the members of a Hamas cell that Israel had failed to kill or capture.[32] A Hamas document titled

'Exclusive and Unique Research: The Detention Philosophy of the Abbas–Dayton Security Apparatuses and Methods of Dealing with Them,' composed by Hamas activists in an Israeli prison, describes in detail the treatment of Hamas activists by Abbas's West Bank regime. According to this document, during the period from Hamas's takeover in Gaza in June 2007 to September 2009, there were 22,000 incidents initiated by the Palestinian Authority against Hamas personnel in the West Bank. West Bank security forces humiliated religious Muslims for observing religious precepts; some were forbidden to fulfill their religious duties and to read the Koran.[33] The Hamas document links these actions to the Palestinian Authority's 'security coordination' with Israel's intelligence agencies. The authors have no doubt that 'the real objective of the Palestinian security forces is to strike a blow to the resistance movement in order to serve the security of the occupation.'[34] Unsurprisingly, people in Bethlehem compare Dayton to Glubb Pasha, the unpopular British commander of Jordan's army until 1957.[35]

However, Israeli security forces continue to operate in areas where Palestinian forces are deployed from midnight to five or six a.m.; Palestinian forces need prior permission to enter Area C to arrest suspects. (Under the Oslo agreements, that part of the West Bank placed under full Palestinian jurisdiction is designated Area A; areas in which the Palestinians exercised civilian control but Israel retained overriding military control were called Area B; in Area C, constituting 60 per cent of the West Bank, territory on which about 150,000 Palestinians live, Israel exercises both civilian and military control.) Israel strictly limits the kind of arms the security forces can wield.[36] 'We now have an excellent subcontractor for dealing with Hamas,' an official on the IDF General Staff admitted in November 2008.[37]

In other words, this delegation of military authority to the Abbas regime did not amount to an Israeli withdrawal that handed power over to an independent Palestinian entity. Rather, Israel delegated certain military functions to a Palestinian protectorate:[38]

Consequently, Palestinian forces are perceived as collaborators that not only serve Israel's interests but are also not able to protect the Palestinian population from Israeli troops. And although the newly-trained forces are much more proficient and professional, they are still perceived by segments of Palestinian society as political tools of the Fatah party and of the old and corrupt Palestinian leadership. Indeed, sometimes they act in ways that validate this perception.[39]

The Israeli control system goes beyond security and policing. A document from the Coordinator of Government Activities in the Territories (COGAT), sent in September 2009 to Beit Sahur municipality, exposes the Israeli control on Palestinian construction all over the West Bank, including in Areas A and B. The COGAT document details the terms and conditions under which the municipality of Beit Sahur can use funds from USAID and the Vatican to build a park. Beit Sahur authorities, the letter said, must obtain COGAT's written approval for the purchase and delivery of construction materials including pipes (especially metal pipes). To get such approval, the Beit Sahur municipality must state whether the proposed construction location is located in Area C, and specify:

(1) the name of the project; (2) where and when the materials were purchased (i.e., name of the factory, city, country); (3) who is the intended recipient; (4) who actually paid for the materials; (5) where the materials will be used; and (6) for what purpose. It is also important to identify who will have custody over any and all building materials procured by the implementing partner and how the materials will be secured from theft or misuse.... When working with Palestinian Authority officials who report that COGAT has approved a

project, the implementing partner must still obtain a copy of the written approval directly from COGAT.[40]

The Israeli authorities want to secure that construction materials will not be used for terrorist activities. But their supervision goes far beyond.

As of 2009, the Palestinians are fragmented politically and geographically and have lost almost all hope of changing their lot through diplomacy. In the above-mentioned March 2009 poll, 73 per cent of the Palestinians said that the chances for a two-state solution in the next five years are zero or low.[41] Moreover, argued Dr. Kahlil Nakhleh in September 2008, there seem to be frightening signs that the Palestinian social fabric is disintegrating. Cultural values are deteriorating; traditional social authorities are losing their standing; education and research quality are regressing; and individuals increasingly place personal needs over national collective ones.[42] 'The days of massive citywide shows of solidarity with families of martyrs have long since passed... Nablus is a broken city,' American–Palestinian historian Beshara Doumani wrote after visiting Nablus in the summer of 2003.[43] Members of the upper and middle classes who can afford to do so leave the West Bank, or move to Ramallah.[44] That Israel's stronger society faces these same challenges is of little comfort to the Palestinians.

Spatial and socio-political fragmentation produces localized and uncoordinated resistance to Israel and criticism of Abbas. Those who lack the political will to resist sink into passivity and despair. Fragmentation also deepens Fatah–Hamas rivalry. Since January 2005, weekly demonstrations in the villages of Bil'in and Na'alin against the expropriation of most of their lands to provide room for the expansion of the nearby settlement city Modi'in Illit and for the Barrier have attracted hundreds of peace activists from Israel, the West Bank, and overseas.[45] They meet every Friday noon to march from these villages to the construction sites. The demonstrations almost invariably escalate into violent confrontations with Israeli soldiers and border police. Bil'in and Na'alin have become symbols of resistance, Palestinian martyrdom and Israeli aggression. While the demonstrations are covered extensively by the regional and international media, they have not been copied elsewhere in the West Bank.[46] Other localities have reacted differently to the Israeli ethno-security regime. The inhabitants of Qalqilya, Tulkarem and Jenin focus on how their individual cities suffer from settlement expansion and the Barrier. Many of Nablus' businessmen and professionals have relocated to Ramallah and Jordan.[47] As Israeli settlers have moved into Hebron's old city center, Palestinians have abandoned it. East Jerusalem, disconnected form its natural hinterland by Jewish settlements and the Separation Barrier (which here takes the form of a wall), has become a slum. Many of its inhabitants find succor by supporting extreme Islamic movements. Observers report on growing support for Hizb al-Tahrir al-Islami (the Islamic Salvation Party) and other radical religious organizations. East Jerusalem poverty and slums are breeding grounds for criminals—a fact that actually benefits Israeli authorities. East Jerusalem residents claim that Israel offers immunity to criminal gangs in exchange for their collaboration and provision of intelligence. In 2002, Faisal Husseini, East Jerusalem's leading political leader, died, shortly before Israel shut down his Orient House, which served as the unofficial headquarters of the PLO in the city. Since then, East Jerusalem has lacked political leadership and institutions. Sheikh Ra'id Salah, head of the Northern Branch of the Islamic Movement in Israel, has stepped into this breach, becoming the most visible campaigner for protecting al-Haram al-Sharif and maintaining East Jerusalem's Palestinian identity. Locals now refer to him as the Sheikh of Al-Aqsa or the Palestinian Mayor of Jerusalem. He provides financial aid to families who have lost their homes to settlers and organizes solidarity tours to Jerusalem for Israeli Palestinians. Since 2001, Palestinian Israelis have made over two million visits to Islam's third-holiest site, with visitors coming in about 600 buses a month, the vehicles carrying around 30,000 people. They not only visit the Islamic holy sites on al-Haram al-Sharif but also go shopping in the bazaar, to display their solidarity by giving business to East Jerusalem tradesmen. In response Israel arrested Sheikh Raid, barred him from entering Jerusalem, and closed the Islamic Movement's media and charity operations in the city.[48]

Ramallah's inhabitants call their city a 'five-star prison,' home to the Palestinian Authority's headquarters, many NGO professionals, and to the offices of international organizations. The city is host to a new globalized, secular, urban middle class living a Western lifestyle. Ramallah has managed to maintain the socio-economic and cultural profile that developed there after 1948, despite Israeli restrictions. This has continued to be the case since Israel eased up travel restrictions between it and other major West Bank cities excluding Jerusalem. No other city in Palestine has so long boasted such an eclectic and heterogeneous population. Its many private schools ensure that its young people learn foreign languages. Emigration rates are high, meaning that the city is not burdened with an ossified and immovable elite.[49]

American Policy

The Bush Administration

With the exception of its veto of the implementation of a plan to expand Ma'ale Adumim and connect it to Jerusalem (the E1 plan), the administration of President George W. Bush did next to nothing to halt Israeli settlement construction. In the absence of sanctions, its repeated statements that settlement construction was detrimental to the peace process were interpreted by Israeli decision-makers as an implicit green light to proceed with expansion. Moreover, the Bush administration did not press Israel to implement its promise to the US not to expand settlements beyond certain lines and parameters. Israel protested these constraints and the US did not enforce the limitations.[50] A US study group asserted that the Bush administration disengaged from active Arab–Israeli peace-making. Likewise, the American administration failed to argue strongly against Israeli practices: 'In March 2002 Bush demanded publicly that Israel pull back from Palestinian cities it had reoccupied, but then dropped the demand and soon after called Sharon "a man of peace."'[51] Later in 2004 and 2005, Bush allowed Sharon to dictate the scope of the Gaza disengagement. He did not compel Sharon to couple the Gaza withdrawal with a significant one from the West Bank as well, which would have countered charges that the disengagement operation was little more then Israel's way of ridding itself of the burden of Gaza.'[52] Indeed, the study group concluded, the Road Map was effectively set aside by Sharon. Moreover, there were moments when American policy was shaped too much by Israeli officials. The Bush administration soon abandoned its commitment to monitor the implementation of the Road Map, including the evacuation of West Bank settlements. Finally, at the end of his term, Bush made final status commitments to Israel regarding the settlements without consulting meaningfully with the Arab states and the Palestinians.[53]

In an article he wrote for the *Washington Post*, former Israeli Prime Minister Ehud Olmert maintained that his predecessor, Ariel Sharon, had reached the following understandings with the Bush administration:

• No new settlements would be constructed;

- No new land would be allocated or confiscated for settlement construction;
- Any construction in the settlements would be within current building lines;
- There would be no provision of economic incentives promoting settlement growth;
- The unauthorized outposts built after March 2001 would be dismantled.[54]

Olmert admitted in his article that Israel did not implement the last provision. But Akiva Eldar, an Israeli journalist and expert on the history of the settlements, argued in July 2009 that Israel also violated other items of the Sharon–Bush understanding.

1. The building line: A few weeks ago the former US ambassador to Israel Daniel Kurtzer published an op-ed in *The Washington Post* in which he claimed that this restriction was never implemented and never agreed to by the Israeli military representative to talks with the United States, Brig. Gen. (ret.) Baruch Spiegel. Kurtzer said that shortly after the November 2007 Annapolis summit, Olmert himself approved the construction of Agan Ha'ayalot, a new neighborhood west of Givat Ze'ev.
2. Incentives: Although there is no line item in the state budget for 'support for settlements,' settlement beyond the Green Line enjoys support via 'priority areas' and other allocations.
3. Land expropriation: In May 2008 final approval was given for expropriating 60 dunams (15 acres) to expand Ariel's industrial area. The same month about 100 dunams north of Kiryat Arba was declared 'state land' for building about 100 residential units. At least four additional orders have been issued to appropriate land for West Bank settlements.

Eldar concluded that 'it is hard to believe that the Americans and Palestinians interpreted these understandings as a license to dramatically accelerate the rate of settlement construction. According to Israel's Central Bureau of Statistics, in the year following the summit there were 2,122 new building starts in the settlements, up from 1,487 in 2007 (excluding East Jerusalem).'[55] The Bush administration did not call Israel to account.

The Obama Administration

At first, the Obama administration seemed to pursue a different strategy. But, by the end of the new president's first year in power, he had not changed much on the ground; in practice, the Democratic administration practiced the same conflict management strategy as its predecessor. Obama told Joe Klein of *Time*:

I think it's fair to say that for all our efforts at early engagement, it is not where I want it to be.... And I think that we overestimated our ability to persuade [the Israeli and Palestinian leaders] to do so when their politics ran contrary to that.... I think it is absolutely true that what we did this year didn't produce the kind of breakthrough that we wanted, and if we had anticipated some of these political problems on both sides earlier, we might not have raised expectations as high.[56]

The Obama administration came in with a clear demand: as a confidence-building measure toward resuming talks with the PA, Israel should freeze all settlement construction, including in East Jerusalem. 'The United States views East Jerusalem as no different than an illegal West Bank outpost with regard to its demand for a freeze on settlement construction.'[57] In parallel, Arab countries were asked to demonstrate that they were willing to end the conflict by implementing small normalization measures, such as letting El Al aircraft fly over Saudi Arabia, or reopening Morocco's and Qatar's interest offices in Tel Aviv. Obama's policy, then, was oriented toward process. Yet, following his speech in Cairo on 5 June 2009, many in the Arab world had expected Obama to achieve results through bold diplomacy.[58] Neither Israel nor the moderate Arab states would have accepted the American strategy. Israel's current Prime Minister, Binyamin Netanyahu, has rejected the American demand to freeze Jewish construction in East Jerusalem. Under American pressure, however, he agreed to accept the concept of a two-state solution, and to negotiate with the US on the terms and conditions of a settlement freeze in the West Bank.[59] The US and Netanyahu agreed, in November 2009, to halt settlement construction for ten months—excluding construction in Jerusalem and excluding about 3,000 housing units that were already in construction all over the West Bank. In addition, Defense Minister Barak approved the construction of a further 490 residential units, most of them to the east of the Barrier.[60] 'Analysis of the situation on the ground suggests that there will be nearly no change in settlement construction, at least not in the coming months,' concluded *Ha'aretz* correspondent Amos Harel.[61] According to his findings, 'Hundreds of new housing units are in the process of construction.... While it is true that the Netanyahu government has not been generous in approving plans for construction, mostly in areas far from the separation fence, there is still a significant amount of new construction in the territories.'[62] Indeed, as of 1 January 2010, hundreds of residential units were under construction in the West Bank despite the freeze. Most of these were to the east—that is, on the Palestinian side—of the Barrier and were begun not earlier than late November 2009, when warrants on the forthcoming freeze were issued.[63]

In December 2009, Israel published plans to construct hundreds of houses in Jerusalem (see below). The White House condemned this move, which coincided with US efforts to re-start Israeli–Palestinian peace talks:

The United States opposes new Israeli construction in East Jerusalem. The status of Jerusalem is a permanent status issue that must be resolved by the parties through negotiations and supported by the international community. Neither party should engage in efforts or take actions that could unilaterally pre-empt, or appear to pre-empt, negotiations. Rather, both parties should return to negotiations without preconditions as soon as possible. The United States recognizes that Jerusalem is a deeply important issue for Israelis and Palestinians, and for Jews, Muslims, and Christians. We believe that through good faith negotiations the parties can mutually agree on an outcome that realizes the aspirations of both parties for Jerusalem, and safeguards its status for people around the world.[64]

This declaration did not, however, mollify the Palestinians, who watch as East Jerusalem is changed by Israeli construction.

The Israeli–American understanding on a temporary, partial settlement freeze left the Palestinian side very disappointed. President Obama seemed initially to be in tune with President Abbas, demanding a total freeze of Jewish settlement in the West Bank and terming the settlement project illegal. The Americans also continued to insist that Hamas fulfill the conditions laid down by the 'Quartet' (a body consisting of the US, EU, Russia and the UN, which promotes an Israeli–Palestinian accord). This put Abbas in the driver's seat, in no hurry to reach an agreement with the radicals on a national unity government or to hold new elections for the Palestinian Authority.[65] Given these favorable circumstances, Abbas even acceded to a request from the administration not to press for a UN debate on the Goldstone report (see above). In return, Abbas expected that sustained American pressure on Israel would give him the diplomatic achievement he needed to convince a skeptical Palestinian public that the path he had chosen would lead to Palestinian independence. That has not materialized. Instead, what the Palestinian people see is ongoing settlement expansion that predetermines the outcome of negotiations. Moreover, although the Palestinian Authority is successfully containing Hamas in the West Bank and imposing law and order there, it has received no diplomatic quid pro quo for doing so. When the Obama administration deferred to Netanyahu on construction in the settlements, the Palestinians started asking themselves: if the Americans have failed to impose a temporary settlement freeze on Israel, how will they be able to force it to withdraw from most of the settlements permanently? Abbas and his aides acknowledged that their hopes regarding the Obama administration had proven false. In November 2009, Abbas announced that he will not seek re-election and that he was even considering resigning from his role in the PLO and Fatah positions before the elections he called for 10 January 2010.[66] 'I think he is realizing that he came all this way with the peace process in order to create a Palestinian state but he sees no state coming,' said Saeb Erekat, the chief Palestinian negotiator. Moreover, he argues, President Abbas has come to the conclusion that the Palestinian Authority is no longer a relevant institution.[67]

But politicians don't rush to resign or to admit failure; instead they seek a Plan B.[68] Abbas and his colleagues are looking for a game-breaking initiative that will radically alter the diplomatic balance of power with Israel. They have decided to launch a diplomatic campaign during which they will ask the Security Council to recognize the 1967 lines as the borders of a future Palestinian state. The Palestinian initiative is based on a proposal by Javier Solana, the European Union's foreign policy commissioner, according to which 'after a fixed deadline, a UN Security Council resolution should proclaim the adoption of the two-state solution.... It would accept the Palestinian state as a full member of the UN, and set a calendar for implementation. It would mandate the resolution of other remaining territorial disputes and legitimize the end of claims.'[69] The Palestinian initiative does not aim to impose a comprehensive solution, but rather to achieve international recognition of the 1967 borders as the borders of the future Palestinian state. The point would be to nullify the effects of Israel's settlement expansion and to impose terms of reference from which productive negotiations can begin. At the time of writing, the PA initiative was supported by Arab countries only. Both the US and the EU had rejected it.

In early 2010 the USA changed its policy and tone regarding settlements expansion. In March 2010 Israel approved the building of 1,600 residential units in Ramat Shlomo, East Jerusalem, at the time when Vice President Biden visited Jerusalem and the US tried to open proximity talks (indirect negotiation) between Israel and the PA. A few days later the Jerusalem Municipality approved the building of twenty residential units in Sheikh Jarah, Jerusalem, just as Netanyahu was set to meet with President Obama to discuss the previous case of approving the 1,600 units. The American diplomatic reaction was quite tough. President Obama demanded that Israel reverse the decision, include Jerusalem in the settlements freeze, make substantial gestures toward the Palestinians, and declare that all core issues, including the status of Jerusalem, be on the table when talks resume.[70] 'Israel needs a wake-up call. Continuing to build settlements in the West Bank, and even housing in disputed East Jerusalem, is sheer madness.... Mitchell's and Netanyahu's aides struck an informal deal: If America got talks going, there would be no announcements of buildings in East Jerusalem, nothing to embarrass the Palestinians and force them to walk. Netanyahu agreed, US officials say, but

41

made clear he couldn't commit to anything publicly,' thus Tom Friedman reflected Washington's anger.[71]

The Palestinian leadership of late 2009 seems to be attentive to those who argue that it is time for the Palestinians to regain the political initiative. In the summer of 2008, a group of intellectuals, professionals and political activists drafted a strategic document in which they offer ways to overcome current Israeli strategy and end the occupation. First, they wrote, the Palestinian leadership should reject and not cooperate with each of following moves that Israel might make to keep the Palestinians from achieving their national goals: prolonging negotiations indefinitely while maintaining the status quo; establishing a Palestinian state with provisional borders while postponing the decision on Jerusalem and refugees, on the grounds that a state with provisional borders would be geographically truncated, divided into separate enclaves, and dependent on Israel; unilateral separation; and bringing in Egypt and Jordan, the first to control the Gaza Strip and the second to supervise the West Bank.[72] It should be noted that Jordan has rejected the idea of returning to the West Bank. 'There are certain elements in the Israeli government that are pushing for Jordan to take a role in the West Bank. That is never going to work and we have to be very clear that Jordan absolutely does not want to have anything to do with the West Bank. All we will be doing is replacing Israeli military with Jordanian military,' stated King Abdullah II.[73] Fatah's sixth conference, in August 2009, adopted the study group's guidelines. The conference also elected new leadership that is more focused on settlement expansion. A number of speakers there criticized Abbas for relying solely on negotiations to resolve the conflict.[74]

The strategy study group suggests reorienting Palestinian policy in four directions. First, it advocates closing down the Oslo and Annapolis negotiations, since these frameworks are not leading to the results the Palestinians seek. Second, it proposes reconstituting the Palestinian Authority so that it will not serve Israeli interests. Instead, it should become the Palestinian Resistance Authority. Third, 'smart' resistance should be given precedence over negotiations as the main means of achieving independence, alongside the establishment of a national unity government with Hamas and a reformation of the PLO. For this to succeed, international and regional support would be essential. Fourth, in case Israel refuses to accept the two-state solution as proposed by the Arab League in the Arab Peace Initiative of 2002, the study group suggests shifting Palestinian preference from a two-state outcome to a single state. The single state would be a 'one man, one vote' polity or a binational state in which power is shared between collectives in a federation or confederation. The confederation could be established at a later stage, once the two states, Israel and Palestine, live securely next to each other.[75] Unwilling to declare that their strategy had failed irrevocably, Abbas and his colleagues in the Palestinian ruling elite have been very selective in accepting these four proposals. They continue to seek a new foundation, in the form of the UN Security Council, for the political process that they have led since the PLO accepted the two-state solution in 1988. Neither are they willing to compromise with Hamas. Marwan Barghouti, however, is ready to go beyond his leadership's position. From his jail in Israel, the popular leader, who plans to run for PA president in the next elections, has stated:

In the shadow of the failure of negotiations and the absence of an Israeli partner for peace, the necessary strategy is firstly ending the division and restoring national unity.... There is no excuse in the world that prevents national reconciliation, especially in light of the latest developments and the blocked horizon for negotiations.... Betting on negotiations alone was never our choice. I have always called for a constructive mix of negotiation, resistance, political, diplomatic and popular action against settlements.[76]

Abbas and Israel have given him a clear response. Abbas declared: 'As long as I am in office I will not allow anybody to start a new Intifada. Never.'[77] It should be noted that Prime Minister Fayyad supports unarmed activity against Israeli occupation. Fatah senior leaders, Jibril Rajub, Kadura Faris and Mahmoud al-Alul, together with two ministers in Fayyad's cabinet, demonstrated in late March 2010 along with hundreds of Palestinian citizens against the arrest of their colleague Abbas Zaki by Israel. At that time, Rajub called Fatah seniors to lead a new phase of popular resistance.[78]

Throughout 2009, Israel used force to suppress popular demonstrations that could have developed into what Barghouti seeks. One Palestinian was shot dead and twenty-nine were wounded by IDF snipers while demonstrating against the Separation Barrier. Since June 2009, Israel has arrested thirty-one inhabitants of Bil'in (5 per cent of its population); ninety-four inhabitants of Na'alin (7 per cent of the population) have been arrested since May 2008.[79] In January 2010, Israel's immigration police, which operate under the aegis of the Interior Ministry, entered Ramallah to arrest and deport activists of Czech citizenship who live in that city and who have participated in the demonstrations in Bili'n.[80] When these steps did not help, the IDF declared on March 2010 a closed military zone for six months of the Bil'in and Na'alin areas where the weekly demonstrations against the Separation Fence take place.[81] Since December 2009, police have used force to prevent Israelis from applying the model of the weekly demonstration in Bil'in in the Jerusalem neighborhood Sheikh Jarah, where they have protested against a new settlement inside that Arab neighborhood.[82]

In August 2009, Prime Minister Salam Fayyad presented another proactive state-building plan, aimed at establishing a

Palestinian state within two years.[83] The program seeks to foster strong governing institutions despite the occupation, bringing about the establishment of an independent Palestine by acting positively from the bottom up. Good governance, accountability and transparency are the principles on which the de facto state institutions would operate. Fayyad's first priority is to establish an effective public sector in five core areas: unifying and modernizing the legal system; reorganizing government services; introducing information and communication technology; improving the management of financial and economic resources; and developing human resources. Fayyad seeks to engage with the international community and secure the backing of Arab states. He realizes that his ambitious program is unachievable without collective Palestinian commitment. It requires the involvement of all social sectors, government and civil society organizations, and national unity with Hamas. However, the deep division between Hamas and the PLO factions, first and foremost the Fatah movement, which rules the West Bank, and the sharp divergence of their political agendas, does not favor the implementation of this technocratic plan. Palestinian society is fragmented and skeptical, and the Fayyad initiative does not offer ways to overcome those factors that it identifies as obstacles to its success. Finally, Israel is unwilling to cooperate, and the international community has not signaled its readiness to force Israel to accommodate to Fayyad's strategy. Israel seems ready to let the West Bank government improve its performance and transportation links inside areas A and B, but will not allow the Palestinian Authority to expand into Area C. Thus, Israel favors a stronger autonomous Palestinian Authority that governs about 40 per cent of the West Bank, but is unwilling to allow a de facto Palestinian state to operate over close to 100 per cent of the area.

3

THE SETTLEMENT—SECURITY SYMBIOSIS

The Development and Cost of the Settlements

In the 1930s, the labor movement, then the leading Zionist ideology of the Yishuv (as the pre-state Jewish community in Palestine called itself), viewed the establishment of Jewish settlements throughout the Land of Israel (as they called Palestine) as an essential preparation for future Jewish sovereignty in the country. The placement of settlements, the movement believed, would determine the borders of the future Jewish state and help defend them once they had been established. The Yishuv's Jewish immigrant society reinvented itself as a native society by cultivating land and defending its settlements.[1] After winning its independence in 1948 and until its victory in the 1967 war, the state of Israel continued to pursue a policy of settlement within its borders, in the framework of an ethnic democracy that privileged Jews over Palestinian citizens. Externally, it sought agreements that would turn the armistice lines with neighboring Arab states to internationally-recognized borders. But, following the war of June 1967, when it occupied the Sinai Peninsula, the Golan Heights, the West Bank, and the Gaza Strip, Israel reverted to its pre-independence settlement strategy. The new territories became frontiers for the establishment of Israeli settlements and army bases as beachheads for an expansion of its borders. The state encouraged Jews to move to these settlements.

The first such settlement was founded quietly in the Golan Heights just a month after the war, in July 1967, with the tacit assistance of government officials and army officers. Its first settlers were young Israelis affiliated with the labor movement. The first West Bank settlement, Kfar Etzion, was established by Orthodox Israelis that September, this time with public fanfare. It was openly backed by the government, led by the Labor party.[2] In the decade that followed, Israel built settlements cautiously and tried to interest Jordan in taking back part of the West Bank, which it had lost in 1967. Alternatively, Israel looked for local leaders who would accept autonomy for the territories under Israeli rule. Labor government peace proposals accorded with the outlines of what came to be known as the Alon Plan. First put forward by Deputy Prime Minister Yigal Alon, it called for Israeli annexation of strategic parts of the West Bank, including the Jordan River Valley, Hebron, the Etzion Block between Jerusalem and Hebron, and East Jerusalem. But settlement was not restricted to these areas. In 1974–75, Israel established Ma'ale Adumim, to Jerusalem's east, now the largest Israeli settlement geographically (covering some 4,800 hectares/11,860 acres) and the third largest in population.

[I]n late 1974 the government decided to build Jerusalem's new industrial zone in Mishor Adummim, as well as a workers camp nearby. A few months later, in 1975, Israel expropriated 3,000 hectares to build Ma'ale Adummim. More land was subsequently expropriated to enable the settlement's expansion, to pave roads, and to develop other public infrastructure in the city. The expropriation procedure used in Ma'ale Adummim is unprecedented in the settlement enterprise. Expropriation of land for settlement purposes is forbidden, not only under international law but also according to the long-standing, official position of Israeli governments. Most settlements were built on area that was declared state land or on land that was requisitioned—ostensibly temporarily—for military purposes. It appears that in Ma'ale Adummim, the government decided to permanently expropriate the land because it viewed the area as an integral part of Jerusalem that would forever remain under Israeli control.[3]

Viewing these regions as essential for Israel's security, history and national interests, the government believed that Jewish settlements were a necessary prerequisite for subsequent annexation, and for suppressing Palestinian aspirations for independence. When Israel failed to find an Arab partner for the Alon peace plan, it began to expand settlements. With the Likud party's accession to power in 1977, it carried Labor's policy much further. Likud governments established settlements in areas of dense Palestinian population that Labor had left alone. In May 1977, when Labor was defeated by the Likud, there were 40,000 Israelis in annexed East Jerusalem and about 11,000 in the rest of the settlements. Thirty years later there were about 500,000 settlers, almost half of them in Arab Jerusalem.[4] By 2009, the Etzion Block settlements, which were established on the grounds that the Jews who had lived there before the 1948 war had a right to return to their land, occupied an area 700 per cent larger than that of the Jewish settlements that had been overrun by Arab forces.[5] Ma'ale Adummim's built-up area covers only 400 hectares only, but it has been granted a jurisdiction twelve times that size, in order to allow its future expansion.[6]

Rather than halting the Israeli settlement enterprise, the 1993 and 1995 Oslo Accords and the 2008 Annapolis peace conference actually intensified it. Israel sought to predetermine the outcome of peace negotiations by establishing as many facts on the ground as it could. The purpose was to impose its positions on the weaker Palestinian side. As of 2006, the biggest settlements were East Jerusalem, where 180,000 Jews live in Jewish neighborhoods;[7] Modi'in Ilit with 38,000 inhabitants; Ma'ale Adumim with 33,000, and Betar Ilit with 32,200.[8] The Israeli Defense Forces' Civil Administration reported in July 2009 that 304,569 settlers lived in the West Bank, excluding East Jerusalem. This constitutes an increase of 2.3 per cent since January 2009. Most of the growth has been in the ultra-Orthodox settlements Modi'in Ilit (a 4.5 per cent increase), and Beitar Illit (3.1 per cent). The average Israeli Jewish population's rate of natural increase in 2008–2009, in contrast, was 1.6 per cent, one-third of population growth in the settlements.[9] An International Crisis Group report suggests that the religious communities are today the spearheads of the settlement enterprise. Ultra-orthodox and national religious settlers account entirely for the 37 per cent increase in the settlement population between the years 2003–2009.[10]

Although the Israeli authorities have never published comprehensive reports on their budget investments in settlements, the available evidence is sufficient to prove that, over the years, the settlements became the country's largest collective endeavor.[11] By 2004, Meron Benvenisti has estimated, Israeli governments had spent a total of $40 billion on this project,[12] while Macro Center for Economics estimated in 2010 that private homes in the settlements excluding Jerusalem are worth a total of $9 billion, apartments are worth $4.5 billion, roads are worth $1.7 billion, and public institutions, synagogues and bathhouses combined are worth $0.5 billion. According to the study, Israeli settlements are home to 868 publicly owned facilities occupying 488,769 square meters. As for residential units, the total number of apartments stands at 32,711 spread over a space of around 3.27 million square meters, as well as 22,997 private homes over 5.74 million square meters.[13]

The Israeli European Network report of 2009 estimates that in forty years of settlement expansion some $18 billion has been spent just on the construction of buildings in the West Bank. According to this study, municipalities in Israel proper received, in the years 2002–2008, an average of 34.7 per cent of their funding from the government, with the remaining 64.3 per cent coming from their own revenue sources. However, settlement municipalities obtain 57 per cent of their funds from the government and only 42.8 per cent from their own sources. In this context, it is important to note that the average income of settler families is 10 per cent higher than the Israeli average, and this despite the fact that a third of settlers are ultra-Orthodox, the poorest Israeli Jewish sector.[14]

The data on employment in Israel's Gaza Strip settlements in the summer of 2005, on the eve of their evacuation, illustrates another aspect of the Israeli government's involvement in the settlement enterprise. A full 65 per cent of the settlements' labor force of 2,300 worked in the public sector, as employees of the Gaza Coast Regional Council or of the Ministry of Defense's Civil Administration. In Israel proper, inside the Green Line, only 30 per cent of the labor force works in the public sector. Furthermore, the state paid its settler employees in Gaza Strip 25–60 per cent more than comparable civil servants inside the Green Line. In addition, the state subsidized Gaza Strip settlers' expenses. For example, a year's preschool tuition in these settlements cost on average 30 per cent less than inside the Green Line; settlers in Gaza Strip paid 30 per cent less local taxes than did Israelis living within the jurisdiction of the adjacent Ashkelon Coast Council, within the Green Line. The Gaza Coast Council received annually from the Interior Ministry an additional budget of NIS 2,356 per capita, whereas the poorest city in Israel, Bnei Brak, received only NIS 187 per capita, a twentieth of Gaza Strip settlements. The state also subsidized public transportation, afternoon classes in community centers, and the cost of water.[15] With their evacuation, the Gaza Strip settlers faced financial crisis in addition to other material and psychological problems.

Another way of looking at this is that 4.1 per cent of Israeli government allocations to municipalities go to settlements, even though they are home to just 3.1 per cent of the total Israeli population.[16] According to the Adva Center, in 2006 settlements received governmental grants of $248 per capita, as compared to $83 per person inside Israel; the government funded 53 per cent of construction starts in the settlements, as compared to 20 per cent inside Israel. This has been done by placing settlements in the highest-priority category for development grants, mortgage aid, tax rebates, and subsidized land sales. According to Peace Now, in the government's two-year 2009–10 budget, nearly NIS 1 billion ($278 million) are explicitly allocated to settlements on dedicated budget lines. This amounts to 8.9 per cent of transfers from the central government to localities.[17] On 25 July 2009 the government of Israel decided to allocate in the following year's budget, through Settlement Department of the World Zionist Organization, another NIS 25 million shekels ($7 million, 34 per cent of that department's total budget for the year) for West Bank settlements.[18] To supplement state funding, settlers have established their own fundraising organizations, many of which operate as charities that benefit from tax break abroad. The ICG reports, for example, that in 2008–2009, U.S. citizens donated $500,000 to buy land for outposts, and approximately $1.5 million per year to support the Jewish settlement inside Hebron.[19]

Israel uses four legal and bureaucratic mechanisms to seize lands for settlements: expropriation for public needs; forced requisition for military use; declaring as 'state land' properties not fully registered as privately-owned (including property for which the process of such registration had nearly been completed); and declaring any land belonging to a person who was not in the West Bank or Gaza Strip on 7 June 1967 (the day Israel occupied these areas) as abandoned property. The last two categories were placed in the hands of a the Custodian for State and Abandoned Property in the Ministry of Defense.

The custodian enjoys broad authority. If he determines that a parcel of land is state property, that classification holds unless proven otherwise. Moreover, Section 5 of the Order Regarding Government Property (No. 59) includes the following provision:

[N]o transaction undertaken in good faith by the Custodian and another person in any property which the Custodian believed at the time of the transaction to be government property shall be nullified and it shall continue to be valid even if it is proved that the property was not at that time government property.[20]

For legal reasons, Israel must present the settlements as part of its defense strategy. International law allows an occupier to expropriate land only temporarily, and for security needs (principally to guarantee the security of the inhabitants of the occupied territory). Compensation must be paid to the owners. Once specific security needs have passed, the land must be returned to its owners. Israel has used this provision to implement its expansion plans, seizing land on the grounds that it was needed for military installations and then using it to establish new settlements or expand existing ones. Between 1967 and 1979, Israel confiscated some 50,000 dunams (19 sq. miles) of private land. It also assumed control of another 700,000 dunams (270 square miles) that had been registered as belonging to the Jordanian government, even though much of it was de facto, if not de jure, in private hands. Between 1980 and 1984 Israel designated another 800,000 dunams (200,000 acres) of property with unclear status as state land. All together, this opened about 25 per cent of the West Bank's territory for

Israeli settlement, and in fact most of the settlements were established on these lands. There is no comprehensive data on all the settlements—that is, how much of the land belonging to each settlement was acquired in each of the four ways. In some cases, as in parts of Jerusalem, settlements were built entirely on land confiscated from private owners. In others they are entirely on land seized for military needs, as in the cases of Beit El, Kiryat Arba, Elon Moreh. Other settlements, like Ofra and Shiloh, stand on a patchwork of state land, confiscated private land, and land seized for military needs.[21] By 2005, more than 40 per cent of the West Bank's territory lay within the bounds of Israeli settlements, although less than 3 per cent of the West Bank is built up.[22]

This proliferation of settlements led to Palestinian concern and unrest. The First Intifada, which broke out at the end of 1987, forced Israel to ratchet up its military presence in the West Bank and Gaza Strip and use IDF troops to police the territories. During the Second Intifada, which began in 2000, Israel used settlements as bases for military operations, further tightening collaboration between them and the army.

Settlement Expansion After 2000

In 1992, on the eve of the signing of the first Oslo Agreement, there were 222,000 Israeli settlers in the West Bank (including East Jerusalem) and the Gaza Strip, according to Colonel (ret.) Shaul Arieli. As an IDF officer, Arieli coordinated the implementation of the Oslo agreements, and later headed the Peace Administration in the Office of the Prime Minister. During the nine years that followed, he reports, another 145,000 Israelis took up residence in the settlements. Then, between the years 2001–2009, a further 122,000 Israelis moved into the territories. Thus, under the aegis of the peace process, the number of settlers increased dramatically from 222,000 to 489,000.[23] Basing itself on official Israeli data, the Foundation for Middle East Peace has found that from the establishment of the Barrier in 2003 to 2007, the number of settlers to its east—that is, on its 'Palestinian' side—grew from 53,823 to 66,749 in 2007.[24] If Israeli governments since the Oslo 1993 agreement had not let settlers reside to the east of the Barrier, only 20,000 would now live there. Instead, now, at the beginning of 2010, they number 80,000.[25]

One particular subcategory of settlement has accounted in recent years for much of the geographical expansion of the settlement enterprise. These are the 'outposts,' wildcat settlements set up, often on privately-owned Palestinian land, by young people—many of them second or third-generation settlers. Nearly all of them lie to the east of the Separation Barrier. Illegal even under Israel's loose interpretation of occupation law, they have nevertheless been tolerated and, in some cases legalized ex post facto, by the government. Data collected by Peace Now shows that outpost construction was 250 per cent higher in 2008 than in 2007.[26] This trend continued during the first half of 2009. Construction of 596 new structures in the West Bank began during the first half of 2009, of which ninety-six of these were in outposts. All told, 35 per cent of the structures under construction during this period throughout the whole West Bank were located to the east of the Barrier.[27] Settlements building on that side of the Barrier did not stop when Netanyahu government decided on late 2009 to freeze settlement building for ten months in order to encourage Abbas to return to the negotiation table. Under pressure from the settlers, however, the government granted numerous exceptions to the freeze, and 20 per cent of the these, allowing the construction of homes and other structures to continue, are in settlements located to the east of the Barrier.[28]

Outposts have an importance beyond their small populations. They are situated at strategic points. Some lie on the
margins of Palestinian cities and towns, with the express inten-
tion of constraining Palestinian urban expansion. Others aim
to fill in territorial gaps between settlements, or to control
roads connecting settlements in the West Bank highlands to
those in the Jordan Valley. In other words, they fragment the
Palestinian population and serve, deliberately, as obstacles to
the establishment of a viable Palestinian state.

During the year of the Annapolis talks, 2007–8, Israel continued to expand its settlements in the West Bank, with the
same result. Housing starts in the settlements in the first half of
2008 increased by 1.8 per cent compared to the same period in
2007.[29] During that entire year, 1,518 new structures, including trailers, were built or installed in settlements and outposts,
as compared to 898 in 2007. In 2008 there was also an eightfold increase over 2007 in home construction tenders. By the
end of its term, the Olmert government had overseen the construction of about 7,000 new homes in the West Bank. In his
last week in office, his cabinet expropriated 423 acres adjoin-
ing the settlement of Efrat, in the Etzion Block, for the construction of 2,500 housing units.[30]

According to official data provided to Peace Now by the
Israeli Civil Administration in 2007, a total of 131 settlements
are completely or partially situated on private Palestinian land,
and over 32 per cent of the land falling within the jurisdictions
of the settlements is such private land.[31] Other Peace Now
reports address the size of the settlement project. One published
in July 2007 reveals that 90 per cent of all settlements exceed
their legal boundaries; almost one-third of the total area of settlements lies outside their official jurisdiction. A full 75 per cent
of this annexed land is located to the east of the Separation
Barrier—that is, on the side that, according to those who view

the Barrier as a border-in-the-making between Israel and Palestine, will become the state of Palestine. A second report, issued in the summer of 2008, found that approximately 55 per cent of the structures built in settlements during the first half of 2008 were located to the east of the Barrier.[32] Finally, a Peace Now report of June 2009 found that the built-up area of the settlements on the 'Israeli' side of the Barrier is approximately 7,300 acres, but the total area of that part of the West Bank land that the Barrier de facto annexes to Israel is approximately 148,000 acres, or around twenty times the size of the built-up area of those settlements.[33] In other words, Israel has created facts on the ground by expanding settlements, taking control of as much land as it can to the east of the Barrier,[34] and by changing the demography of that part of the West Bank that lies on the western, Israeli, side of the Barrier.

The policy of settlement expansion is completed by the demolition of Palestinian structures. Concurrent with the construction of settlements, Israel has severely restricted Palestinian construction, planning, and development in Area C, in order to preserve maximum land for settlement expansion. According to a report by the UN's Office for the Coordination of Humanitarian Affairs (OCHA), in 70 per cent of Area C (that is, 44 per cent of the total area of the West Bank), Palestinian building is entirely forbidden, as this land is earmarked for the settlements, the army, nature reserves or is included in the buffer zone on either side of the separation fence. In the remaining 30 per cent, construction is theoretically possible, but getting a permit is so difficult as to render it practically impossible.[35] Effectively, then, Palestinians can build freely on only 1 per cent of Area C, land which is already nearly totally built up.[36] As Robert Fisk reported in *The Independent*:

Even the western NGOs working in Area C find their work for Palestinians blocked by the Israelis... Oxfam, for example, asked the Israelis for a permit to build a 300m2 capacity below-ground reservoir along with 700m of underground 4in pipes for the thousands of Palestinians living around Jiftlik [a village in the Jordan Valley with about 5000 residents—MK]. It was refused. They then gave notice that they intended to construct an above-ground installation of two glass-fibre tanks, an above-ground pipe and booster pump. They were told they would need a permit even though the pipes were above ground—and they were refused a permit.[37]

In 1972, Israel approved 97 per cent of Palestinian building applications in this area, but only 5 per cent between 2000 and 2007. Only fifteen villages out of 149 in Area C enjoy approved master plans.[38] Without approved master plans for Palestinian localities in the West Bank, their residents cannot obtain building permits. The Palestinians thus have no choice but to build without permits; Israel in turn condemns new structures and additions to existing ones as illegal and issues demolition orders against them. According to the OCHA, Israel has, since 2000, torn down hundreds of structures in Area C, the territory available for the natural expansion of densely-populated Palestinian towns and cities in Areas A and B. In 2009, Israel demolished 180 structures, with particular attention to those in or adjacent to the E1 zone, which Israel has designated for the expansion of Ma'aleh Adumim so that it can be linked to Jerusalem.[39]

Jerusalem in Focus

Since 2000, and especially since the Annapolis Conference in late 2007, Israel has been busy augmenting the Jewish presence in East Jerusalem. Expansion of Jewish settlement stifles Palestinian urban growth and makes the prospect of an Israeli–Palestinian accord on Jerusalem even more difficult.[40] Israeli government agencies, the Jerusalem municipality, and civil society organizations have worked to achieve five goals. First,

Israel expands its settlements—the Jewish neighborhoods built after 1967 in East Jerusalem—in order to link them up and create a continuous block of Jewish habitation. The strategic aim is to divide the Palestinian city to several enclaves.

Ir Amim, an Israeli NGO that tracks Israeli operations in East Jerusalem, reports that between 2003 and the end of 2008, Israel issued tenders for 2,768 housing units in the part of the city annexed in 1967. Of these, 1,931 were issued in 2008 (the publication of a tender for construction on state land and/or at the initiative of the government is a critical step on the way to implementing a construction plan). Once these units are completed, about 6,750 Israeli Jews will move into the area. Most of the tenders seek to 'fill in the blanks' between Jewish neighborhoods and to separate Palestinian neighborhoods.[41] That same year, Israel filed for public review plans for the construction of 5,431 residential units in East Jerusalem. (A building plan must be filed for public review; the local planning commission then considers the plan and any objections that are filed. If approved, the municipality may then issue a building permit.) Similarly, final approval was granted for two plans for the construction of approximately 2,730 residential units. In late December 2009, the Ministry of Construction and Housing published tenders for 692 units in Neve Ya'akov, Pisgat Ze'ev, and Har Homa, three large Jewish settlements in East Jerusalem, the first two in the city's north and the latter to the southeast.[42] These construction plans also target open spaces between Israeli and Palestinian built-up areas. It is worth noting that, since 1967, the Israeli government has built about 50,000 residential units in East Jerusalem for its citizens, but fewer than 600 for the city's Palestinian residents, the last of which was built over thirty years ago.

Second, Israeli settlers have moved into Palestinian neighborhoods with the express purpose of preventing the ethno-national division of the city according to President Clinton's parameter of 'Arab areas are Palestinian and Jewish ones are Israeli.'[43] These Jewish enclaves also divide the Palestinian population geographically, making it easier to control. The tactic is reminiscent of the placement of outposts next to centers of Palestinian population in the West Bank. In August 2009, the Jerusalem municipality approved a plan to build a settlement compound called Ma'ale David, consisting of 104 residential units, a sports and recreation facility, a school, and a synagogue in Ras al-Amud, a densely-populated Palestinian neighborhood just to the east of the Old City.[44] The Ma'ale David project includes a bridge to the already existing Jewish enclave of Ma'ale Zeitim on the Mount of Olives.

Ateret Cohanim, a Jerusalem settler organization, published in September 2009 a brochure offering for sale to Jewish families six properties in the Arab quarters of the Old City, with a collective market price of over $7.5 million. According to the brochure, when occupied, the number of Jews living in the Old City's Palestinian neighborhoods will reach 1,000. The brochure also refers to the construction of 300 residential units in Kidmat Zion, a settlement next to the Palestinian Abu Dis neighborhood in East Jerusalem. 'The heart of Jerusalem is calling us....' the brochure states. 'At a time when the United Nations and countries around the world plot to forcibly take away Jerusalem and the holy places from Jewish hands, a steady and strong Jewish presence inside the Old City has become crucial to our ability as a nation to maintain and control this spiritual center.'[45] Ateret Cohanim has already given these properties Hebrew names. Its explicit goal is to prevent partition of Jerusalem or any acknowledgement of East Jerusalem's Palestinian identity.

Purchases of Palestinian buildings for the purpose of settling Jews in them are funded by settlers associations such as Elad and Ateret Cohanim. American Friends of Ateret Cohanim, founded in New York in 1987, is registered in the United States as an organization that funds educational institutes in Israel. It sends millions of American dollars every year to 'redeem land' in East Jerusalem. In 2007 it transferred to Ateret Cohanim in Jerusalem $1.6 million.[46]

In compensation for the massive plans for the expansion of Jewish neighborhoods, the city's master plan offers the construction of a mere 13,000 residential units for Palestinians. Jerusalem municipal planners have labored on this project for over a decade, with the goal of guiding the city's development for the next twenty years. Yet Jerusalem's mayor, Nir Barkat, withdrew the master plan under pressure from right-wing politicians and settlers, who charged that it authorizes far too much construction for Palestinians. They enjoyed the support of Interior Minister Eli Yishai, whose ministry must sign off on master plans. Yishai instructed the Jerusalem district supervisor to block its approval.[47]

Third, Israel intends to add, de facto, further territories to Israeli–ruled East Jerusalem. These are areas that lie between the official city line and that on which the Barrier runs or is planned to run. This is no small amount of land. The territory that Israel annexed in 1967 amounted to about 1 per cent of the West Bank's territory; these additional areas comprise another 3 per cent. It includes the aforementioned E1 zone between Jerusalem and Ma'aleh Adumim, which would create a belt of contiguous Jewish settlement stretching from Jerusalem down to the approaches to Jericho. Infrastructure plans for major parts of the project were completed in 2008, including the expropriation of Palestinian land and the evacuation of hundreds of Bedouin living in the area. The small settlement of Kedar was absorbed by the Ma'ale Adumim municipality, and orders were issued to pave a bypass road for Palestinians, to run to the east of the planed settlement block. The road would separate Israeli and Palestinian traffic, reserving the existing artery for exclusive Israeli use. An eastern bypass road is meant to connect the Palestinian cities located to the north and south of this settlement block. Another road, divided in the middle by high wall, will channel Israeli vehicles into Jerusalem and keep the Palestinian traffic away from the city.[48]

The symbiosis of state and settlers can also be seen in the construction of the headquarters for the Israeli police district responsible for the West Bank (the 'Shai' district) in the E1 area. According to *Yedioth Aharonoth*:

only a small portion of the funding originates from the state. The bulk of the money comes from private organizations with a clear right wing orientation: the Bukhara Community Trust, and the Shalem Foundation—a subsidiary formed by the Jerusalem-based Elad NGO. The funding of the construction by the Bukhara Community Trust was undertaken in broad daylight, as part of an agreement which included the removal of the old Samaria and Judea District Police headquarters in the Ras el-Amud neighborhood in East Jerusalem and handing it over to the Bukharan community, which owned the area prior to 1948. In exchange for the return of the property, the trust financed part of the construction of the new headquarters... The old headquarters in Ras el-Amud in the pre-1948 building was Bukharan property, and after the war remained in Jordanian hands. Events proceeded as follows, according to the response of the Internal Security Ministry as conveyed to *Yedioth Ahronoth*: 'With the renewed seizure of the area by Israel, the state was registered as the owner of the property. The Bukhara Community Trust filed a lawsuit over the confiscation, and a court ruling instructed the state to compensate the trust for the land. However the payment failed to materialize.... Seeing that according to the law, the trust may purchase the land by means of return of ownership, and that the trust sought to do this, an agreement was signed between the Israel Lands Administration and the trust, in which the administration acquiesced to the trust's request to obtain the land in exchange for the trust's agreement to provide alternative construction for the state. In other words, the trust would undertake construction for the police in exchange for the buildings in Ras el-Amud.

In the course of the hearing before the High Court of Justice, the state argued that no funding from any additional private sources had been received, and that the Bukhara Community Trust had alone born the cost. However a more detailed examination reveals that a private company called the Shalem Foundation has funded the construction of the headquarters as well as its surrounding infrastructure, at the cost of millions of shekels....The Shalem Foundation is a subsidiary of Elad—which is considered one of the most powerful and rich right wing NGOs operating today, known for its vigorous activity in the Old City and East Jerusalem. Among others, Elad and the Bukhara Community Trust are involved in operations to strengthen the Jewish enclaves around Mount Olives, one of Jerusalem's most contested areas.[49]

Fourth, Israel wants to divide al-Haram al-Sharif (the Muslim name for the holy site that the Jews call the Temple Mount) from Palestinian residential areas. It works to impose the Jewish historical and religious narrative on the Old City and its surrounding sites (the area referred to as the Holy Basin) and to link their compounds inside Silwan, a Palestinian neighborhood adjacent to the Old City's southern wall, to the Old City's Jewish Quarter. Israel works to achieve these goals by controlling the area beneath the terrain through archeological excavations and on the ground through the establishment of Jewish–Israeli national parks around the city, construction for Jews, the demolition of Palestinian houses, and settler infiltration.

Events in Silwan expose the profound symbiosis between official Israeli government bodies and organs of the ideological right. For example, all the 'State Land in Wadi Hilweh/City of David has been handed over without tender to the organization known as Elad. The control in the national park in Silwan has been handed over to Elad and the entrance fee to the park is paid to Elad. According to the settlers' own reports, about 40,000 IDF soldiers visit the area every year as part of tours led by the settler organizations. All the archeological excavations on the site are carried out under the sponsorship of Elad or in close cooperation with it. ...

In 2008 the excavation/exposure was begun of a tunnel that is designed to lead from the Silwan Pool to the Old City, whose opening is to emerge near the walls of the Temple Mount.... Security control of Silwan, as in the rest of the historical basin, is partly in the hands of private security firms that are in close contact with settlers' organizations. They are financed to the tune of over NIS 40 million annually by taxpayer money.[50]

Special attention should be given to the mix of archeology and political goals in Silwan, argues Dr. Raphael Greenberg, an Israeli archeologist from Tel Aviv University who participated in the past in excavations conducted in the area. Since Silwan lies on top of the biblical city of Jerusalem, the City of David, it is an archaeological site of huge historical, religious, and scholarly importance. However, Greenberg maintains, the proper balance between the archaeological and the political has been disrupted:

[M]ost of the archaeological research in Jerusalem is being driven by pressures from politically interested groups and individuals with the aim of 'proving' our historical rights in the city or clearing an area for construction. The outcome is 'fast archaeology' that satisfies the consumer's hunger but damages archaeological assets under Israel's responsibility.... [T]he most advanced archaeology is also transparent and open to criticism, undertaken in an atmosphere of openness. And here and now, in the Israel of 2009, the opposite is the case.

Much of the archaeology in the center of Jerusalem's 'holy basin' is fast archaeology, swallowing up more than it is capable of digesting. It is no coincidence that the top archaeologists from this country's leading institutes are refraining from taking part in excavations in Jerusalem. I would not send my students to apprentice there. This archaeology is being carried out under time pressure and is subordinate to the desires of landlords who are not scholars; usually these are religious, ideological or tourist organizations, or contractors.

Greenberg concludes that a shallow and brutal archeology is developing in Jerusalem.[51] A Hebrew University professor, Yoram Tsafrir, one of Israel's leading archeologists, publicly condemned the Israeli Antiquities Authority's plan to construct a building over a site near the Western Wall, where a well-preserved Roman road was excavated. The Western Wall Heritage Foundation, which is involved in physical preservation and development of the area, plans a three-story museum with public services. Tsafrir charged that 'Even the most amazing architect will not be able to avoid damaging the find.'[52]

The deep symbiosis between Israeli government agencies and the settlers' organizations extends all over the holy basin, where the conflicting religious narratives of Judaism, Islam and Christianity meet the contending Israeli and Palestinian national narratives. Israel has established nine national parks in the basin, some of which have been fenced in. Ir Amim notes that 'there is a high degree of dovetailing between the various plans and their borders on the one hand and the existing and planned settlements of the right–wing settlers.'[53] According to this organization, the parks bear a significance that goes beyond the fact that they claim pieces of East Jerusalem as Israeli territory. They also impose the official Israeli and Jewish narrative on the Old City and its environs.[54] Israeli motives are evident in the Jerusalem municipal budget for 2010. '[The] tourism budget will increase by 266 per cent in 2010. The municipality increased the budget from 3 million NIS in 2009 to 8 million NIS in 2010. In addition, the municipality raised from the government for the tourism budget an additional 10 million NIS. The overall budget will be about 18 million NIS.'[55] Since tourist services, sites and infrastructure are well-developed in West Jerusalem, it is reasonable to presume that these new funds will be invested in East Jerusalem. Only the grand plan for a ring of national archeological parks, as well as for biking and hiking trails to the east and southeast of the Old City, can justify such a dramatic increase in the tourism budget.

Fifthly, Jewish national–religious groups have pressed to change the status quo at al-Haram al-Sharif/the Temple Mount. They want to force the Islamic Waqf to allow Jews to visit the site freely, and to allow them to pray on the Temple Mount compound. Leading national religious rabbis have called on their followers to ascend to the Temple Mount in order to demonstrate that the site belongs to the Jewish people and to Israel.[56] This call came in parallel to an educational campaign in which national religious institutions sought to enhance the status of the Temple Mount in the minds of their community's members. The campaign includes a monthly procession around Temple Mount's gates and the preparation of sacred items to be used in a rebuilt Jewish Temple.

These five goals have served as a pretexts for demolishing Palestinian homes and for blocking construction plans initiated by Palestinians. Between 2001 and the end of 2008, Israel demolished 556 houses in East Jerusalem, compared to 206 in the years 1992–2000.In the past, Israel's building code was enforced randomly and arbitrary, but since 2007 it has been coordinated with plans for establishing Israeli settlements on the east side of the city.[57] For example, by the end of 2008, some 400 settlers had moved into houses in Silwan, which has a Palestinian population of about 1,600. The houses were purchased by Elad, the settler organization that also manages the archaeological excavations and national archaeological park in the neighborhood, or were expropriated by the state and handed over to the settlers. The state and the settlers call the neighborhood by the biblical name of the City of David, since it lies over the remains of original site of the biblical Jerusalem.[58] To promote the settlement plan, the Jerusalem Municipality plans to demolish approximately eighty-eight Palestinian homes built there without permits. When, in January 2010, the Supreme Court, attorney general, and state prosecutor forced Mayor Barkat to evict the Jewish squatters in an eight-story building built five years earlier without permit in Silwan (where, according to zoning regulations, no more than four stories are allowed), the mayor wrote to the state prosecutor that the municipality would also tear down 200 hundred Palestinian homes slated to demolition. The responsibility for the expected violent response of the Palestinians would be laid at the feet of the officials who ordered the enforcement of the evacuation order in Silwan, he threatened.[59]

It should be noted that the settlers' association operating in East Jerusalem enjoys powerful backing in the municipality and the cabinet. Mayor Barkat delayed the implementation of the legal system's ruling on the eviction of the settlers in this illegal structure in Silwan; and then sought retroactive legal approval for the four excess floors in exchange for legalizing Palestinian construction built without permits. He launched a public relations offensive against the municipal legal counsel, state prosecutor, and the attorney general, the three officials who insisted on the rule of law. When Barkat was unable to help the settlers, Interior Minister Eli Yishai stepped in. He sought to use his powers to thwart the court order by instructing the ministry's District Planning Commission to license the building.[60]

Because of East Jerusalem's sensitivity, it was decided that municipal operations there, and in the Holy basin in particular, would be directed by the national government. This includes law enforcement. Uri Ariel, a member of the Knesset for the extreme national religious National Front party, in December 2009 informed the Knesset Law Committee that the prime minister had issued a directive that all prospective demolitions in East Jerusalem were to be brought to his attention. The commander of the Jerusalem police district, who is directly responsible for carrying out all demolition orders in the city, is to inform the national police chief, who in turn is to inform the prime minister's military attaché.[61] In response to a settler petition to the Supreme Court, seeking an order to enforce municipal law on Palestinian construction in the Muslim Cemetery adjacent to the Temple Mount, the municipality claimed that it lacked the authority to do so. Any such decision, it said, must be made by the leaders of the national government.[62] It should be noted that, in September 1996, Israeli and Palestinian forces clashed over Israel's decision to open to the public the tunnels at the Western Wall, which run adjacent to al-Haram al-Sharif/the Temple Mount. Four days of hostilities left sixteen Israeli soldiers and seventy-four Palestinians dead, and fifty-eight Israelis and over 1000 Palestinians wounded. Four years later, the Second Intifada (called the al-Aqsa Intifada by the Palestinians) erupted following a much-trumpeted visit by Ariel Sharon, then an opposition parliamentarian for the Likud party, to the Temple Mount.[63] Since then, Israel's decisions regarding policy in East Jerusalem are made by the prime minister and his inner cabinet for Jerusalem affairs.

Israel's policy in Jerusalem has long concerned the European Union. In November 2009 Sweden, which then held the chairmanship of the EU Council of Foreign Ministers, drafted a document calling for the division of Jerusalem between Israel and a future Palestinian state. The paper implied that the EU would recognize the 1967 borders as the borders of the future state of Palestine. These statements were toned down in the final decision made by the Council. Their adopted text expresses a readiness, 'when appropriate, to recognize a Palestinian state,' and calls 'to resolve the status of Jerusalem as the future capital of two states.' The Council 'will continue the work undertaken on EU contribution to state-building, regional issues, refugees, security, and Jerusalem.' However, the EU foreign ministers endorsed the rest of the Swedish draft. Their document rejects Israeli policy of annexing East Jerusalem and dividing it from the West Bank:

The European Union will not recognize any changes in the pre-1967 borders including with regard to Jerusalem, other then those agreed by the parties.... The Council of the European Union is seriously concerned about the lack of progress in the Middle East peace process. The Council is deeply concerned about the situation in East Jerusalem.... The Council of the European Union is seriously concerned about the lack of progress in the Middle East peace process.... The Council recalls that it has never recognized the annexation of East Jerusalem.... The Council calls for the reopening of Palestinian institutions in Jerusalem in accordance with the Road Map. It also calls on the Israeli government to cease all discriminatory treatment of Palestinians in East Jerusalem.[64]

Institutional Collaboration

With the exception of East Jerusalem, which Israel annexed, the occupied territories were administered by the military. The IDF became the dominant force in the day-to-day life of their Palestinian inhabitants. As Israel became more ensconced in the territories and broadened its settlement project, the links between the settlements, the army, and the state bureaucracy grew tighter, to the point that it is difficult to make out where one ends and the other begins. The outcome was a military-settlement-bureaucracy complex that stifles the Palestinians inhabitants of the territories.

Oded Haklai argues that the settler movement has managed to penetrate all levels of the state apparatus and forge alliances to gain supporters in influential positions. Consequently, the state has ceased to function as a coherent, unitary institution. Some state agencies have acted in ways inconsistent with official government policies, working to facilitate unauthorized settlement growth. Settlement expansion has been achieved on two interrelated tracks, the first of which works through the legal system and the bureaucracy, and the second of which is illegal and circumvents the bureaucracy. The latter has opened new frontier areas for settlement. Setting up frontier settlements requires different methods than do settlements in established areas. These outposts, illegal even under Israeli law, have been founded since the 1990s by methods similar to those used to settlements that Israel built earlier in what were then frontier zones: Kfar Etzion in 1968, Hebron in 1969, and Ofra and Kedumim in 1976–77.[65] State agencies have overseen the establishment of both authorized and unauthorized settlements.

Many state and non-state Jewish agencies are involved in the settlement project. This includes the Settlement Division of the World Zionist Organization and the Jewish Agency, Israeli government ministries, and the local governments of already established settlements. Each of these provides ongoing material or political support. Sometimes state agencies act with the tacit support but without the explicit sanction of the highest political authorities. The Ministry of Construction and Housing and the Ministry of Defense bear most of the responsibility for developing settlements.[66] The army grants permits for transporting trailers and prefab houses to settlement points and deploys troops to protect settlements. According to international law, the army has the obligation to enforce law and order. Yet the army protects unauthorized settlements, which are illegal even under Israeli law, alongside settlements that, even if the rest of the world sees as illegal, are seen as legal by the Israeli government. In some cases, the military has actively facilitated the construction of unauthorized settlements by providing generators, bulldozing access roads, and supplying building equipment and materials.

According to *Ha'aretz*'s military correspondent, Amos Harel:

Behind every settlement action there is a planning and thinking mind that has access to the state's database and maps, and help from sympathetic officers serving in key positions in the IDF and the Civil Administration. The story is not in the settlers' uncontrolled behavior, though there is evidence of this on some of the hilltops, but rather in conscious choices by the state to enforce very little of the law. Most of the outposts were established during two periods: 1997 to 1999, whose climax came when foreign minister Ariel Sharon, upon his return from the Wye summit, called on the settlers to take over the hilltops; and later, between 2001 and 2003. Those were the terrible years of Palestinian shooting attacks on the roads of the West Bank and murderous infiltrations of settlements to perpetrate acts of slaughter. During those years, the area of the settlements themselves increased....

The settlers' moves were supported by surveillance cameras, protected roads, guards and often by declarations of a 'special security zone.' To prevent infiltration, the area of the settlements was expanded and Palestinians from neighboring villages were prevented from approaching them. However, in the same breath, the moves were exploited for long-term goals, taking over and building on lands that were in large part private.

For nearly twelve years now, I have been intermittently covering the outposts, as part of my coverage of the army. Officially, the IDF doesn't see the connection between the defense establishment and the settlers. Construction in the territories is ostensibly a matter for settlement reporters and nosy activists from Peace Now. In fact, this connection is at the heart of the settlement project. In March 1998, during a tour, I was told by the commander of the Samaria Area Brigade, in an afterthought, that although the Gidonim outposts near Itamar were established without a permit, the Defense Ministry was acting to 'launder' them. On that same day, Eli Cohen, the defense minister's settlement adviser, was also touring the area. Queries put to the ministry by Knesset members were answered with evasive comments, but very quickly all the outposts in the vicinity were connected to all the necessary infrastructures.

Five years later, at the height of the Sharon prime ministership, a senior officer who had recently been demobilized after service in the territories volunteered to explain the facts of life to my colleague Guy Kotev and me. With the patience usually reserved for children who have difficulty understanding, he asked us whether we really believed that the outposts go up without the authorities' knowledge. He related that the director general of the settler organization Amana, Zeev Hever (known by his nickname, Zambish), was visiting the prime minister's residence at night to go over the maps with Sharon. 'And after that you expect that we won't give them guards and we won't hook them up to the water system?' he wondered.[67]

The army is interlinked with the Civil Administration in the Ministry of Defense. The Civil Administration is in charge of civil affairs such as administering state land and development planning; supervising illegal construction and approving the connection of buildings to electricity and water. The head of the Civil Administration is an IDF major general and he, together with the Minister of Defense's assistant for settlements, cooperates with the Ministry of Construction and Housing. In 2004, Prime Minister Sharon appointed a Justice Ministry official, Talia Sasson, to study how such illegal and unauthorized activities took place. She found that the housing ministry had spent at least $16 million (NIS 72,000,000) on illegal settlements from 2000 to 2004. The ministry funded the purchase of mobile homes, helped pave roads, linked settlements to the water and electricity grids, and constructed public buildings and other permanent structures. The Ministry of Housing and Construction funded construction contracts concluded by the local governments of existing settlements. These ministries operated, according to Sasson report, in violation of proper procedures.[68] Sassoon's report documented, in short, systematic abuse and illegality in the construction of outposts, including extensive illegal collusion between settlers and supportive Israeli public servants. Sharon also asked Brigadier

General [ret.] Baruch Spiegel to assemble a data base on settler actions. Sasson's report was shelved, as was Spiegel's comprehensive database on the illegal settlements.[69]

Illegality does not stop at the construction of settlements. The Ministry of Defense failed to implement Supreme Court orders to demolish nine houses in the Ofra settlement that were built on private Palestinian land. 'Illegality is being ignored. Ofra isn't the first instance. There are so many cases up in the air. The impression is that you changed your position about your willingness to demolish,' said Supreme Court President Dorit Beinisch to the state's attorneys.[70]

The Social Profile

The social profile of the settler population explains much about the connection between their faith-inspired motivation, the structure of their community identity, and their geo-political location. The 2008 socio-religious profile of the settlers shows that, out of a total of 289,600 settlers excluding East Jerusalem, 87,495 (31 per cent) live in ultra-Orthodox settlements; 62,769 (22 per cent) live in national-religious settlements, and 44,309 (15 per cent) live in secular settlements. The remainder, 92,156 (32 per cent), live in heterogeneous settlements where there is a variety of religious observance. The Barrier also separates two telling profiles. Of the 67,000 settlers who live east of the barrier, 54 per cent live in national religious settlements, 19 per cent in secular ones, 9 per cent in ultra-Orthodox settlements, and 19 per cent in heterogeneous settlements. Of the 220,000 settlers west of the barrier, 37 per cent live in ultra-Orthodox settlements, 36 per cent in heterogeneous settlements, 14 per cent in secular settlements and 13 per cent in national-religious settlements.[71] In other words, more than half of the settlers who live to the east of the Barrier are national religious Jews who subscribe to an ideology of expanding Israel's border beyond the Barrier line.

Moreover, motivated by their concept of not giving up even an inch of the Holy Land, national religious Jews move into settlements and houses that secular Jews have abandoned in the Jordan Valley and in the northern and central West Bank. Finally, they turn out in large numbers for political action—the demonstrators at rallies against the evacuation of the Gaza Strip settlements were composed almost exclusively of national religious Jews.[72]

In the first decade of the twenty-first century, the national religious community underwent an ideological and generational shift. The young generation that grew up during the Second Intifada and under the trauma of the evacuation of the Gaza Strip settlements in 2005 adopted a radical anti–establishment and sometimes an anti–state, mind-set. The founders of the first wave of settlements believed that the state of Israel was an instrument of God and part of the messianic mission. The younger generation rejects this theology. In lifestyle, dress code, communal life and the kind of education they give to their children, they have adopted many ultra-Orthodox norms. Some of them avoid military service, seek to establish a halachic state, and give preference to Jewish Law and the instructions of their charismatic rabbis over the laws, courts, and democratic institutions of the Israeli state. In late 2009, a group of rabbis who teach at *hesder* yeshivot (where young men pursue religious studies in a program integrated with military service), issued a letter in which they reiterated previous assertions that soldiers must refuse to obey orders to evacuate settlements. The law of the Torah, they asserted, is above that of the Israel Defense Forces. 'Unfortunately, the IDF has been used for purposes unrelated to Israel's defense and directly opposed to God's wishes for quite some time.... We are committed to teach that loyalty to the Lord comes before any other loyalty, whether to the army or to the government.'[73] While the previous generation of settlers legitimized the state and establishment and worked with it to achieve common goals, the younger generation sees the state as part of the problem, not the solution. Since the 2005 evacuation of the Gaza Strip settlements, which the Yesha Council, the organization that represents the settlers, failed to prevent with its traditional, cooperative methods, the established leadership lost its exclusive authority. Other militant settler organizations have arisen since then. They are supported by those in the veteran establishment who have always favored militant actions to prevent any deal with the government on freezing the construction or enlargement of settlements and outposts, or their evacuation. This split could be seen in the summer of 2009, when the Ministry of Defense tried to reach an understanding with the Yesha Council on the evacuation of unauthorized outposts. By their own estimate, they have the loyalty of 17,000 activists out of the approximately 70,000 Jews living to the east of the Barrier. The establishment, they argue, represents there no more than 3,000 persons.[74]

Indeed, the younger generation is divided between those who support anti–establishment operations and those calling for comprehensive regime change. Unlike the ultra-Orthodox, who wait for the Messiah to establish the Torah state, national religious radicals have absorbed the Zionist ethos of self-reliance and activism. They have no compunctions about using violence against Palestinians, in particular in retaliation for the evacuation of outposts. To a lesser degree, they attack Israeli policeman and soldiers.[75] The generational divide is also ecological and geographical. While the old guard lives in comfortable settlements, the young guard prefers isolate hilltop outposts deep in the West Bank, where they can demonstrate their dissident identity. The young generation's attitude toward the Palestinians is also more radical than that of their parents. From the start, the settlement movement's spiritual leaders dismissed any Palestinian right for self determination. They denied that the Palestinians had a legitimate claim to their land or any collective rights on it. The best that they could hope for, argued the original settlers, would be to receive individual rights from Israel. In the terms of the Torah, they would be 'resident aliens,' inhabitants who receive individual rights if they fully recognize the hegemony of the Jewish nation and its exclusive sovereignty over the Land of Israel. With the ascendancy of the radical young generation, more extreme views spread from the far right into the mainstream. Prominent settler rabbis call for ethnic cleansing. 'We must cleanse the country of Arabs and resettle them where they came from, if necessary by paying. Unless we do it we will never enjoy peace in our land,' declared Rabbi Dov Lior, the chief rabbi of Kiryat Arba.[76] Others liken the Palestinians to the biblical Philistines or to Amalek, a nation that, in the Torah, God commands the Israelites to expunge. The IDF rabbinate distributed material advocating these views to IDF soldiers during the 2009 invasion of the Gaza Strip.[77] In this atmosphere, it is easy for extremist settlers to stage attacks on peaceful Palestinians. Aiming to 'keep them away' or to take revenge for IDF evacuations of outposts, they organize offensives that they call 'price tag' operations, meant to show the government, the army, and the Palestinians that any move against the settlements will cost their enemies dearly. They torch fields, uproot olive groves, pull down tents, steal or poison sheep, throw stones, shoot, and desecrate mosques and Muslim graves. A correspondent for *Ha'aretz* offered this account of a 'price tag' attack on Bayt Illu, a village located next to Givat Menachem, an outpost that the army demolished in January 2010:

The crowd of rioters reached a house at the edge of [Bayt Illu], which overlooks the nearby settlements. The house belongs to the Mazar family. Some of the teens approached the back of the house and threw stones at the windows. Other approached the car at the front and tried to set it on fire. One of the seats did catch fire, but the residents managed to put it out. Two other members of the household tried to escape in another car. The rioters surrounded them and pelted them with stones. Mohammed Mazar, who was visiting his grandmother, was hit in the head and began to bleed. Another relative was also injured, and both were evacuated to a local clinic. All of this occurred in no more than two minutes. The rioters then quickly escaped, leaving behind destruction, casualties and an unsettled village.[78]

Settlers have also attacked soldiers guarding Palestinians gathering in their olive harvest. Beyond expressing their anger, their aim is to deter Israeli authorities from dismantling outposts, and perhaps also to induce Palestinians to leave the area.[79] The IDF counted 551 settler's attacks in 2007 and 429 in the first half of 2008.[80] In December 2009, following the Israeli cabinet decision to freeze most settlement construction and expansion for ten months, settlers set fire to a mosque in the village of Yasouf, leaving behind Hebrew graffiti declaring that 'we will burn you all.'[81] The general of the IDF Central Command described these attacks:

There has been a rise in Jewish violence in Judea and Samaria [the West Bank]. In the past, only a few dozen individuals took part in such activity, but today that number has grown into the hundreds.... These hundreds are engaged in conspiratorial actions against Palestinians and the security forces. It's a very grave phenomenon. We have to divert our efforts to there from other issues. The margins [in the settler community] are expanding, because they are enjoying a tailwind and the backing of part of the leadership, both rabbinical and public, whether in explicit statements or tacitly.[82]

These attacks are followed by Palestinians attacking settlers in revenge. These 'shepherds' wars' occur in the rural areas of the West Bank, whereas in Hebron they take the form of urban ethnic clashes.[83]

National religious extremists do not stop there. They also target IDF commanders and left-wing activists. They termed Major General Yair Naveh, who oversaw the dismantling of four West Bank settlements in the summer of 2005, a collaborator [*moser*, a highly-charged term in Jewish religious law]. And they have advocated the use of force against IDF soldiers and other Israeli law-enforcement authorities. Rabbi Lior told his followers: 'If they use violence against us we have to use force against them.'[84] Rabbi Avigdor Neventzhal was quoted as saying, 'anyone who wants to give away Israeli land is as a *rodef* [a pursuer, another charged halachic term; a pursuer may be killed by the person he is pursuing without due process]. Rabbi Elyakim Levanon heads the yeshiva at Elon Moreh, near Nablus, which also has a *hesder* program enrolling soldiers. He signed a rabbinic ruling stating that, as a matter of halachic principle, Naveh could be killed as a *rodef*.[85] Rabbi Yitzhak Shapira, head of the yeshiva at Yitzhar, another settlement near Nablus, is the author of a book, *The King's Torah*, in which he writes that it is permissible for Jews to kill 'non-Jews who demand the land for themselves' and who engage in hostile blasphemy, as well as, apparently meaning other Jews, 'those who, by speech, weaken our sovereignty.' Shapira has termed his book a theoretical study, and he does not explicitly state that the non-Jews referred to are today's Palestinians or Arabs. But, he writes, 'One is permitted to kill any citizen who supports the war or the fighters or expresses satisfaction with their deeds—his killing is permitted.'[86]

'Based on the way in which Yesha [the Hebrew acronym for Judea and Samaria, the term used by the settlers and their supporters to designate the West Bank] rabbis are currently leading their students at the outposts ... their students currently understand that they have the green light to resort to any means in this struggle. Every day that goes by without anyone dying in this struggle is a miracle,' Rabbi Yoel Ben Nun, himself one of the founding figures in the settler movement, has warned.[87] In 2009, Jack Teitel, a West Bank settler, was arrested and charged by the Israeli security services with the murders of two Palestinian civilians and of planting a pipe-bomb, which exploded and injured its target, at the home of a prominent anti–settlement Israeli public intellectual, Zeev Sternhell.[88] Anonymous rightists have offered financial reward for the killing of the leader of Peace Now.[89] The head of the Israel's General Security Service (GSS—the secret internal espionage organization also known as Shabak or the Shin Bet), Yuval Diskin, was quoted as saying in a cabinet meeting on November 2008 that 'our investigation found a very high willingness among this public to use violence, not just stones but live weapons, in order to prevent or halt a diplomatic process.'[90]

Prime Minister Olmert and Minister of Justice Daniel Friedmann denounced as a pogrom an attack by settlers on Palestinians in December 2008. But national authorities are slow to take action against such crimes. And those national religious leaders who condemn them prefer to voice their critiques within their communities rather than in public—Rabbi Ben-Nun, quoted above, is a notable exception.

A generational change is also evident in the ultra-Orthodox community, one that can be attributed in part to this community's high birth-rate. But also to its absorption of new members, especially among Israel's Mizrahi (Sephardi) community. The ultra-Orthodox community has grown eightfold since 1948. In 2009 it comprised about 10 per cent of Israel's population. In earlier times, the ultra-Orthodox preferred to defend their community identity from state and secular pressures by securing autonomous institutions. But, more recently, they have begun to evince a growing interest in national policy. Ultra-Orthodox parties have participated in most governing coalitions since the Likud's historic upset victory of 1977. Political integration led to increasing social integration. Young ultra-Orthodox Israelis share public spaces such as shopping centers and coffee shops with the broader public. They, too, were victims and shared the traumas and insecurities of the Second Intifada. They hike in Israel's countryside and visit national parks and nature reserves. Increasingly, they are entering the labor force. The community's baby boom and rising apartment prices in main Israeli cities led Prime Minister Netanyahu, during his first administration in the late 1990s, to offer the ultra-Orthodox subsidized houses in settlements of their own. His proposal came just as the community gradually integrating into the Israeli society, and gave them, for the first time, a vested interest in the settlement enterprise. It should be noted that ultra-Orthodox settlers are both of Ashkenazi and Sephardi origins. Unlike the national religious community, which is motivated by a nationalistic messianic ideology, ultra-Orthodox support for settlements is largely pragmatic. About 90 per cent of ultra-Orthodox settlers live to the west to the Barrier, in Modi'in Ilit, population 38,000, and Betar Ilit, population 32,200. A new ultra-orthodox city is planned adjacent to the northern part of Arab Jerusalem. All the three are in areas adjacent to 1949 armistice line.[91]

The ICG reports a further recent change. Ultra-Orthodox settlers are now increasingly relocating into settlements east of the Barrier that were previously dominated by national-religious or secular Israelis.[92] Moreover, as they have established their own settlements, they have developed a stronger commitment to the political and theological principles of the settler movement. Ultra-orthodox rabbis now preach about the sacred nature of the Land of Israel in terms reminiscent of the national religious discourse. They and their constituency have increasingly adopted the hawkish views of the Israeli right, for example that the settlements are critical means in the war on terror. In December 2008, ultra-Orthodox youths participated in demonstrations in protest against eviction of a national religious settler from his house in Hebron.[93] In July 2009, in one of his weekly public talks, the spiritual leader of the ultra-Orthodox Sephardi movement, Rabbi Ovadia Yosef, slammed U.S. President Barack Obama and other western leaders for pressuring Israel to freeze construction in the West Bank and East Jerusalem: 'You can't build here, you can't build there'—it's as if we were their slaves,' the rabbi protested. 'We are being ruled by slaves,' he said, in an apparent reference to the president's race, and added that, 'Our messiah will come and throw them out.' Rabbi Yosef also bemoaned the status quo on the Temple Mount: 'Where is our Temple? There are Arabs there!' He then promised that the messiah 'will throw all these evil ones out of here.'[94] Using more diplomatic language, Israel's Sephardi chief rabbi, Shlomo Amar, called on American Jews 'to take advantage of your strength and power to influence the authorities in the U.S. … the Torah commands the Jewish people to live in [the Land of] Israel. And we hear that the U.S. is putting pressure on the Israeli government to prevent Jews from living or building their homes in large parts of the Land of Israel. This is being done at a time when every person is allowed to live wherever he wishes to live in every area of the world, while here in Israel [Americans] want to create a [Palestinian] state in which it will be prohibited for Jews to live. And even expanding existing settlements is prohibited.'[95]

The theology of Shas's leaders nevertheless differs from that of national religious rabbis. The former advocate passivity, and call on the messiah to bring the changes they hope for. The latter call for human actions, here and now. The common ground of the two theologies is that they expect Jewish ethnicity and religion to determine Israeli policy toward the Palestinians. Rabbi Israel Rosen, a settler from Etzion Block and head of the Conversion Authority in the Office of the Prime Minister, has gone much further. In January 2010 he wrote in a popular pamphlet distributed to synagogue worshippers on the Sabbath that:

the time has come 'to declare war' on the Israeli Arabs, and of course on the Palestinians of Judea and Samaria, who are not loyal to the state, using clear tests to determine this, and to designate them as enemies… Taking away rights, also collectively (such as travelling on major arteries), as long as they do not meet the test of loyalty to the state. Also the right to vote for the Knesset, and certainly the right to be elected, are not 'God-given rights' and may be encroached on due to disloyalty, and certainly for security reasons, and to protect ourselves from those who would harm us.…The reason for our inability to implement this 'war' lies with our 'internal enemy.'… Our brethren, the Jews of the left, head by some of the High Court justices who prefer human rights and humanism for our enemies to the security of the state and its citizens.[96]

The ultra-Orthodox presence in the West Bank brought them closer to the front lines with the Palestinians. Modi'in Illit is located next to Bil'in, and some of the land it occupies was expropriated from the inhabitants of the village. The settlement's residents can hear or see the clashes that occur at the weekly anti–expropriation demonstrations, and their cars are targeted by Palestinian stone-throwers. By settling in the West Bank, the this community has come to feel they are part of the general project of building the Land of Israel and defending the state. This, in conjunction with their ethnic theology, which views the Jews as God's chosen people, explains why 'polls suggest that of all Israel's communities the ultra-Orthodox currently are most opposed to negotiations with the Palestinians and further withdrawals, transforming their voters from anti–to ultra-nationalists.'[97]

West Bank settlers are supported by their sister religious communities and family members who live in Israel proper. It is difficult to assess the extent to which the radical young generation enjoys this same backing. Revolutionary and anti–establishment attitudes apparently are weaker in the state centre then in its West Bank hilltop periphery. However, in February 2006, through the autonomous state-sponsored national religious school system, national religious youth movements and synagogues networks, radical settlers were able to mobilize thousands of such Israelis to protest against the dismantling of nine buildings in the Amona outpost and the evacuation of one building in Hebron. In the violent clashes between protestors and security forces at Amona, eighty policemen and soldiers and 120 settlers were wounded.[98] In other words, the distance between center and periphery is short and bridgeable, and the boundaries between them are flexible.

The IDF's Dilemma

In no few cases, IDF officers have aided settlers in confrontation with Palestinians all over the West Bank. They have opened fire on Palestinians, used tear gas against protestors, confiscated workers' tools at the demand of settlers, and protected settlers during their violent attacks on Palestinians.[99]

Moreover, many soldiers serving in the West Bank come from the same social background, have received the same education, belonged to the same youth movement, and share friends with the settlers and are ideologically sympathetic to their enterprise. Their rabbis are either Gush Emunim settlers themselves or staunch supporters of the settler movement. Rabbi Avichai Rontzki, who served as IDF chief rabbi from 2007 to the beginning of 2010, broadened the army rabbinate's mission. Once limited to providing for the religious needs of soldiers who wished to maintain their observance in the army's secular environment, Rabbi Rontzki took it upon himself to educate combat troops in national religious views. Pamphlets distributed by the IDF rabbinate under his command include quotations from articles by settlement rabbis that reject Palestinian nationalism. In one such pamphlet, Rabbi Shlomo Aviner, the spiritual leader of the settlement of Beit El, compares the Palestinians to the Philistines 'because the Philistines of the past were not natives.… They invaded the Land of Israel, a land that did not belong to them and claimed political ownership over our country.… Today the problem is the same.' The same pamphlet stated that there is 'a biblical ban on surrendering a single millimeter of [the Land of Israel] to gentiles through all sorts of impure distortions and foolishness of autonomy, enclaves and other national weaknesses.'[100] Another pamphlet, addressed to soldiers going into battle during the Gaza invasion, called the operation a holy war, in which no mercy should be shown to the enemy.[101]

According to Yagil Levy, a political sociologist, 'The bias of the army is naturally in favor of the settlers, over the Palestinians. This bias was strengthened by the deployment of the military force in three circles. The first circle is regional defense, reserve units, made up of settlers.… The army has limited control over the activity of these militias, under whose aegis settlers harm Palestinians, seize control of land, and the like.'[102] The ICG's report provides some data on this regional defense. The army formed these reserve units in the mid-1990s, but since the outbreak of the Second Intifada in 2000 their number has grown. As of 2009, there were some 200 such units manned by over 2,000 reservists who volunteered to transfer from their previous postings to these units operating in West Bank settlements and outposts. The army provides rifles, but the squads buy for themselves extras such as telescopic sights.

With both financial aid from the state and overseas donations, they also buy armoured landrovers, ammunition and hire private security companies to train them. One such company is run by a settler and trains mainly national religious and some ultra-Orthodox settlers.

The same circle of settler defense also includes civilian security coordinators who work together with the army. As of December 2009 there were almost 150 such officials. They enjoy broad powers—they may stop individuals and inspect their identification papers, and detain people until army or police officials arrive. They are settlers and their salaries are funded by the state through local councils. Many of them have been involved in large numbers of conflicts with Palestinians living near their settlements. They have asserted their powers in nearby illegal outposts as well, as well as in areas around the settlements in which the ownership of property is in dispute. In some instances they have expelled Palestinians from such land on the grounds that they posed a security threat, thereby enabling settlers to move in.[103]

'The second circle,' Levy continues:

is composed of the six policing battalions.... The regular deployment of a military force within a civilian community that it is supposed to protect blurs the boundaries between the settlers and the soldiers. The blurring is physical, since many settlers serve in these units as well, some of the units are deployed in the settlements themselves, settlements have been built on army bases, etc. But it is also cultural, insofar as the commanders try to maintain proper relations with the settlers. In addition, a significant percentage of the soldiers in the policing battalions are graduates of yeshivas whose ideological bias is clear, and who are subject to external rabbinical influence.... The third circle is that of other units, reservists and regular army, who reinforce the activity in the territories. About half of the graduates of the officers training school Bahad 1 are religious; the graduates of the Orthodox *mekhinot* (pre-army programs combining study and military preparation) and the *hesder* yeshivas (combining study and military service) constitute over 10 per cent of the army's combat force; the settlers constitute about 5 per cent of combat soldiers (some overlapping the previous statistic), 1.3 times their proportion of the general population. A large percentage of these groups man the infantry brigades, which occasionally carry out activity in the territories.'[104]

The ICG estimates that 30 per cent of the officer corps of the standing army are national religious soldiers; the proportion is even higher in combat units and those that are deployed regularly in the West Bank units. Many of them are graduates of one of the fifty-six *hesder* yeshivot, or of the sixteen religious pre-army academies. These institutions graduate about 2,500 religious soldiers each year.[105] They are important socialization institutions for the national religious community, promoting, perpetuating, and spreading communal norms and doctrines accordingly to which there is an identity between the Jewish religion, the Jewish state, Jewish nationality and the Land of Israel. Students are encouraged to serve this ideology through army service, living in a settlement, and spreading these doctrines through formal and informal education. The anonymous sources interviewed by the ICG displayed a range of opinions about where the primary loyalties of these soldiers lay. Top GSS officials have expressed concern about how trained, well-organized, armed and highly motivated settler units will react if settlements have to be evacuated. For this reason, the army and the GSS at one time considered not conscripting radical national religious activists.[106] At the time of the evacuation of the Gaza Strip settlers in 2005, the army command decided not to use the Golani and Givati infantry, which were generally deployed there. The reason was apparently the high proportion—50 per cent—of company commanders who are religious.[107] Officers gave the settlers early warnings about the army's preparations for the evacuation of the Amona outpost in February 2006. Consequently, when a decision was made to evacuate settlers from a disputed house in Hebron in December 2008, it was classified. Army personal suspected as collaborators with settlers were kept in the dark.[108]

It seems to have been this problem that led Chief of Staff Gabi Ashkenazi to say, on 27 July 2009, that 'wherever possible' police units would be assigned to evacuate civilians from outposts.[109] Two days later, the police indeed evacuated an outpost near Hebron.[110]

IDF commanders are aware on the problem they may face if the government orders to evacuate settlements. In mid-2009 the commander of the Judea and Samaria division, Brig. Gen. Noam Tibon, wrote a memo in which he estimates that up to one-third of soldiers and commanders might refuse the implementation of 'cabinet decisions that are in the public discourse,' as opposed to 'pure security issues.' He suggests commanders not assign soldiers with connections to outpost residents to evacuations, calling for 'a sensitive policy toward commanders or soldiers with family or social relationships in the evacuated population.' Until orders are refused, commanders should treat soldiers with sensitivity, but once an order is refused, unambiguous action should be taken, the memo states.[111] More worried is Maj. Gen (res.) Giora Eiland, who headed the National Security Council at the time of the evacuations in the Gaza Strip. He is convinced that Israel is incapable of evacuating settlements on the West Bank. In his testimony before the state commission of inquiry on the handling of the Gaza Strip evacuees, Eiland said: 'On the level of the state, is the state capable, yes or no, of taking steps which are certainly politically controversial—the answer is certainly not. We are a neutralized country. What, that isn't clear?'[112]

In late 2009, Rabbi Eliezer Melamed, the head of Har Brachah *hesder* yeshiva, declared his support for soldiers who refuse orders to evacuate settlements. He made his statement in reference to the cases of nine soldiers involved in three incidents over the space of about two weeks of November–December 2009. Soldiers from the Kfir and Nachshon Brigades were sentenced to jail for holding up signs at a military ceremony declaring that their units would not evacuate settlements. Two of the soldiers in question had also refused to carry out an assignment to man roadblocks aimed at preventing right-wing activists from reaching the settlement of Negohot, where the Civil Administration was demolishing two buildings. IDF commanders became worried by the possibility of large-scale refusal to obey orders should the army be tasked with evacuating illegal outposts.[113] Based on the IDF's recommendation, Defense Minister Ehud Barak ruled that the Har Bracha yeshiva would no longer be allowed to participate in the *hesder* program, meaning that its students could not intersperse a shortened period of army service with studies at the yeshiva. In response, rabbis from most other *hesder* yeshivot signed a statement supporting Rabbi Melamed's right to speak his mind.[114]

In late 2009, the army moved to delineate clearly the responsibilities of civilian security coordinators in West Bank settlements. No such clear demarcation of their authority had ever been made before. The move came in the wake of a petition filed by attorney Michael Sfard on behalf of the Yesh Din human rights organization. The IDF defined the geographical limits of the coordinators' powers. It gave each of them a map displaying the zone in which he is authorized to act. The zones are limited to the territory of the respective settlements and do not include adjacent highways, access roads, or nearby Palestinian land. The coordinator may under some circumstances act in nearby illegal outposts, but the IDF order provides that civilian security squads from the settlements may not operate in the outposts without the presence of the coordinator.[115]

4

THE ISRAELI CONTROL SYSTEM

The Principles

Israel developed its current control system over the West Bank in the years 2000–2002, as the Israeli–Palestinian conflict was transformed from a border struggle to a purely ethnic one. Although this system incorporated elements from its previous regimes over its Arab citizens after 1948 and over the Palestinians in the territories after 1967, it was fundamentally different. The change resulted from the combination of a much greater number of settlements and settlers, scattered more widely, with the military measures taken to battle the armed Palestinian uprising. During the confrontations of the Second Intifada, Israel deployed some 100,000 troops in the West Bank and Gaza Strip, far more than it ever had before.

But, under the new structure, Israel does not control the West Bank only by military might, bases and security zones. It also uses its settlements and a network of roads reserved exclusively for Israelis. The Barrier is another element of the system. The Barrier is not simply a border demarcated unilaterally by Israel, as some have claimed, because Israeli settlers live and soldiers are based on its far, 'Palestinian' side. Therefore, instead of being a border, the Barrier serves as a tool of annexation and control. Israel also rules by recruiting collaborators, interrogating detainees, granting or denying work, construction, and other permits as it sees fit, and by managing the population registry. This latter function gives it the power to deny residency rights in the West Bank to Palestinians who leave the territory. It also means that these Palestinians must register their personal information and changes in personal status with Israel, through the PA.

The quantity of Israeli army and settlers created a qualitative change. Military operations and settlement activity were loosely connected before 2000, but became coordinated parts of a single machine thereafter. This system is, however, a stratified one, and stratification is one of the principles on which it is based.

Controlling Movement

In Operation Defensive Shield of 2002, launched in response to the Palestinian uprising that began in 2000, Israel effectively rendered the Palestinian Authority powerless. For all intents and purposes, Israel now controls every aspect of the lives of the West Bank's Palestinians and makes all major policy decisions for them. For example, to travel from one part of the West Bank to another requires passing through checkpoints, and this cannot be accomplished without an Israeli permit. Neither can goods be transported from one area to another without Israeli sanction. Israel supervises population registration, determines which roads Palestinians can use, and what hours Palestinian policemen can operate in the few cities in which Israel allows their deployment. The only functions under the sole purview of the Palestinian Authority are health and education.

In September 2008, the United Nations Office for the Coordination of Humanitarian Affairs (OCHA) counted 630 roadblocks (ninety-three of them manned, the remaining 537 being unmanned earthworks and obstructions) constraining internal Palestinian movement. This number did not include sixty-nine obstacles in the Israeli–controlled center of Hebron (the H2 zone). Almost three-quarters of the main routes leading into the eighteen most-populated Palestinian cities and towns are either blocked or controlled by Israeli army checkpoints.

Israel prohibits Palestinian access to vast areas of the West Bank, such as military zones (21 per cent), settlements (3 per cent), and Greater Jerusalem (4 per cent). Palestinians wishing to travel from their homes to other parts of the West Bank (or to Israel) must receive Israeli permits. Their use of about 200 kilometers (125 miles) of main roads is severely restricted, rendering these arteries largely out of bounds for Palestinians. Israel also imposes curfews; stops and inspects Palestinians at dozens of ad hoc checkpoints; and imposes travel restrictions on members of specific demographic profiles, in particular males aged sixteen to thirty-five.[1] It should be noted that, in December 2009, the Israeli Supreme Court handed down a precedent-setting ruling that voided the military order forbidding Palestinian movement on Route 443, which connects Tel Aviv and Jerusalem via the West Bank. The court instructed the IDF to open the road to Palestinians, after an interim period of a few months during which the army will find methods to provide security to Jewish and Palestinian travellers.[2]

Israel also imposes its will by recruiting collaborators and interrogating detainees. Since 2000, Israel has incarcerated between 8,000 and 11,000 Palestinians at any given time.[3] Israel also uses biometric data to monitor the Palestinians in the West Bank. Beginning in 2005, photographs, handprints and fingerprints have been coded into the magnetic card that Palestinians must present, together with their ID card, when they apply for permits to enter Israel or to travel through parts of the West Bank under its direct control. Together with the Palestinian population registry (recording birth date, address, marital status and number of children), which the Israeli Ministries of Interior and Defense control and validate for the Palestinian Authority, the biometric data serve as a powerful tool of supervision and surveillance.[4]

As Israel intensifies its control over its subject Palestinians, it can collect more information about them. It can make them even more dependent on its government agencies than they ever were before. It thus serves as a way of deterring revolt, and imposing collective punishments that go far beyond the form of Israeli control prior to 2000. More than ever, Israel sees the Palestinians as a collective, not as individuals.

In other words, Israel fully controls, almost without exception, the entire area of what once was British Mandatory Palestine, from the Jordan River to the Mediterranean Sea. 'What was once justified by the Israeli authorities as a short-term military response to violent confrontations and attacks on Israeli civilians appears to developing into a permanent system,' charges OCHA.[5]

Israel's policy of keeping the Palestinians fragmented by controlling their road system applies to Jerusalem as well.[6] Its main goal is to disconnect East Jerusalem from its hinterland in the West Bank through twelve checkpoints that operate along the Security Barrier, such as the Qalandia and Shu'afat refugee camp in the north, on the Mount of Olives and in Hizme in the east, at Rachel's Tomb, and on the 'tunnel road' to the south. To supervise the crossing from Palestinian areas of the city into Jewish neighborhoods, Israel uses less obtrusive methods, such as spot inspections of Palestinians and mobile checkpoints. Israeli Palestinians enjoy full freedom of movement.

No control system is sustainable if there are not people who benefit from it. In keeping with the 1993 Oslo agreement,

Israel grants VIP cards to senior Palestinian Authority officials, political figures and selected NGO activists. The cards entitle their holders to pass through special, faster lines at checkpoints and border crossings; to travel freely to other Palestinian areas; and to receive more easily permission to enter to East Jerusalem or Israel. Holders of VIP cards belong to the upper middle class, and resist the system less than do ordinary people who suffer more. The latter's frustration and anger is directed not only against Israel but also against the VIPs. Such resentment intensified with the collapse of the Oslo agreements and Israel's imposition of its ethno-security regime in 2000–2002. The populace views the VIPs as corrupt collaborators.

In June 2009, under heavy pressure from the Obama administration, Israel agreed to remove roadblocks and ease access to the major Palestinian cities, with the exception of East Jerusalem and the Israeli–controlled area of Hebron. Israel also agreed to allow the Palestinian Authority's police force to operate freely within the city limits of Bethlehem, Tulkarem, Ramallah, Jericho and Qalqilyah, except between the hours of midnight and 5 a.m. This came in the wake of more determined and forceful actions by Palestinian security forces against the Hamas and Islamic Jihad infrastructure in these West Bank areas, including arrests and the closure of Hamas-affiliated charitable organizations.[7]

The roadblocks surrounding Nablus, a city that had been under complete siege, were lifted in the summer of 2009. The trip, for a patient with a permit, by hospital bus from Nablus to East Jerusalem took four to five hours in 2006; in July 2009 it took approximately two hours.[8] Roadblocks have also been removed from the roads leading to Jericho, Qalqiliyah, Tulkarem, Jenin and Ramallah. In some of these places, Israeli soldiers conduct spot checks on Palestinians, while in others Israeli soldiers deploy roadblocks to prevent the entrance of cars with Israeli license plates, but allow Palestinians to pass freely. Since the beginning of September 2009, one of the four checkpoints controlling access to the Jordan Valley is manned only sporadically, easing access between the northern West Bank and parts of the Jordan Valley. Searches and the checking of documentation at a number of other checkpoints along key routes are now also performed on a random basis, and most people are able to cross after short delays of only five to ten minutes. Such is the case at key spots like Wadi Nar, on the main route between the southern and the central West Bank; Tapu'ah, on the main route between the central and northern areas; Huwwara, at the southern entrance to Nablus; and Enav, at the eastern entrance to Tulkarem.[9] Based on the GPS coordinates provided to OCHA by the IDF, supplemented by its own field work, OCHA was able to confirm the removal of 35 of the roadblocks on the IDF's list of 100. On 29 September 2009, OCHA counted 592 movement obstacles in the West Bank, down from 630 a year earlier. Of these, sixty-nine were permanently manned, twenty-three were intermittently manned, and 500 were unmanned obstacles.[10] During October the number of obstacles decreased further, to 578. However, most of Area C remained off limits to Palestinians, and access to the Jordan Valley, to the Israeli–controlled zone in Hebron (H2), to East Jerusalem, and to the part of the West Bank to the west of the Barrier remained severely restricted.[11]

But this new freedom of movement has been enabled, para-doxically, because Israel actually erected more entrenchments and obstacles, with the purpose of shifting Palestinian traffic to separate or alternative roads. Palestinians can travel where they do not use or cross roads used by Israelis. Palestinian movement is also facilitated thanks to bypass and underpass roads that have been paved on expropriated private and public land to create separate Israeli and Palestinian road networks.

The change has thus occurred within the Israeli control system rather than as part of its amelioration, easing the effect of the fragmentation of the Palestinian territories without ending it. OCHA maintains that the most important factor affecting Palestinian movement and access restrictions are Israeli settlements. 'This is reflected in the significant degree of overlap between the location of access restrictions (including the Barrier) and the location of settlements and settlers' routes.'[12]

Freer movement and the improving security environment in the West Bank have had a positive impact on economic and commercial activity. By August 2009, preliminary figures indicated that unemployment in Nablus had dropped to 13–15 per cent, from 28–32 per cent at the beginning of 2009. Nablus is regarded as the West Bank's economic center, with a third of its businesses and some 23 per cent of its GNP. Businessmen and companies who had left Nablus for other cities began returning, although many kept a foothold in their other locations out of a lack of confidence that the new Israeli policy would continue. A no less significant indication of an improved economic climate is the large number of Israeli Palestinians who come to shop in the city on Saturdays. As part of its change in policy, Israel permitted them to enter the city in their private cars on this day; as a consequence, sales rocketed.[13] However, a July 2009 report on Jenin found that the IDF continues to operate in that area at night, albeit at reduced levels, especially in the refugee camp next to the city and in some villages. No major checkpoint has been removed from this area, only a few roadblocks, and Palestinian Israelis are not allowed to enter by car, except on Saturdays. In this part of the West Bank, as a consequence, an economic upswing was not yet evident at the end of 2009, and a high level of uncertainty still prevailed.[14]

In September 2009, the Word Bank forecast that the new ease of travel could produce the first per capita GDP growth in the West Bank economy in years. However, it qualifies this statement by noting that 'much of the growth appears to have been generated by donor spending, which rose significantly in response to Israel's recent military operation in Gaza, and may not be sustainable.'[15] Both the World Bank and the International Monetary Fund stress that real GDP growth depends on pushing forward the peace process. Moreover, the World Bank states that 'much of the administrative system that undermines investor confidence and restricts access to natural resources, such as Area C land (which constitutes some 60 per cent of the West Bank), water, and telecommunications frequencies, remains in place.'[16] Therefore, in order to achieve the goals of the Palestinian Authority program of 25 August 2009, 'Palestine: Ending the Occupation, Establishing the State' (known also as the Fayyad Plan), Israel must revamp its regime in line with Palestinian institution-building.[17] Israeli economists also agree that the West Bank's improved economic climate following the removal of these transportation restrictions will be limited in scope, so long as there is no full freedom of access to local and foreign markets, only a very small number of laborers are allowed to work in Israel, and uncertainty persists regarding the creation of properly functioning Palestinian governing institutions.[18]

Five Palestinian Groups

Israel's ethno-security regime controls the Palestinians (in both Israel and the occupied territories) by implementing differential levels of state supervision, security control, bureaucratic rules, civil rights and citizen benefits. The fundamental and most visible division is the territorial/legal one that divides Palestinians into five groups: Israeli Palestinians; Jerusalem Palestinians; Palestinians who reside between the Security Barrier and the

Green Line; Palestinians in the rest of the West Bank; and Gaza Strip Palestinians.

Israeli Palestinians: Israel's 1,195,200 Palestinian citizens, constituting 15 per cent of the country's population of 7,050,000,[19] enjoy the greatest rights and benefits. As citizens, they are represented in the Knesset, and they are influenced by Jewish Israeli culture, standards and norms. For nearly two decades following the establishment of Israel, they lived under military rule. Although the military regime was abolished in 1966, these Palestinian citizens of Israel are nevertheless subject to systematic and institutionalized discrimination by the Jewish majority. Jews dominate the state bureaucracy, and the Israeli Palestinian minority is not treated equally in development plans, budgets, land allocations, education, housing and zoning. Few Arabs hold positions of state power, such as membership on government committees and senior ministerial posts.[20] A study published by Hebrew University Professor Sorel Cahan shows that the Education Ministry's budget for special assistance to students from low socio-economic backgrounds severely discriminates against Israeli Palestinians. The average per-student allocation in Israeli Palestinian junior high schools amounts to only 20 per cent of the average in Israeli Jewish junior highs. Ordinary classroom hours are allotted to schools strictly on a per-student basis. But the special assistance budget, which totaled NIS 150 million in 2009, is by nature differential, as its purpose is to give extra assistance to schools with a large proportion of students from low socio-economic backgrounds. The ministry's 2009 data on the percentage of high school students in each locality who passed their high school graduation exams show that, once again, most Israeli Palestinian communities were at the bottom of the list.[21] Moreover, 'Officials said it has been known for some time that state security services wield tremendous influence within the Arab community's education system, particularly in terms of selecting people to fill top posts.'[22]

The General Security Service also intervenes in the appointment of Muslim clerics.[23] The state claims this is necessary to prevent advocacy of resistance to Israeli law in schools and mosques. But Israeli educators and rabbis who have called on their students and followers to resist government decisions to evacuate settlements in the occupied territories (see above) have not been stripped of their positions and salaries.[24]

According to a report by Adalah, a Palestinian–Israeli human rights organization, Israel's law enforcement agencies pursued a no-tolerance and anti–democratic policy toward Israeli Palestinian demonstrators who opposed the Israeli invasion of the Gaza Strip in 2008–9. Moreover, the report shows that the police followed different standards in cases where Israeli Jews were involved.

The police detained 832 people during the operation; 34 per cent of them were minors under the age of eighteen. Some 80 per cent of those detained were kept in custody until the end of the proceedings against them, 54 per cent of whom were minors. The authors wrote that, while they worked on their report, President Shimon Peres accepted the recommendation of the then Justice Minister Daniel Friedmann to pardon fifty-nine citizens who had committed criminal offenses during protests against the Israeli unilateral disengagement from the Gaza Strip in August 2005. Peres declared that the pardons were being granted in consideration of the young age of the protestors and anawareness that this was an unusual, historic event. But, the Adallah writers stated, 'court decisions [regarding protestors against the war] in which the authorities took into consideration the reason the war opponents were angry.' They stated:

The hundreds of dead, the injured, the destruction, the tragedy and the damage the Israeli army against brought upon Gaza's residents are not mentioned anywhere in any remand decision. The detainees were presented as lawbreakers and criminals who should be treated harshly due to 'the situation,' unconnected from the political climate of their protest.[25]

Courts made their decisions not on the basis of each individual suspect's actual actions, but rather on the basis of his or her collective identity. All of those arrested in Israel's northern police district were detained until the end of the proceedings; 94 per cent of those arrested in the Jerusalem district were kept in custody until the end of the proceedings on their cases. These were predominantly Palestinian citizens of Israel and Palestinians with permanent resident status. No person from the Tel Aviv district was so remanded. Notably, Tel Aviv's inhabitants are overwhelming Jewish citizens of the state. State prosecutors confirmed that the detentions were designed 'to send a deterrent message to the public as a whole and to the rioters in particular.'[26] The GSS summoned dozens of political activists for interrogation. With the backing of the attorney general, the GSS officers asked political questions and threatened these people with prosecution. GSS agents also told the activists that they would be charged with any crime committed at the demonstrations, even if they were not personally involved. The ethno-security perspective of the law enforcement authorities rings clearly in the Ministry of Justice's response to the Adalah report: 'Court rulings, throughout the October 2000 events, called for detaining rioters—including minors—who were involved in nationalistically motivated disturbances that posed a threat to passersby and security forces.'[27]

East Jerusalemites: On the next rung below Israel's Palestinian citizens are the 260,500 Palestinians of East Jerusalem (who, as of 2007, comprised 35 per cent of the city's total population of 747,600).[28] In June 1967, when Israel annexed Jordanian Jerusalem and its surroundings, the Palestinians in this territory were granted permanent resident status rather than citizenship. They enjoy the right to move and work in Israel, as well as health care and national insurance benefits, as long as they can demonstrate that they have not left the annexed area. Nevertheless, East Jerusalem Palestinians enjoy fewer rights and are subject to greater legal and administrative restrictions than are Palestinian citizens of Israel.[29] For example, Mayor Barkat decided in December 2009 to cut funding to open a well baby clinic in the East Jerusalem neighborhood of Silwan, while approving funding for such a clinic in the Old City's Jewish Quarter. The municipality's professional staff recommended opening the center in Silwan, which would serve about 100,000 inhabitants of south-east Arab Jerusalem. The clinic in the Jewish Quarter will serve only about 7,000 people.[30] Based on its own data for 2006, the Association for Civil Rights in Israel (ACRI) found that:

Sixty-seven per cent of the Palestinian families in East Jerusalem and 77.2 per cent of East Jerusalem children live in poverty, compared with 21 per cent of the city's Jewish families and 39.1 per cent of the city's Jewish children.... [T]rash piles up in the streets.... The postal service barely functions. Welfare services—with insufficient funding and ongoing discrimination in comparison with those on the western side of town—are on the brink of collapse. This is particularly serious in light of the socioeconomic situation of the population. In the area of education, there is a disgraceful shortage of 1,500 classrooms in the state school system. As a result, the system has no room for some 40,000 East Jerusalem children who have to study in expensive private schools or simply drop out. Almost no preschool programs exist.... In the field of planning, East Jerusalem suffers from glaring discrimination whose purpose is clear: to limit legal construction by the Palestinian population and constrict the space available for the development of Arab neighborhoods. The reality of life in East Jerusalem is therefore an ongoing cycle of neglect, discrimination, and poverty. These, combined with cutting off the West Bank through construction of the Separation Barrier, have brought economic and social ruin to some parts of the city. The vast majority of residents in this area does not receive and are unable to purchase the most basic services and their right to a dignified existence and an adequate standard of living is severely compromised.[31]

Two West Bank Groups: The 2007 Palestinian Authority census counts a total population of 3,767,126 in the West Bank and Gaza Strip, 2,350,583 (62.3 per cent) in the West Bank and 1,416,543 (37.7 per cent) in the Gaza Strip.[32] Israel has physically divided the Palestinians of the West Bank into several geographical units and, as mentioned above, severely restricts movement between them.[33]

Israel supplies the Palestinians of the West Bank with almost half of their water, a World Bank Report found in early 2009. The Palestinians extract only about one-fifth of the water resources of the Mountain Aquifer, the major aquifer that straddles the Green Line.[34] Average Israeli water consumption per capita is four and half times higher than that of the Palestinians in the West Bank and Gaza. Adding industrial water use, Israel's per capita consumption is five and half times higher than that of the Palestinians.[35]

As noted, one of Israel's most important instruments for controlling the West Bank is the Separation Barrier. The Barrier places 9 per cent of the West Bank on its Israeli side and either disconnects or heavily restricts the access of 500,000 Palestinians to their cultivated lands and to the urban centers where their educational, health, social and financial services are located. The legal status of about 250,000 of these Palestinians, those who live outside annexed Jerusalem, differs from that of other West Bank Palestinians. While the latter need permits to leave their places of residence, the former require an Israeli permit to reside in their own towns and villages. Israel has declared the area between the Green Line and the Barrier a closed security zone. The Palestinian inhabitants of this zone receive temporary ad hoc permits to remain in this zone, whereas Jews, Palestinian Israelis, tourists and West Bank Palestinians who work in West Bank settlements can enter it freely. In other words, the zone is closed to its permanent residents but open to the occupier, its guests and its servants.[36]

The Gaza Strip: The Palestinians of the Gaza Strip are the worst off. They endure a blockade, which Israel imposed in response to Hamas's victory in the Palestinian Authority elections of 2006. They were also the targets of Israel's military operation of 27 December 2008–18 January 2009.[37] Israel seeks not only to retaliate against Qassam rockets fired on its civilians from Hamas-controlled territory, but also to put pressure on Hamas to release Gilad Shalit, an Israeli soldier it holds prisoner. Colonel Oded Iterman, an officer in the office of the Coordinator of Government Activities in the Territories (COGAT), explained the policy as follows: 'We don't want Gilad Shalit's captors to be munching Bamba [a popular Israeli snack food] right over his head.'[38] Moreover, since mid 2009 Israel has hoped that people in the Gaza Strip will see how living conditions are improving in the West Bank under the Abbas administration and draw the appropriate political conclusions. In other words, Israel wants to topple the Hamas regime by showing the Palestinian populace that Hamas can neither defend them nor provide for their material well-being. The supply of fuel for power stations, cooking, automobiles and public transportation is heavily restricted by Israel. Basic services such as electricity, cooking gas and water pressure sufficient to reach upper floors are provided only intermittently.[39] Israel has defined sesame paste, plastic sheeting, toys, books, refrigerators, washing machines, light bulbs, shoes, musical instruments, blankets, candles, cups, mattresses and canned tuna as luxuries, and therefore does not allow these goods into the Gaza Strip in the framework of humanitarian aid. In early 2009 it reversed its previous ban on toilet paper, diapers, sanitary napkins, detergent, hand soap and shampoo (but not on hair conditioner). Margarine, salt and artificial sweetener were also placed on the permitted list at that time, but 'delicacies' such as cherries, kiwis, green almonds, pomegranates and chocolate were expressly prohibited. As of April and May 2009, pumpkin, tea, coffee, sausages, semolina, milk products in large packages, frozen food and most baking products were still not allowed in. The Coordinator of Government Activities in the Territories, General Amos Gilad, arbitrarily determines the list of permitted items. He has refused the PA's request to update them in writing on changes in the list. He insists on providing the information only by telephone. A total of only thirty to forty household commodities were allowed into the Gaza Strip in May 2009, as compared to 4,000 approved items prior to the blockade.[40] In early November 2009, Israel allowed in only 3 per cent of the Gaza Strip's cooking gas needs.[41]

The application of the blockade changes weekly, even daily. Some changes result from international pressure exerted upon Israel. Israel agreed to allow in pasta and other food items in response to specific appeals from Secretary of State Clinton and Senator John Kerry in February 2009. The following July, further US pressure prompted Israel to allow hundreds of tons of cement and other construction materials into the Strip. In order to bypass the Hamas regime, these goods were transferred directly to the United Nations Relief and Works Agency (UNRWA), expressly for the purpose of rebuilding a flour mill and a sewage treatment plant destroyed by Israel during its invasion the previous winter.[42]

Other changes are made to mollify Israel's powerful agricultural lobby. Agriculture Minister Shalom Simhon and Deputy Defense Minister Matan Vilnai are sensitive to farm interests and intervene accordingly.

In a discussion that took place in the office of Deputy Minister Vilnai, it was decided that every day, fifteen trucks filled with agricultural produce would be brought in. 'The problem right now is the emphasis on melons and fruit in general,' Agriculture Ministry Director General Yossi Yishai said at the meeting. At the conclusion of the discussion, Vilnai instructed that three trucks with melons be brought into Gaza each week, 'so as not to cause a market failure in Israel.' Another document, from the end of April, signed by Vilnai's public information officer, says: 'Israel's policy at the crossings is set at various times in accordance with a number of considerations.... Economic considerations, including the agricultural establishment, are at the basis of the policy considerations.'

Meir Yifrah, secretary of the Vegetable Growers Organization, also tries to exert influence on the decisions of COGAT and the Defense Ministry, with occasional success.

Once a month or so, I send a text message to [Agriculture Minister Simhon] Shalom saying the situation in the market is very tough, the growers need to send produce to Gaza, see what you can do with the Defense Ministry, so they'll bring in what's needed.... Last year I had a bad situation with onions. A lot of growers were stuck with their stock. We pressed the Agriculture Ministry and then they increased the onion quota from five to eight trucks at the end of last year.' According to him 'The farmers' interest is to find other markets, so we can increase profitability for the grower, by creating demand in Israel and avoiding surpluses.[43]

The Israeli blockade has had a devastating impact on Gaza Strip living standards and employment. In the summer of 2009, OCHA estimated that over 40 per cent of the Gaza Strip workforce was unemployed, and that approximately 75 per cent faced food insecurity. There is a protracted energy crisis; much physical infrastructure, including the water and sewer networks and the health system, is deteriorating and some facilities were damaged or destroyed by Israeli strikes during the recent invasion.[44]

Interestingly, the Israeli blockade benefits Hamas and local interest groups. They reap the profits of a new industry—the construction and operation of tunnels under the Gaza–Egyptian border, which are used to smuggle goods into the Strip. The Hamas government levies customs payments from the entrepreneurs who build and manage the tunnels. Israeli security officials told Avi Issacharoff of *Ha'aretz* that, during the summer of 2009, between 300 and 800 tunnels were in use, employing at least 4,000 people directly and providing a livelihood for tens of thousands more. It costs about $100,000 to excavate a tunnel about 15 meters under the ground and 250 meters long. The job takes two to three months and involves up to 100 diggers a day. Digging is very well-paid work, relative to Gazan salaries. Teams of diggers bid in a kind of tender process to excavate tunnels of a specified depth and length, by a given deadline. The owners' return on their investment depends on the type and price of the goods smuggled. Owners levy a 15 per cent surcharge on merchants or individuals who move goods or people through their tunnel. At a minimum of $2,000 a head, people are the most lucrative commodity to transport. More than 100,000 litres of kerosene move through the tunnels daily, equal to the amount Israel allows in to the Strip through the border crossings. Other products that come in through the tunnels are those that Israel has banned, such as cigarettes and certain foods, electrical goods and livestock, as well as cement. The huge amount of tunnel traffic has led to a growth in ancillary professions—crane operators, carpenters, mechanics, porters and traders, and even real estate agents eager to cash in on the high demand for property along the border. The tunnel industry has also had a social impact on the

Gaza Strip. On the one hand, the tunnels' owners have become the *nouveaux riches* of Gaza. On the other hand, it has created tension with those who suffer from the system. Some residents of Rafah complain that Hamas encourages smuggling despite the fact that criminals are also using the tunnels to bring in drugs and alcohol. People in Rafah are also furious about the outrageous prices that the tunnels' owners charge for their use, as well as their importation of bogus products. In response, the Hamas government established a 'tunnel administration' to supervise the operations.[45]

Israel has nevertheless failed to achieve its strategic goals with these policies. Despite criticism of its shortcomings in running the Gaza Strip and resisting the Israeli invasion, Hamas enjoys grassroots support. Hamas runs the Gaza Strip government and a network of welfare institutions, as well as a bank. Through these institutions, Hamas pays salaries to its employees and pensions to the unemployed; it also pays the young activists of its armed wing.[46] In some respects, Hamas has ruled the Gaza Strip more successfully than Fatah has governed the West Bank. In August 2005, Israel unilaterally evacuated its Gaza Strip settlements and army bases, deciding that it would control the Strip from the outside. Despite its evacuation, however, Israel imposes by fire a no-go zone that amounts to about 6.6 per cent of the Gaza Strip's territory.[47] But beyond this, Palestinians are free to move within the Gaza Strip, in contrast to the restrictions in force in the West Bank. Hamas's armed struggle forced Israel to evacuate all its settlements in the Gaza Strip, whereas settlements continue to proliferate in the West Bank. In the Gaza Strip, Hamas's effective police force has maintained public order,[48] in contrast to the West Bank. There the police are only now gradually establishing control, operating under Israeli and American supervision. In addition, despite Israel's refusal to legitimize Hamas rule, the organization has compelled Israel to negotiate with it, indirectly, over ceasefires and prisoner exchanges.

In the face of Hamas's success, Israel has tightened its blockade of the Gaza Strip. As of November 2007, Israel has required Palestinians whose registered address is in Gaza to apply for temporary permits to remain in the West Bank. This applies even if they have lived in the West Bank for many years and have established their homes there; in some cases this policy has been applied even to Palestinians who were born in the West Bank but whose families came originally from the Gaza Strip. Moreover, in 2007–8 the Israeli military took active measures to locate and expel Palestinians from the West Bank to the Gaza Strip under the pretext that they were 'illegal aliens.' Israel forces families in which one parent comes from the West Bank and one from the Gaza Strip to move to Gaza permanently. In addition, Israel requires Palestinians wishing to enter Gaza to sign an undertaking never to return to the West Bank. Palestinians from Gaza wishing to enter the West Bank for medical treatment, family visits, and other such purposes are required to deposit a large sum of money to guarantee their return to Gaza.[49]

In June 2009, Israeli human rights organizations petitioned the Supreme Court against new Israeli restrictions imposed on Palestinians living in the Gaza Strip who want to live in the West Bank. According to these new regulations, no Palestinian living in Gaza is allowed to apply for residency in the West Bank except under exceptional circumstances, and only if the applicant does not have a 'security impediment.' Eligible to apply are: someone who suffers from a chronic medical condition and who has no other family member (not necessarily of the first degree) in Gaza to provide care; and a minor under the age of sixteen living with one parent in Gaza who dies and another living in the West Bank, on condition that there is no relative in Gaza to look after the minor. Even if he or she does have such relatives, Israel may allow the move, depending on the nature of the relationship with the living parent; a person over the age of sixty-five who is in a 'needy situation' and has a 'first-degree relative' in the West Bank who can help him, conditional, in part, on not having relatives in the Gaza Strip. Anyone who meets one of these criteria and is allowed to move will receive a temporary permit, renewable each year, for seven years. After seven years, if the person has security clearance he or she may be entered in the West Bank population registry.[50]

Methods of Rule

Land and Individual Status: The territorial–legal division is based on differentiations between the status of the land and the status of the Palestinians residing on it. During its first decade, Israel established a land ownership system that placed under Jewish possession, control and management 96 per cent of the state's real estate. Nearly all this land is managed by the Israel Lands Authority (ILA), formed in 1960, which controls 93 per cent of the state's land. The Jewish National Fund (JNF) owns about 13 per cent of the land—but half the members of the ILA's executive board are JNF representatives.[51] A large portion of this land was taken from Palestinians during the 1948 war, including from 'internal refugees' who fled their land and homes to other places inside Israel and who are Israeli citizens. Some was confiscated by the state later on. Israel distributed these lands to Jewish settlements established before the 1948 war, or used them to build new settlements to absorb the large number of Jewish refugees from Europe and the Middle East who arrived in Israel in the early 1950s. In 1962, the government made a pact with the JNF under which the latter would lease its land to Jews only, through the Israel

Lands Administration. The ILA can only lease land under the terms and conditions set by the JNF. This enabled the JNF to pursue its mission to purchase and develop land for Jewish settlement. According to the agreement, the ILA would compensate the JNF with equivalent alternative land whenever the former leased to non-Jews.

In reality, however, it was very hard for non-Jews to lease such ILA land. In 1994, the Ka'adan family requested a permit to build a home in Katzir, a Jewish settlement in central Israel. The request was rejected because the Ka'adans are Arabs. Katzir is situated on land that the ILA has leased to the Jewish Agency for the purpose of establishing an exclusively Jewish settlement. In 1995, the family and the Association for Civil Rights in Israel petitioned the Supreme Court to order a reversal of the decision. In March 2000 the court ruled that state resources cannot be allocated in discriminatory ways. Such a policy, the Court ruled, violates the country's Basic Law on Human Dignity and Freedom (in lieu of a constitution, Israel has a set of basic laws to which other legislation must conform). But the ILA, the Jewish Agency and Katzir's local council sought not to implement the Supreme Court ruling. In September 2003, ACRI filed a second petition, which it withdrew in mid 2004 when the ILA stated that it will allocate land to the Ka'adan family in Katzir.[52] The Israeli authorities, however, did their best to make sure that the Ka'adans would be an exception. In September 2004 a similar petition was brought before the Supreme Court in another case. The petitioners asked the Court for a preliminary order instructing the ILA to allow Arabs to participate in the tender at issue or to suspend it pending the Court's ruling. In the meantime, the ILA and Jewish politicians drafted legislation to circumvent the Court's ruling. In June 2007, the Knesset sent to committee a bill that would allow the JNF to lease lands to Jews only.[53]

In mid 2009, two Jewish community settlements weighed changes in their bylaws. Manof's inhabitants considered requiring prospective residents to declare loyalty to 'Jewish and Zionist values'; Yuvalim's residents discussed the possibility of requiring applicants to affirm their commitment to Israel as a Jewish and democratic state, 'values of the Zionist movement, Jewish heritage and the settlement of the Land of Israel.' They also proposed that new residents be required to participate in the effort to enlarge the Jewish population of Misgav, the regional council to which these two settlements belong. Misgav is located in Upper Galilee, near many Israeli Palestinian villages and towns. Such participation would involve 'creating and maintaining communal Zionist settlement,' 'marking traditional Jewish holidays together, encouraging the children of residents to join in the Zionist youth movement and IDF service [sic], and participating in immigrant absorption.'[54] Mitzpeh Aviv, another Misgav settlement, in November approved new bylaws underlining the settlement's Jewish and Zionist character, which was not mentioned in the previous bylaws. According to the rules, new members must share the basic worldview and goals of the settlement association, which are: 'settlement; Zionism; the heritage of Israel; the values of the State of Israel as a Jewish and democratic state in the spirit of the vision of the State of Israel's Declaration of Independence; tolerance; and human dignity.... [T]he community's Israeli Zionist essence is emphasized in daily life, by celebrating Israeli holidays communally, organizing activities for the youth in connection with their bar-mitzvah year and having members' children join Zionist youth movements, all while taking part in the Zionist enterprise.'[55]

In accordance with the new trend in Gush Segev, the Knesset in December 2009 sent to committee a bill that would allow the admissions committees of communal settlements to check whether candidates' worldviews are compatible with the community's beliefs and mores. The parliamentarians who drafted the bill said that their proposal aims to preserve the 'Zionist vision.'[56] In other words, the new bill aims to circumvent the Supreme Court's ruling in the Ka'adan case and legalize segregated settlements on public land. In reaction, Ahmad Tibi, a member of the Knesset for the Ra'am–Ta'al faction, which lies on the other end of the political spectrum, drafted a bill proposing that the state enforce equal allocation of land to Jews and Arabs. As expected, the Ministerial Committee for Legislation rejected his proposal.[57]

Moreover, since March 2002, the Interior Ministry has not processed any new applications for resident status submitted by Palestinians in Israel. This policy was formalized by a cabinet decision in May 2002, and in 2003 by the Knesset when it passed the Law of Citizenship and Entry into Israel (Temporary Order), which the Knesset later extended until mid 2010. The law applies to Israeli citizens or legal residents who marry people from the territories who are not Israeli citizens (that is, excluding settlers) or elsewhere outside Israel. It prevents the non-Israeli spouses from receiving legal status in the country.[58] Petitions claiming that the extension of the law is unconstitutional have been submitted to the Supreme Court. In response, forty-four members of the Knesset have signed on as co-sponsors of an amendment to Israel's Basic Law on Human Dignity and Freedom so that it cannot be construed to annul the Citizenship and Entry to Israel Law.[59]

In its annual report on the state of Human Rights in Israel and the Occupied Palestinian Territories 2008, the Association for Civil Rights in Israel stated that:

The trend towards racist legislation, which we pointed out in our 2007 State of Human Rights Report, has continued this year. This trend is manifest in draft bills and laws that fuel the de-legitimization of Arab citizens and reflect an attitude towards them that is more akin to the attitude towards an enemy than towards citizens with equal rights.... Land distribution and planning is one of the areas in which Arab citizens of Israel suffer from the most severe deprivation and discrimination. Since the establishment of the State, the Arab population has increased sevenfold, but the State has expropriated half of the lands that were under Arab ownership and has not established a single new Arab town (apart from the Bedouin towns in the Negev that were built on Bedouin lands). In stark contrast, during the past sixty years, more than 600 new Jewish towns have been built. Whereas Arab citizens in Israel account for 20% of the population, the area of jurisdiction of all Arab authorities covers only 2.5% of the area of Israel. Social and institutional barriers have led to a situation in which Arab citizens are effectively prevented from acquiring land or leasing it in more than 80% of the State's territory. In the existing Arab towns and villages, outline plans fail to meet the needs of the population, including its natural growth rate.[60]

On 27 May 2009 the Knesset permitted the submission of legislation that would make it a crime publicly to deny Israel's right to exist as a Jewish state. The right-wing parliamentarian who introduced the bill explained that his purpose is to test the loyalty of Israeli Palestinians. That same week other bills in the same spirit were introduced, including one to outlaw the commemoration of the Nakba (a term meaning 'catastrophe' in Arabic, that the Palestinians use to designate their defeat in the 1948 war). Palestinians commemorate the Nakba annually on 15 May, the date on which the state of Israel was declared in 1948. (Israel's Independence Day is celebrated according to the Hebrew calendar, and thus only occasionally falls on 15 May.) A public and political outcry led its sponsors, in July, to soften its language. In its current form, it would deny state financial support to institutions that publicly commemorate the Nakba. The first reading passed in the Knesset in March 2010. Another decision regarding the Palestinian commemoration of their Nakba was also made in July by the Minister of Education Gideon Sa'ar, of the Likud. He ordered all references to it removed from textbooks written for Israeli Palestinian schoolchildren.[61] Another bill implying that Israeli Palestinians are prima facie disloyal was a proposed amendment to the Basic Law—the Knesset. It would add to the current oath, taken by members of that body, language committing them to uphold the state's Jewish, Zionist and democratic character and to respect and promote its symbols and values.[62] The Ministry of Education did not wait for the end of the legislative process. Its listings of positions open to non-Jews include, as a perquisite, 'a positive view toward the values of Israel's society and culture.' In a job posting for director of the ministry's Tel Aviv district, the criteria are even more detailed: 'A positive attitude toward the values of society and Judaism, as well as the wider Israeli culture.'[63]

The differentiation between the legal status of land and that of the people living on it can also be seen in Jerusalem and the West Bank. In June 1967, Israel annexed Jordanian Jerusalem and its surroundings, making them part and parcel of the sovereign territory of the state. Yet the Palestinians living in this newly-added territory were not granted citizenship, the status granted to the country's Palestinian inhabitants after the creation of the state. Instead, they were given a lesser status, that of permanent residents. Their legal status is that of nationless residents of Israel who bear Jordanian travel documents: Jordanian nationals who live in Israel. With this status, they do not enjoy the rights of citizens. They cannot, for example, purchase an apartment in most of the city's Jewish neighborhoods. Most homes in Jerusalem (and elsewhere in Israel) are built on land belonging to the ILA, which leases the land to homeowners for a renewable period of forty-nine years. Article 19 of the ILA lease specifies that a foreign national cannot lease ILA land. The only way such a person can purchase an apartment built on ILA land is to demonstrate that he is eligible to immigrate to Israel under the terms of the Law of Return, which grants all Jews the right to move to Israel and receive citizenship. Yet Jews can buy land and homes in Jerusalem's Arab neighborhoods, and are even given incentives to do so by state agencies. The few East Jerusalem Palestinians who have moved into Jewish areas have either rented apartments or have bought homes but have refrained from registering their property.[64]

Furthermore, the Interior Ministry strips East Jerusalem Palestinians who have moved outside the city's boundaries of their residency rights. By law, permanent residents lose their standing automatically if their 'centre of life' lies outside the city's boundaries. During the first forty years of Israeli rule over East Jerusalem, from 1967 to 2007, the ministry deprived 8,558 Arabs of their residency rights. But in 2008 alone the ministry revoked residency rights from 4,577 East Jerusalem Palestinians.[65] Concerned about the demographic balance between Jews and Arabs in its capital, the Israeli administration does its best to identify and take action against Palestinian Arabs who have moved out of the city. In the late 1990s, the Jerusalem municipality and the Interior Ministry estimated that between 50,000 and 80,000 of East Jerusalem's Palestinian inhabitants had moved out to the suburbs, although their lives continued to be centered on Jerusalem.[66] Following the construction of the Barrier, which severely hampers travel between the city and its Palestinian suburbs, many of these people—by both Israeli and Palestinian estimates—thousands have moved back into the city.

In the 1980s Israel began to use for its own purposes the Jordanian legal category of 'state land.' Any property lacking a locally registered, known owner was declared abandoned and expropriated by the state. Large tracts of this land were allocated for Jewish settlements, enabling Israel to redouble its project of moving Jews into the West Bank.[67]

Political Participation: Palestinians enjoy only limited participation in ruling institutions. Although represented in the Knesset, no Muslim or Christian Palestinians attained cabinet rank until January 2007. Then, for the first time, a Muslim Palestinian citizen of Israel, representing the Labor Party, was appointed a government minister. Nearly all East Jerusalem Palestinians boycott municipal elections and have no voice in the decision-making institutions that manage their daily lives. About 128,000 of them had the right to vote in the November 2008 municipal elections, but fewer than 2,000 exercised this right, a 1.7 per cent turnout, the lowest since 1967.[68]

The Palestinians of the West Bank and the Gaza Strip enjoyed political empowerment in 1996 when, under the provisions of the Oslo Accords, they voted for their autonomous parliament and presidency. But, as I have noted, Israel effectively divested the Palestinian Authority of its power through its invasion of the West Bank in 2002. Since then, Israel has held Palestinian independence in check and made all major policy decisions in the West Bank, in a process that excludes those who are affected by these decisions. At best, the Palestinians can ask international actors and human rights agencies to put pressure on Israel to modify its policies. The popular electoral support for Hamas in the PA's 2006 elections can be seen as a protest vote against this state of affairs—an attempt to find an alternative combination of political power and identity that could replace Fatah and overcome Israeli–imposed fragmentation.

Regulations: Israel has, since 2000, frequently revised the regulations that govern the daily lives of Palestinians in the West Bank and Gaza Strip. Israeli Palestinians enjoy status stability as citizens. But, as I noted above, thousands of East Jerusalem Palestinians have, since 1996, faced the threat of losing their residency rights when they moved out to the city's eastern Palestinian suburbs. Israel encouraged such moves by not granting such people permits to build and enlarge homes in the city; furthermore, housing in the suburbs is cheaper and of higher quality. Under the new enforcement regime of the residential law, these people are presumed not to be Jerusalemites unless they can prove otherwise. As a result, those lacking acceptable proof are cut off from their urban center by the Separation Barrier—which in Jerusalem takes the form of a massive wall cutting through the middle of neighborhoods that straddle the municipal boundary.[69] Worse is the situation of the Palestinians in the West Bank and Gaza. Since 2000, they have been subject to frequent changes in Israeli military regulations, which fragment their territory and control their time. These changes are made deliberately in order to create uncertainty among the population, which Israel sees as sheltering terrorists.[70] Typically telling is the case of prohibiting, since mid-January 2010, Palestinian lawyers and the relatives of Palestinian detainees from reaching a military tribunal via the Beitunia checkpoint west of Ramallah. The court lies 300 metres south of the Beitunia roadblock. When the military court was moved in 2004 from Ramallah to the Ofer facility next to the checkpoint, the roadblock was opened so that lawyers and relatives of the accused could get to the court. However, at this writing the Israeli police require Palestinians wishing to reach this military tribunal, located in the West Bank, to use the Qalandiyah crossing, which lies 20 kilometers away. There they need an entry permit into Israel, a request which can be rejected or takes weeks to process.[71]

Uncertainty reaches its peak in the Gaza Strip, where Israel has tightened its blockade.

Differentiation: is a fundamental instrument of the Israeli ruling system. It helps the Jewish institutions to maintain and sustain the system by mitigating its negative aspects. By awarding formal citizenship to one group of Palestinians and residency rights to another, Israel can claim to be a democratic state in its sovereign territory while defending itself in the Occupied Palestinian Territories. On the other hand, in limited times and places, Israel can use massive force and commit brutal acts against Palestinians. For instance, in May 2004 Israel retaliated against the killing of thirteen of its soldiers in the Gaza Strip with a large-scale military action in the city of Rafah, in the southern part of the Strip. A total of 116 Palestinian houses were destroyed and 1,160 people made homeless. Altogether, during the first half of 2004, Israel demolished 284 homes in Rafah, leaving 2,185 people homeless.[72] During the Israeli offensive against the Hamas regime in the Gaza Strip, December 2008–January 2009, Israeli forces killed 1,414 Palestinians. (The numbers are Adalah's; B'tselem counted 1,387 Palestinians killed. Nine Israelis died in the clashes.) Over 5,300 Palestinians were injured, according to B'tselem.[73] According to UN figures, Israel destroyed more than 3,500 residential dwellings and 20,000 people were left homeless.[74] The combined result of these two elements can explain the sustainability of the Israeli system.

Indeed, the strategy of differentiation stands on two pillars: creating commonalities while at the same time maintaining differences. For example, Jewish and Palestinian citizens of Israel share formal citizenship status, a base on which they achieved gains and improved their citizenship status. But this commonality is a weak one because of the ethnic basis of the Israeli citizenship, the shift of the conflict since 2000 and due to the overriding role of security as a criterion for the operation of state agencies. Simultaneously, the commonality of different Palestinian groups is empowered by the Israeli containment of the occupied territories. In other words, there is a reciprocal relationship between exclusion and inclusion, both of which change over time.

5

THE CHANGING PATTERN
OF THE CONFLICT

Back to 1948?

From 1882 until 1988, the Israeli–Palestinian conflict was a zero-sum game between two national movements struggling for exclusive ownership of the same land. The Palestinian national movement was able to build power centers only outside Israeli–ruled areas, which it struggled to infiltrate. The First Intifada of 1987 and the subsequent Oslo agreement of 1993 started a process that was leading toward the establishment of a Palestinian state in the West Bank and Gaza Strip. This promised to turn the dispute into a border conflict rather than an existential struggle between two forces, each of which denied the other's right to the land between the Jordan and the Mediterranean. But Israel continued to construct settlements extensively even after the Oslo accords were signed, creating a paradox. The aim of the settlements was to impose a border to Israel's liking on the emerging Palestinian state. In other words, Israel continued to pursue its old strategy of expansion precisely at a time when a diplomatic process sought to stop it. By the time the Camp David negotiations of 2000 terminated fruitlessly and the Second Intifada broke out, the ground had already been prepared for Israeli rule over the entire land—what Israel called the Land of Israel and the Palestinians Palestine. The Oslo agreements' tripartite division of the West Bank and Gaza Strip into zones where the Palestinian Authority had different powers was not, as it first promised to be, a step along the way to an extension of full Palestinian rule over all this area. Instead, it ended up ensconcing de facto Israeli rule over divided Palestinian territories.

Israel was, and remains, the strong side in this asymmetric conflict. But, as the weaker side, the Palestinians exercise a veto over any permanent resolution of the dispute. Israel has thus had no choice but to invest ever more resources in its occupation and domination of the entire area west of the Jordan River. Israel retains control over the entire land so that it can combat the Palestinian uprising. The Palestinian people is divided into several groups with different gradations of rights, living under different security regimes. Israel hopes that a differential system can prevent international criticism or keep it at a tolerable level.

The de facto unitary state and the lack of a border between Israel and the Palestinians have presented Israel with an acute dilemma: an unfavorable demographic balance between Jews and Arabs. According to Sergio Della Pergola, a demographer at the Hebrew University of Jerusalem, the territory that was once Mandatory Palestine—the territory between the Jordan River and the Mediterranean Sea—was, in 2000, inhabited by 5,168,000 Jews and 4,151,000 Palestinians.[1] In other words, Jews constituted 55.5 per cent of the total population in this area. He projects that the proportion of Jews will decline to something in the range of 50.2–54.9 per cent by 2010 and 44.3–51.9 per cent in 2020. Within Israel proper, that is, Israel within its borders prior to the 1967 war, Della Pergola projects that the proportion of Palestinians will increase from 18.6 per cent in 2000 to 20.6–20.9 per cent in 2010 and 22.8–23.6 per cent in 2020.[2] In a few years' time, given current demographic trends, if no alternative solution is found, a Jewish minority will rule by force over a Palestinian majority. It should be noted that Israel faces a similar demographic problem in Jerusalem. As mentioned above, Jerusalem's population at the end of 2008 was 35 per cent Palestinian and 65 per cent Jewish. Israel has, since 2003, tried to shore up its diminishing majority by creating a Greater Jerusalem, augmenting the city with West Bank territory that remains on the Israeli side of the Security Barrier. This land measures about 225 square kilometers (87 square miles). It contains about 286,000 Israeli Jews and 243,000 Palestinians—53 per cent Israelis versus 47 per cent Palestinians.[3]

The means of control that work within Israel and which allow it to control the Palestinians who constitute about a fifth of its citizens is unlikely to work for long when there is near-parity between the two populations, or even worse, when the Jews become a minority. When that happens, it will be difficult to paper over the hard problems that this uneasy fact will produce with soft solutions, such as giving limited civil rights to select Palestinian communities, invoking Israeli security needs, and pursuing partial and temporary measures. The sustainability of the Israeli ethno-security regime is built on thin ice. It can hold only so long as the ice is not melted by the spotlight of criticism.

Today, Israel finds itself facing the same inter-communal conflict with the Palestinians that it faced sixty-two years ago. Rather than a conflict between two neighboring states, it finds itself embroiled in a domestic conflict between two or more ethnic communities under one government. However, Israel is much more powerful than it was in 1948. Furthermore, now, at the beginning of the twenty-first century, the Arab world is willing to accept Israel and establish peaceful and normal relations with the Jewish state, provided that it withdraws to the pre-June 1967 borders and agrees to find a just solution to the plight of Palestinian refugees. In 2002, the Arab states challenged Israel with a peace proposal that contradicts the Arab rejection of the United Nations partition plan of November 1947. In 1947, the Arabs refused to accept the establishment of a Jewish state on the part of Palestine, but today they are prepared to recognize Israel and establish normal relations. The change came in the wake of the unprecedented Israeli victory of 1967. Egypt and Jordan accepted UN Security Council Resolution 242 of November 1967, hence implicitly accepting Israel within its pre-June 1967 borders.[4] All partial Israeli–Arab settlement plans and accords are based on Resolution 242. They mark significant steps away from the complete rejectionism of 1947. Further down this road stand Israel's peace accords with Egypt and Jordan, the Oslo agreements, and the Arab League peace plan.

Yet one similarity between the two periods is striking. In both periods the Palestinian national movement was weak and domestically divided. In 1948 its weakness helped the Jews expand their territory and change the demographic balance between them and their Palestinian rivals. Similarly, the Palestinians since 2000 are too weak and divided to resist Israeli rule over all of Mandatory Palestine.[5]

Are the Palestinians facing a second Nakba? This question was posed frequently in Palestinian public and private discussions during 2008, and in December 2009 it was still very much on the Palestinian mind. A joint survey of Israeli and Palestinian public opinion, conducted by the Truman Institute of the Hebrew University in Jerusalem and the Palestinian Center for Policy and Survey Research in Ramallah, found that 53 per cent of the Palestinians fear that Israel aspires to a Jewish Greater Israel and will thus expel the Palestinians. Another

23 per cent believe that Israel plans to annex the West Bank while denying political rights of Palestinians; only 11 per cent believe that Israel wants to guarantee Palestinian security and withdraw from all the territories occupied in 1967. As for the Israelis, 40 per cent fear that the Palestinians plan to overrun the state of Israel and annihilate its Jewish population. Another 14 per cent think that the Palestinians 'only' want to conquer Israel, while 26 per cent think that the Palestinians' aim is to gain control of the West Bank and Gaza Strip. Only 14 per cent of Israelis believe that Palestinian aspirations in the long run will be satisfied by gaining control of a part of the West Bank and Gaza Strip. These mirror-image perceptions, or mis-perceptions, of mutual hostility engender pessimism. In December 2009, a full 65 per cent of Israelis and 67 per cent of Palestinians thought that a final status agreement was out of reach for the time being.[6]

Acutely aware of the political fracture between Hamas and Fatah, on top of the physical and legal divisions that Israel imposes, Palestinians are cognizant that their current circumstances resemble those they faced in 1937–47. That latter period of division and infighting presaged the collapse, in 1948, of their military forces and civil society and the loss of large amounts of Palestinian-owned land to Israel. They also note that, as Israel grapples with its demographic problem, it continues to expand and divide Palestinians from their lands. Can Israel repeat its actions of 1948 on a smaller scale in the face of an international consensus that ethnic cleansing and apartheid are unacceptable? Are the Palestinians not too weak to gain international support? These questions crossed the Palestinians' mind as they commemorated the sixtieth anniversary of their Nakba.

As I have noted, the Israeli–Palestinian conflict has shifted backward from being a border conflict into an ethnic struggle between Israeli Jews and Arab Palestinians within a single state. In such a conflict, the Green Line is of little importance; what counts are ethnic affiliation and community origins. The frontier line is not an internationally recognized border but rather an ethnic divide.

The Israeli public in fact accepts a two-state solution in principle, as has been demonstrated in many public opinion polls, among them surveys conducted by the Hebrew University's Truman Institute and the Palestinian Center for Policy and Survey Research.[7] However, the majority of Israelis also reject a return to the Green Line—the border that preceded the war of June 1967. In 2008, most Israelis maintained that the chances for achieving a two-state solution in the near future were weak or non-existent.[8]

The transformation of the conflict has brought many in both constituencies to accentuate their religious identities and perspectives on the Israeli–Palestinian struggle. For these people, the conflict is an ethno-religious one, a clash between Jewish and Islamic civilizations. The ethnic foundation of Judaism is increasingly used to justify the system of Israeli control. Growing numbers of Jews interpret the concept of a Jewish state in exclusively ethnic terms, rejecting any obligation to respect minority rights. The Tami Steinmetz Center for Peace Research's Peace Index of March 2008 found that 55 per cent of Jewish Israelis define the West Bank as 'liberated territory,' while only 32 per cent prefer the term 'occupied territory.' Moreover, 57 per cent maintain that the Green Line should not constitute the future border between Israel and the Palestinians, and that a new boundary should be drawn, one that will place most settlements on the Israeli side, while placing Israeli Arab communities adjacent to the West Bank on the Palestinian side. Only 23 per cent of the Jewish public favors the Green Line as the future border with Palestine. Finally, 75 per cent of Israeli Jews oppose the idea of a bi–national state as an alternative to the two-state solution.[9] In other words, a majority of Israeli Jews reject the concept of 'one man, one vote,' and want to establish a polity based on an ethnic divide between Jews and Palestinians. Yet acceptance of the 4 June 1967 border is a Palestinian and pan-Arab prerequisite for peace agreement. Only by accepting it in principle can Israel release itself from controlling the Palestinians by force.

It is not unrealistic to assume that, despite their weakness and domestic divisions, the Palestinians will not tolerate this new state of affairs for long, just as Israeli settlement expansion, occupation and discrimination impelled them to launch the 1987 Intifada. Most likely, a significant number of Israeli Palestinians will not simply observe such an uprising from the sidelines, in particular if the Israeli response is brutal. Indeed, Israel received powerful reminders of the implications of Israeli Palestinians' growing ethnic awareness. In October 2000, thousands of them violently protested against Israeli killings of Palestinians in the West Bank and Gaza Strip during the first days of the Second Intifada. As mentioned above, the Islamic movement in Israel acts to preserve Temple Mount as an Islamic holy site, in opposition to Israeli religious–national extremists who seek to establish a new order and secure Jewish worship there.

Since the late 1990s, according to Honaida Ghanim, the intellectual discourse of Israeli Palestinians has been divided into three schools. The first sees their liminal status as a privilege with which they can bridge between modern Western Jewish society and an underdeveloped Arab society. This school dominated between 1948 and 1967. The intellectuals who hold this approach view Israel as a model for the Arabs. The second school prefers to identify with the land of Palestine and disregards the state of Israel. Intellectuals who belong to this school look back to golden ages in Arab history in order to escape from the painful present. This approach offers no solutions to current problems, and as such is not popular. The third school developed in the 1990s, and since 2000 has led to a shift in the discourse among Israeli Jews and Arab Palestinians. It calls for ending the liminal status of the Palestinians who live in Israel by turning Israel into a bi–national state or a state of all its citizens, regardless of ethnic origins. When Israel becomes a liberal democracy, in this view, its Palestinian citizens will resolve the conflict between their homeland and their state. The third school is highly critical of the first one. It argues that, with its discriminatory Zionist ideology, Israel estranges the Palestinians.[10]

During the Israeli offensive against the Gaza Strip's Hamas regime in December 2008 and January 2009, tens of thousands of Israeli Palestinians participated in demonstrations against the war; the Israeli police arrested 832 persons who participated in acts of violence.[11] In March 2010 when Hamas called for a 'Day of Rage' following Israeli settlement expansion in East Jerusalem, Palestinian violence spread to Jaffa and the Negev—the Israeli South area—where public buses and private cars were stoned.[12]

In 2006–7, three NGOs founded and run by Israeli Palestinians published political documents that challenge the ethnic foundations of the state of Israel. The most comprehensive is *The Future Vision of the Palestinian Arabs in Israel*, published by the National Committee of the Heads of the Arab Local Authorities in Israel.[13] The principal demand put forward by its authors is for the state to:

recognize the Palestinian Arabs in Israel as an indigenous national group (and as a minority within the international conventions) that has the right within their citizenship to choose its representatives directly and be responsible for their religious, educational and cultural affairs.... The State has to acknowledge that Israel is the home-land for both Palestinians and Jews (the Israeli future constitution and state laws should reinforce this point by adding an introduction [sic] paragraph).... Israel should refrain from adopting policies and schemes in favor of the majority. Israel must remove all forms of ethnic superiority, be that [sic] executive, structural, legal or symbolic. Israel should adopt policies of corrective justice in all aspects of life in order to compensate for the damage inflicted on the Palestinian Arabs due to the ethnic favoritism policies of the Jews. The State should cooperate with representatives of the Palestinian Arabs to search the possibility of restoring parts of their lands that Israel confiscated not for public use. Israel should also dedicate an equal part of its resources for the direct needs of the Palestinian Arabs.[14]

Palestinians inside and outside Israel saw this document as inviting the Jewish majority to a dialogue about the paper and about ways to improve Israeli democracy.[15] Most Israeli Jews, however, viewed it as a threat to the Jewish character of the state and as a watershed leading into a new and worse era of relations with the country's Arab citizens.[16] Yuval Diskin, the head of the General Security Service, defined the new trends among Israeli Palestinians as a strategic threat, and stated that his organization will operate against anybody seeking to harm Israel's Jewish or democratic character, even if that activity was carried out by legal means.[17] 'The Shin Bet's position,' wrote Diskin to Attorney General Mazuz, 'is that the term "subversive" can include attempts to change the fundamental values of the state by nullifying its democratic or Jewish character and can be regarded as undermining the arrangements of the democratic regime and its institutions.... As for activity that is not illegal when that activity "rubs up against" injury to the arrangements of the democratic regime and its institutions, it is the Shin Bet's duty to collect and analyze information regarding this activity so as to guarantee that it does not spill over into illegal activity and is not camouflaged to hide illegal activity. When there is a basis for suspecting that there is sub-versive activity going on that has secret elements, such activity may justify using information-gathering techniques such as wiretapping.'[18]

Simultaneously, the Israeli Jewish majority adheres more strongly to its ethnic origins. The Tami Steinmetz Center for Peace Research's Peace Index of October 2007 found that a majority of Israeli Jews still voice support for democratic val-ues. Yet its status has declined considerably since June 1996, while the status of Jewish nationality has strengthened.[19]

The 2009 Democracy Index, published by the Israel Democ-racy Institute in early August 2009, revealed that 53 per cent of the Jewish public supports encouraging Israeli Palestinians to emigrate from Israel. It also found that 38 per cent of the Jewish public thinks that Jewish citizens should have more rights than non-Jewish citizens,[20] and that only 19 per cent of the Jewish public opposes the statement, 'Agreement of a Jew-ish majority is required on decisions fateful to the country.' These figures point to broad support for denying political rights to Israel's Arab minority.[21]

Of course, both Hamas and Gush Emunim (the Block of Faithful, the movement behind most of Israeli settlements in the Occupied Territories) were founded long before 2000—the former in 1987 and the latter in 1974. They are national–reli-gious movements created in reaction to the Israeli occupation of 1967 territories. Both were afraid that the Oslo process would lead Israel and the PLO to make concessions, and both movements acted separately to stymie the diplomacy pursued by their national leaderships. But as reflected in 2006 Palestin-ian and 2009 Israeli elections, the current stage of the conflict's transformation has led many more in both constituencies to adopt conservative national-religious identities and perspec-tives on the Israeli–Palestinian struggle. On the Palestinian side, Islam is not only a replacement for the failing secular identity represented by the PLO. Political Islam is also a uniting identity, a tool for bridging over the socio-geographical divisions that Israel imposes, as well as a divine guarantee of a better future. With the national–political structure of the Palestinian Authority in ruins, Palestinian society has taken up political Islam as an alternative identity, as well as a source of power and a symbolic center. The strong Jewish side does not need to use religion as a source of power and hope. It rather uses Judaism's ethnic foundations to empower and justify the Israeli control system. A growing number of Jews understand the concept of a Jewish state in exclusive terms rather then as an inclusive obligation to respect minority rights. Judaism is seen less as a value system with a universal cast and more as an exclusive ethnic order.

Colonial Practices in the Service of an Ethno-Security Regime

So far, the Israeli government has largely been reluctant to take strong measures against settlers who violate the law.[22] The authorities have evacuated settler houses and halted their construction projects only when forced to do so by Israeli courts, US pressure, or, as was the case in the Gaza Strip, Palestinian violence. If territorial expansion and containment of Palestinian land is detrimental to Israel's interest, why does Israel persist in these counterproductive policies? Why does the state not reverse the process, reinstate the 4 June 1967 border, and make it the basis for an accommodation with the Palestinian national movement? What can bring about such a change?

Israel is a regional power that uses imperial methods and colonial practices to pursue its national struggle with the Palestinians. (This does not mean that it is a colonial power, only that it has adopted some of the methods used by such powers.) Israel expands through settlements, denies egalitarian integration of its Palestinian citizens into the Jewish state, and maintains colonial economic relations with the Palestinians of the West Bank and Gaza Strip. The Israeli military displays its power through the deployment of both real and symbolic force, bringing the Palestinians to internalize Israel's superior strength and to behave accordingly. When the Palestinians choose rebellion over subservience, Israel uses brutal imperial methods to combat the uprising, in order to reiterate the asymmetric power balance between the sides.[23] Why does Israel find it so difficult to choose, for its own benefit, a policy of territorial devolution and decolonization?

Haklai suggests[24] that the settlers have infiltrated the state bureaucracy. He shows that all state agencies, from the top political echelon down, were not passive but rather active in promoting the settlement project. In fact, the ideology and practice of expanding borders through settlements goes back to the early days of Zionism, as does the correlation between settling on the land and armed defense of it. Given this correlation, and its zealous advocacy by the national religious public, Israel's political and military leadership are profoundly concerned that national religious soldiers and officers will refuse to carry out a government decision to evacuate settlements and that pro-settlement civilians will engage in civil disobedience to protest such a move. 'I pray and hope that the State of Israel will know how to make difficult and heart-rending decisions without a civil war,' Prime Minister Olmert said at a cabinet meeting on outpost evacuation.[25]

Yet there are reasons to believe that future evacuations in the West Bank will be even more difficult than were those in the Gaza Strip. The Israeli public by and large did not see the Gaza Strip as part of the Land of Israel, so could be persuaded to support the evacuation. Furthermore, the settler leadership at the time kept the protest within the bounds of civil disobedience. Violence was delegitimized. While this approach was opposed by the radical young generation, they did not want to split with or revolt against their leaders. But hard-liners did say then that they would use harsher methods in any future evacuation. Thirdly, the socio-economic profile of the typical Gaza Strip settler was different from that of those in the West Bank settlements. Many Gaza settlers were the children or grandchildren of immigrants who had come to Israel in the 1950s from the Islamic world. Many of them had been born in the Negev, not far from their settlements. They were not part and parcel of the hard core of the ideological Gush Emunim settler movement, as are many West Bank settlers.

A comparison of the Israeli–Palestinian conflict with that of the French in Algeria can be instructive, despite some disparities between them. The two cases differ in the physical distance between the colony and the home country, the time frame, and the legal status of the colony. Israeli settlements are very close to the state's major population, economic and symbolic centers, and no sea separates the metropolitan and the colony. Israeli settlements are younger than were those of the French in Algeria; and the Occupied Palestinian Territories were never annexed de jure to Israel as Algeria was to France. During the Algerian war, the French army and the Pieds Noirs (the ethnic Europeans living in Algeria) plotted against the Fourth and Fifth Republics. Given the differences, however, Ian Lustick surmises that Israeli settlers will most likely not seek to prevent their evacuation from the West Bank by attempting a violent overthrow of the Israeli regime.[26] Lustick also argues that Israel is a smaller country than France and is thus much more dependent on maintaining good relations with other countries; first and foremost the US. Israel cannot afford a confrontation

131

with its allies if they decide to impose sanctions to compel it to relinquish the Palestinian territories.[27] But Lustick published his book before the assassination of Prime Minister Yitzhak Rabin, in November 1995. Rabin was murdered by a radical religious–nationalist student in reaction to his signing of the Oslo II Agreement just a few weeks previously. When it came out, Lustick was correct that the IDF, unlike the French army, 'does not contain elite units or any units with a particular political coloration.'[28] But this is no longer the case, following the changes in the composition of the IDF's combat troops and officer corps described above.

Despite the differences, in both cases the powerful side expanded into the colony through the construction of settlements and the exercise of military force, and the chief power-holders in the home country were committed to the colonial project. They and their constituencies perceived the colony as an integral part of their national territory, closely tied to its glorious past, essential for preserving the nation's heritage. In both cases, furthermore, leaders and the citizenry maintained that control of the colony was vital for the home country's defense. The French argued that, if decolonized, Algeria would fall to Communist forces. Israel, for its part, argues that Hamas, and through it Iran, would take control of the West Bank if Israel were to leave—just as Hamas took over the Gaza Strip after Israel left that territory. In both cases, the political leadership generally gave the army a free hand to crack down the insurgents, and no serious international pressure was brought to bear on the colonial power to withdraw. It is certainly true that the French army in Algeria used means far more brutal than anything done by the IDF in the West Bank. But this is largely due to the IDF's self-restraint, deriving from its own moral standards and operational constraints, as well as the norms of the society it serves. The government itself has not placed limits on the army. Beyond this, in both cases political rhetoric was often not backed up by action—despite their declarations of the vital importance of the colonies, the home countries were reluctant to increase national investment in the war. What finally defeated the French colonial project in Algeria, Gil Merom argues, was the domestic debate in France over the moral cost of the colonial enterprise. The French army was not defeated by the FLN, the Algerian independence movement. Rather, criticism of the war's morality and its real value to the home country, voiced by intellectuals and the media, led to a change in public perceptions and thus to the erosion of popular support for the war.[29] If this can be taken as a model, the current state of affairs in Israel will prevail as long as the majority of its citizens support the ethno-security regime and its repressive methods and do not criticize its moral and political costs.

Lustick offers another answer. In his comparative study of Britain and Ireland, France and Algeria, and Israel and the West Bank and Gaza Strip, he concludes that when a regime considers withdrawing from an occupied or annexed territory it has to cross, first, a threshold of civic upheavals, violent disorder and delegitimization. Second, it faces the task of crossing the hegemonic ideological threshold that prohibits questioning the future of the territory. Once the widespread belief that the occupied or annexed territory is an integral and necessary part of the homeland breaks down and its future is under debate, the government is likely to cross the political threshold.[30] Thus, according to Lustick, the major forces behind the status quo are hegemonic ideology and the readiness of the political elite to confront those elements that hold veto-power and act as spoilers for any accommodation. Unless the leadership sizes its power and leads the change, the current state of affairs prevails.

Hendrik Spruyt offers a wider perspective based on his analysis of the end of empires.[31] He argues that the more fragmented the decision-making process in the core of the empire, the greater the resistance to changes in territorial policy. Such fragmentation creates multiple veto opportunities that interest groups exploit to preserve their status and privileges. Settlers are not the only group that stands to lose material and status privileges from a relocation of the state's borders. Israeli manufacturers have, since 1967, maintained a trade surplus with the Palestinian territories, making them important large markets for Israeli products.[32] Furthermore, business interests stand to lose investments, as well as economic and financial benefits they have enjoyed as part of the imperial–colonial enterprise. Politicians worry about losing public support and failing in re-election bids. In addition, the military has an institutional interest in maintaining its opportunities for career advancement, its budget, and the high status it enjoys as the nation's defender and the key instrument of the creation and maintenance of the empire. In countries in conflict, the army often enjoys a dominant political role; in such cases, this role frequently constitutes a necessary and sufficient explanation for the persistence of the colonial territorial configuration. Like the settlers themselves, the defense establishment argues that control of the territories is vital to state security. If the civilian leadership exercises only weak oversight, the military will set policy, in particular in cases of territorial dispute.

Spruyt's model is most pertinent for the case at hand. Israel has a powerful military–security establishment, a fragmented political system, and weak civilian leadership. Moreover, civil society has little capacity to limit the security establishment's enormous clout in decision-making and in shaping social values.[33] Indeed, the defense establishment is committed to defending Israel and does so according to its best professional judgment. Unsurprisingly, it resists compromises that, in its view, would place Israel at a strategic disadvantage. But military leaders are not impersonal automatons—they also have institutional, budgetary and status interests that are served by maintaining the colonial system. The army not only helped to establish and maintain the settlements but also uses them as bases in its repression of Palestinian unrest.

As a consequence, when politicians consider withdrawing from Palestinian land, many actors exercise their veto-power. This happened on a small scale in 1979, when Israel signed a peace treaty with Egypt and withdrew from the Sinai Peninsula. At that time, however, Israel enjoyed the strong leadership of Prime Minister Menachem Begin. Furthermore, he enjoyed the support of Foreign Minister Moshe Dayan and Defense Minister Ezer Weizman, both of whom had been celebrated military commanders before entering politics. These three men together had the political cachet to overcome the vetoes of the defense establishment and the settler movement and its supporters. Moreover, Israel's investment in Sinai and the number of settlers there were smaller than in the Palestinian territories. Israel's pullback from southern Lebanon in 2000 was also different. Israel had no settlements in southern Lebanon, and most of the military work was carried out by a proxy, the South Lebanon Army. Israeli investment and direct involvement in southern Lebanon were lower then they are in the Palestinian areas. Therefore, when the IDF failed to keep the area under control at low cost, it was easy for forces in civil society and Prime Minister Ehud Barak to rally public support for withdrawal.

From a Two-State Solution to a One-State Problem

'At this juncture,' Robert Malley and Hussein Agha argued early in 2008, 'a two-state solution... has been stripped of what made it valuable' for the Palestinians: liberation, self-determination, dignity and respect. Moreover, they wrote, 'at present it is not just that neither Israelis nor Palestinians believe an agreement will be reached; it is that they hardly care. They have become familiar almost to the point of indifference with the possible solutions, endlessly promised, endlessly deferred.'[34] Similarly, Nathan Brown argues that the peace process has come to an end. The formula of land for peace 'is rapidly passing the point at which it is even feasible ... it's time to stop pretending that there is a meaningful diplomatic process leading toward a two-state solution.'[35] Bernard Chazelle has reached the same conclusion, maintaining that while the two-state solution was once the only realistic road to peace, it is now a challenge likely to be beyond Israel's capabilities.[36]

Indeed, there has recently been a resurgence of interest in a one-state resolution. By the early 1980s Meron Benvenisti had already concluded that the Israeli settlement project was irreversible, and that a single state was inevitable.[37] But his analysis found few adherents until recently. Now there is growing intellectual interest in the one-state model. It was the historian Tony Judt who inaugurated the current discourse, in an essay he published in 2003 in *The New York Review of Books*.[38] Plenty of books, research reports and articles have followed.[39] Radicals among the advocates of a single state hope to revive their old vision of an undivided Palestine under Palestinian majority rule—a vision that disappeared from the political agenda when the PLO declared its support for a two-state solution. The pragmatists in this group use advocacy of a single state as a tactic aimed at forcing Israel to accept, in the face of the demographic threat, a partition along 1967 lines. The one-state solution has also been tabled in Israeli–Palestinian talks as the Palestinians' plan B. Ahmed Qurei, the Palestinian chief negotiator, told his Israeli counterparts at the Annapolis talks in June 2008 that if Israel continues to create 'facts on the ground' by force, he will tell his people 'that we spent thirty years persuading Palestinians to accept a two-state solution, and if we do not succeed in achieving it, we will return to the idea of one state.'[40] And in November 2009, Saeb Erekat recommended that Mahmoud Abbas tell his people the truth—that with the continuation of settlement activities, the two-state solution is no longer an option.[41] Erekat made this statement in response to the Obama administration's acquiescence in Israel's refusal to freeze all its settlement expansion. Although the administration had originally demanded that Israel halt all construction in the settlements pending negotiations with the Palestinian Authority, in the end it agreed to a temporary ten-month freeze that included numerous exceptions. Under this understanding, Israel continued with the construction of 2,500 housing units in West Bank settlements. Furthermore, the US acceded to Israel's demand that the construction moratorium not apply to East Jerusalem.

According to the Palestinian pollster Khalil Shikaki, the one-state paradigm is supported by around 25 per cent of Palestinians, mainly young people and left-wing intellectuals.[42] Those who demand a single non-ethnic state based on the principle of 'one man, one vote' believe that current circumstances have created the foundation for this solution. But given the exacerbation of ethnic conflict, it is unrealistic to expect that the two rival communities can live together in a liberal democratic state. Each of the ethnic entities comprises a collective that extends beyond the community residing on its territory. Israel is the state of all Jews, and Palestine is to be the state of the Palestinian diaspora as well. It will be difficult, if not impossible, for each of them to sever its ethnic ties and reverse its decades of struggle for the establishment and maintenance of a separate nation-state. A state founded on citizenship alone will not satisfy the ethnic–national needs of either community. Can Israelis and Palestinians 'overcome their dislike of each other such that they can contemplate living together in one state whether binational, federal, cantonal or unitary?' wonders Rashid Kahlidi.[43] Within such a state, Jewish and Palestinian citizens would jockey constantly for the upper hand. Who could and would dominate in such a case, the Palestinian numerical majority or the stronger, more advanced and powerful Jews? A single state, Nathan Brown has concluded, 'will not be based on coexistence but on a relationship of naked domination and brutal resistance.'[44] In other words, in the absence of a dramatic and unexpected shift in the national consciousnesses of both peoples, the land between the Jordan River and the Mediterranean Sea will head not toward Swiss-style federation but toward Balkanization. While the two-state solution is beyond the sides' current capabilities, a state of individuals whose national, historical, cultural, linguistic and religious roots and identifications take second place to the abstractions of Western-style liberal democracy will never be achieved.

The Israeli ethno-security regime is sustainable as long as the political asymmetry between the Israeli and the Palestinian sides remains overwhelmingly in Israel's favor. It will end only when the external forces that help to maintain it, even if unintentionally, cease to cooperate. According to Meron Benvenisti:

This explosive status quo survives due to the combination of several factors: fragmentation of the Palestinian community and incitement of the remaining fragments against each other; enlistment of the Jewish community into support for the occupation regime, which is perceived as protecting its very existence; funding of the status quo by the 'donor nations,' which cause corruption among the Palestinian leadership; persuasion of the neighboring states to give priority to bilateral and global interests over Arab ethnic solidarity; success of the propaganda campaign known as 'negotiations with the Palestinians,' which convinces many that the status quo is temporary and thus they can continue to amuse themselves with theoretical alternatives to 'the final-status arrangement'; the silencing of all criticism as an expression of hatred and anti–Semitism; and psychological repugnance toward the conclusion that the status quo is durable and will not be easily changed.[45]

Benvenisti's conclusions are not all that different from those of Smooha, who wonders whether Israel's ethno-democracy within the Green Line is stable. Despite its non-Western nature and its discrimination against its Arab minority, Smooha argues, Israel's ethnic democracy is viable and stable. The main factors accounting for its sustainability include a firm commitment to democracy, a permanent and large majority, a highly threatened majority, a manageable minority and an international environment that is incapable or unwilling to intervene and to force a change of regime. These conditions enable Jews to impose a self-serving ethnic democracy and keep the Arab minority from undermining the regime. Israel is a strong, highly developed state that effectively curbs all threats, whether external or internal.[46]

The ethno-security regime persists also because of Israel's unwillingness to pay the necessary price for an accommodation with the PLO—principally, one Palestinian state that will comprise the entire West Bank and Gaza Strip. Even those who acknowledge that Israel rules over the entire area from the Jordan to the Mediterranean using methods similar to those used by white-ruled South Africa, among them a current government minister, Dan Meridor, prefer to manage the conflict until the Palestinian side accepts Israel's terms:

We must disabuse ourselves of the illusion that the present situation between us and the Palestinians can be permanent, that it can continue into infinity. This is a grave mistake. We're essentially trying to normalize an anomaly.... Even if we're not a minority, even if we comprise up to 55 per cent. That's no longer a Jewish state with an Arab minority, that's a state of two peoples who share the govern-

139

ment. If we then want to maintain a situation in which only we have rights and they don't, that's what Begin meant by 'Rhodesia.' ... Begin didn't want to say South Africa openly, in the Knesset, but in closed deliberations of the Ministerial Committee on Security Affairs he said South Africa. In the Knesset he said Rhodesia, presumably because he didn't want to offend the South African regime.... One thing that worries me is that if Abu Mazen said no even to Olmert's supposedly very far-reaching offers, when Olmert really wanted an agreement, then how will we reach an agreement? Does anyone think that we'll give more than Olmert gave? It's inconceivable. Therefore, on the other side I don't see the leadership, the leadership ability, and the leadership's ability to impose an agreement. If the Palestinians accept our conditions for a final status accord, I'm ready to sign it tonight. I have no reason to drag things out. I have nothing to gain from that. But what's the problem? Looking at it realistically, that's not how it is. Because there are the tough questions, and Jerusalem is the toughest of them all, because we are not prepared—I am not prepared—to view Jaffa Gate as being abroad. Absolutely not.... I want very much to reach an accord and I'm ready to take chances, but going beyond what I'm proposing would mean a security gamble and a breaking of the historic Zionist ethos. If it's not possible to reach an accord in the foreseeable future, then we need to find breathing room so we can manage this conflict until the other side is ready.[47]

Based on its success in ruling the West Bank through the proxy of the Palestinian Authority, the Israeli defense establishment has not recommended to the cabinet that it make a comprehensive deal with Abbas. Rather, in late 2008 it strongly recommended continuing the policy of confronting Hamas and preventing elections in the Palestinian Authority, even at the cost of a confrontation with the US and the international community.[48] Similarly, in January 2009, at the end of Israel's incursion into the Gaza Strip, a senior military official offered an authoritative explanation of his government's war aim. The Palestinians, he declared, will remain bifurcated between what he called Hamastan in the Gaza Strip and Fatahland in the West Bank for many years more, just as Germany was divided during the Cold War. 'The idea,' concluded the *Wall Street Journal*'s Bret Stephens, who interviewed the official, 'is that a Hamas state in Gaza—somehow deterred from mischief—could become a kind of useful negative example to the Palestinians of the West Bank.'[49]

The de facto single state that currently exists changes the status of security issues in the Israeli mind and the interrelations between the main final status issues. During the period of the Oslo Accords, when the sides negotiated over a border, they divided final-status subjects into technical and symbolic categories. They considered Jerusalem and the refugees to be issues that were more symbolic than technical, because both were dominated by national narratives, value systems, collective traumas and hopes for redemption. Security, on the contrary, was perceived first and foremost as a technical problem, and hence easier to solve. However, with the establishment of Israel's ethno-security regime, security considerations have gained weight in the Israeli mind. Israel perceives security as related primarily to its identity. Security policy is based on the combination of Jewish demographic anxiety and the need to control the Palestinians. These two elements touch on Israel's self-definition as a Jewish and democratic state. Israelis see the military policies of the ethno-security regime as safeguarding the Jewish state. The division of the 'other' into five subgroups helps the diminishing Jewish majority rule over the Palestinians—and it also assuages the Israeli mind regarding the contradiction between the Jewish ethno-security regime and democracy.

However, today's reality is not necessarily that of tomorrow. True, the road toward two states living side by side seems to have grown longer, and the cost of reaching such a settlement may well be higher than it was just ten years ago. But there is a consensus that Israeli rule in its current form cannot and must not last. Even Meron Benvenisti, who has long described (but not prescribed) Israeli rule over the occupied territories as a single state, played in the 1990s with the idea of a two-state solution. More recently, he has sought to bridge the differences between the one-state reality and the two-state model by promoting a constitutionally vague concept of a bi–national state with soft borders.[50] The advocates of the 'one man, one vote' approach also assume that the present state of affairs is malleable. If so, the question is: what could best replace today's problematic single regime? As long as the majority on each side rejects the joint state in favour of its own nation state,[51] there is a hope of revitalizing the two-state solution. As soon as the economic, diplomatic and military costs of ethnic conflict become too high, Israel will inevitably exert itself once again to achieve a two-state accommodation. It is the contradiction between the future that neither side wants and the current reality that keeps alive the option that, for all its elusiveness, remains the only really viable solution: two ethnic states, Israel and Palestine, with the Green Line as their border. Then Israeli Jews, who according to the demographers will enjoy a solid 80 per cent majority in their country, no longer need fear losing their Jewish state. At that point, they will be able to reach agreements with their fellow Palestinian citizens on the minority's collective rights.[52]

NOTES

ACKNOWLEDGMENTS

1. Menachem Klein, 'One State in the Holy Land: Dream or Nightmare?' *The International Spectator*, Vol. 43 No. 4, December 2008, pp. 89–102.
2. Menachem Klein, 'Settlements and Security' in Daanish Faruqi (ed.), *From Camp David to 'Cast Lead': Essays on Israel, Palestine and the Future of the Peace Process*, Lanham, Md.: Lexington Books, 2010.

INTRODUCTION

1. Hussein Agha and Robert Malley, 'Obama and the Middle East,' *The New York Review of Books*, Vol. 56 No. 10, 11 June 2009, http://www.nybooks.com/articles/22731.
2. Agha and Malley 2009.
3. See Aaron David Miller, *The Much Too Promised Land: America's Elusive Search for Arab–Israeli Peace*, New York: Bantam Dell, 2007; Menachem Klein, *A Possible Peace Between Israel and Palestine: An Insider's Account of the Geneva Initiative*, New York: Columbia University Press, 2007.
4. The Road Map is the short name for a document called 'A Performance-Based Road Map to a Permanent Two-State Solution to the Israeli–Palestinian Conflict,' presented by President Bush in June 2002 and endorsed by the EU, Russia and the UN. The document can be found at http://www.un.org/media/main/roadmap122002.html.

5. Jeff Halper, 'The Key to Peace: Dismantling the Matrix of Control,' http://www.icahd.org/eng/articles.asp?menu=6&submenu=3.

6. Ghazi Walid Falah, 'The Geopolitics of Enclavisation and the Demise of the Two-State Solution to the Israeli–Palestinian Conflict,' *The Third World Quarterly*, Vol. 26 No. 8, 2005, pp. 1341–72.

7. Leila Farsakh, 'Independence, Cantons or Bantustans: Whither the Palestinian State?' *The Middle East Journal*, Vol. 59 No. 2 Spring 2005, pp. 230–45.

8. Sari Hanafi, 'Spacio-cide and Bio-politics: The Israeli Colonial Conflict from 1947 to the Wall' in Michael Sorkin (ed.), *Against the Wall: Israel's Barrier to Peace*, New York: The New Press, 2005.

9. Lisa Taraki, 'Enclave Micropolis: The Paradoxical Case of Ramallah/al-Bireh,' Journal of Palestine Studies, Vol. 37 No. 4, Summer 2008, pp. 6–20.

10. Baruch Kimmerling and Joel S. Migdal, *The Palestinian People: A History*, Cambridge, Massachusetts: Harvard University Press, 2003, pp. 203–13.

1. HISTORICAL AND THEORETICAL BACKGROUND

1. Gershon Shafir, 'Israeli Society: A Counterview,' *Israel Studies*, Vol. 1 No. 2, Fall 1996, pp. 189–213. Quotation from page 192.

2. Gershon Shafir, *Land, Labor and the Origins of the Israeli–Palestinian Conflict 1882–1914*, Cambridge: Cambridge University Press, 1989.

3. Israel Ministry of Foreign Affairs, 'The Declaration of the Establishment of the State of Israel 14 May 1948,' http://www.mfa.gov.il/MFA/Peace+Process/Guide+to+the+Peace+Process/Declaration+of+Establishment+of+State+of+Israel.htm.

4. Palestine Media Center, 'Palestinian Declaration of Independence, 15 November 1948,' http://www.palestine-pmc.com/details.asp?cat=11&id=27.

5. Robert Satloff, *From Abdullah to Hussein: Jordan in Transition*, New York: Oxford University Press, 1994; Avi Shlaim, *Lion of Jordan: The Life of King Hussein in War and Peace*, London: Allen Lane, 2007.

6. Itamar Rabinovich, *The Road Not Taken*, New York: Oxford University Press, 1991; Avi Shlaim, *Collusion Across the Jordan: King Abdullah, the Zionist Movement and the Partition of Palestine*, Oxford: Clarendon Press, 1988, pp. 111–67.

7. Adam Garfinkle, *Israel and Jordan in the Shadow of War: Functional Ties and Futile Diplomacy in a Small Place*, New York: St. Martin's Press, 1992; Menachem Klein, 'Rule and Role in Jerusalem: Israel, Jordan and the PLO in a Peace-Building Process' in Marshall J. Breger and Ora Ahimeir (eds.), *Jerusalem: A City and its Future*, Syracuse: Syracuse University Press, 2002, pp. 137–74.

8. Glenn E. Robinson, *Building a Palestinian State: The Incomplete Revolution*, Bloomington and Indianapolis: Indiana University Press, 1997.

9. On the Camp David talks, see Jeremy Pressman, 'Visions in Collision: What Happened in Camp David and Taba,' *International Security*, Vol. 28 No. 2, Fall 2003, pp. 5–43, http://belfercenter. ksg.harvard.edu/files/pressman.pdf; Clayton Swisher, *The Truth About Camp David: The Untold Story About the Collapse of the Middle East Peace Process*, New York: Nation Books, 2004; Gilad Sher, *The Israeli–Palestinian Peace Negotiations 1999– 2001, Within Reach*, New York: Routledge, 2006.

10. The best recent summary of this debate is in Ariella Azoulay and Adi Ophir, *This Regime Which Is Not One: Occupation and Democracy between the Sea and the River 1967–*, Tel Aviv: Resling, 2008, pp. 353–93 (in Hebrew). Also worthy of note is David Kretzmer, *The Occupation of Justice: The Supreme Court of Israel and the Occupied Palestinian Territories*, Albany: State University of New York Press, 2002; Elisha Efrat, *The West Bank and Gaza Strip: A Geography of Occupation*, Abingdon: Routledge, 2006; Neve Gordon, *Israel's Occupation*, Berkeley: University of California Press, 2008; Leila Farsakh, *Palestinian Labour Migration to Israel: Labour, Land and Occupation*, London: Routledge 2005; Eyal Weizman, *Hollow Land: Israel's Architecture of Occupation*, London: Verso, 2007.

11. Jeff Halper, 'The 94 Percent Solution: A Matrix of Control,' MERIP 216, Fall 2000, http://www.merip.org/mer/mer216/216_halper.html.

12. Jeff Halper, 'Dismantling the Matrix of Control,' MERIP, 11 September 2009, http://www.merip.org/mero/mero091109.html.

13. Azoulay and Ophir 2008.

14. Gordon 2008, pp. 2–46.

15. Sammy Smooha, 'The Model of Ethnic Democracy' in Sammy Smooha and Priit Järve (eds.), *The Fate of Ethnic Democracy in Post-Communist Europe*, Budapest: Open Society Institute, 2005, pp. 5–60, http://soc.haifa.ac.il/~s.smooha/download/SmoohaJarve BookEthDemoPostCommunistEurope.pdf. The quotation is from pp. 21–2.

16. Oren Yiftachel, *Ethnocracy: Land and Identity in Israel/Palestine*, Philadelphia: University of Pennsylvania Press, 2006, p. 3. In his discussion of Yiftachel's concept, Smooha notes that ethnocracy is not a *Herrenvolk* (master race) regime. It maintains selective openness to democracy, mostly to obtain international legitimacy. Smooha 2005, p. 19.

17. Julie Peteet, 'Beyond Compare,' *Middle East Report*, 253, Winter 2009, http://merip.org/mer/mer253/peteet.html.

18. Peteet 2009.

19. Human Science Research Council of South Africa, *Occupation, Colonialism, Apartheid: A Reassessment of Israel's Practices in the Occupied Palestinian Territories Under International Law*, Cape Town: May 2009, http://www.hsrc.ac.za/Media_Release-378.phtml.

20. United Nations, International Convention on the Suppression and Punishment of the Crime of Apartheid, New York: 30 November 1973, http://untreaty.un.org/cod/avl/ha/cspca/cspca.html.

21. Baruch Kimmerling, 'Boundaries and Frontiers of the Israeli Control System' in Baruch Kimmerling (ed.), *The Israeli State and Society: Boundaries and Frontiers*, Albany: State University of New York Press, 1989, pp. 265–84.

22. Sami Smooha, 'Has Indeed the Occupation of the Territories Permeated Inside? The Modest Contribution of Israeli Sociology to the Study of Occupation Issues,' *Sociologia Yisraelit* 9, 2, 2008, pp. 255–62 (in Hebrew).

23. Smooha 2008.

24. Nadim Rouhana, *Palestinian Citizens in an Ethnic Jewish State: Identities in Conflict*, New Haven and London: Yale University Press, 1997.

2. A COMPLETE ISRAELI VICTORY?

1. Meron Benvenisti, *Son of the Cypresses: Memories, Reflections and Regrets from a Political Life*, Berkeley: University of California Press, 2007, p. 191.
2. Final Statement of the International Donors' Conference for the Palestinian State, Paris: December 2007, http://www.diplomatie. gouv.fr/en/country-files_156/israel-palestinian-territories_290/ peace-process_2155/international-donors-conference-for-the-palestinian-state-17.12.07_10439.html.
3. Mohammed Yaghi, 'The PA Financial Crisis: Causes and Implications,' Washington Institute for Near East Policy, http://www. washingtoninstitute.org/templateC05.php?CID=3084.
4. Ma'an News Agency, 'EU Pledged 160 Million Euros to PA,' 19 January 2010, http://www.maannews.net/eng/ViewDetails.aspx? ID=255218. This report notes that the EU is the largest single donor to the PA. Since 2007 it has provided total assistance to the Palestinian people, including civil society organizations and refugees, averaging more than €500 million annually.
5. Yaghi, ibid.
6. Karin Laub, 'US Transfers $200 Million in Aid to Palestinians,' Associated Press, 24 July 2009, http://www.google.com/ hostednews/p/ article/ ALeqM5jw6c6W7D_lf3F_aBJvrojp0NKUWQD99L1JB00.
7. Ma'an News Agency, 'Donors Pledge 400 million USD for PA Shortfall,' 27 September 2009, http://www.maannews.net/eng/ ViewDetails.aspx?ID=227388.
8. Ibid.
9. *Ha'aretz*, 3 March 2009.
10. Tovah Lazaroff, 'The World Bank to Give Palestinians $33.5 M in Aid,' *Jerusalem Post*, 14 July 2009, http://www.jpost.com/ servlet/Satellite?cid=1246443808810&pagename=JPost%2FJPA rticle%2FShowFull.
11. Akiva Eldar, 'We are running out of time for a two-state solution,' *Ha'aretz*, 17 August 2008, http://www.haaretz.com/hasen/spages/ 1011859.html.
12. Yezid Sayigh, 'Inducing a Failed State in Palestine,' *Survival*, 49, Autumn 2007, pp. 7–40; similarly see Rashid Khalidi, 'Palestine:

Liberation Deferred,' *The Nation*, 8 May 2008; International Crisis Group reports on the Palestinian Authority, http://www. crisisgroup.org/home/index.cfm?l=1&id=1271&sr=1.

13. US Department of State, 'Secretary Rice, Palestinian President Abbas in Amman, Jordan,' 31 March 2008, http://www.america. gov/st/texttrans-english/2008/March/20080331190345xjsnomm is0.2582666.html.

14. Kevin Peraino, 'Olmert's Lament,' *Newsweek*, 13 June 2009, http://www.newsweek.com/id/201937. His map is in Aluf Benn, '*Ha'aretz* Exclusive: Olmert's Plan for Peace,' *Ha'aretz*, 17 December 2009, http://www.haaretz.com/hasen/spages/1135699.html.

15. Avi Issacharoff, 'Abbas to *Ha'aretz*: Peace Possible in 6 Months if Israel Freezes All Settlements,' *Ha'aretz*, 16 December 2009, http://www.haaretz.com/hasen/spages/1135431.html.

16. *Ha'aretz*, 12, 14, 25 August 2008; *al-Quds*, 29 August 2008; Foundation for Middle East Peace, 'Report on Israeli Settlements in the Occupied Palestinian Territories, November–December 2008,' http://www. fmep.org/reports/archive/vol.-18/no.-6/olm-erts-final-status-map; *al-Hayat*, 14 December 2008, http://www. alhayat.com/arab_news/levant_news/12–2008/Article-20081213 –31f94b21–c0a8–10ed-0088–d0c18c7d7244/story.html; Mahmoud Abbas, 'Israel and Palestine Can Still Achieve Peace,' *Wall Street Journal*, 19 September 2008, http://online.wsj.com/article/ SB12217862440645 5063.html?mod=googlenews_wsj; Menachem Klein, 'Nothing New in Jerusalem: Jerusalem in the Current Final Status Talks,' *Bitterlemons 35*, 8 September 2008, http://www.bitterlemons.org/previous/bl090908ed35.html; Menachem Klein, *The Jerusalem Problem: The Struggle for Permanent Status*, Gainesville: University Press of Florida, 2003.

17. Aluf Benn, 'Renewing Israeli–Palestinian Talks is Obvious Way to End Impasse,' *Ha'aretz*, 15 January 2010, http://www.haaretz. com/hasen/spages/1142741.html.

18. Benn, ibid.

19. *Ha'aretz* service, 'Ex–US Envoy: Livni Told Palestinians to Reject Olmert Peace Offer,' *Ha'aretz*, 22 October 2009, http://www. haaretz.com/hasen/spages/1122879.html.

20. Quartet Statement, 9 November 2008, Sharm El-Sheikh, http:// www.jmcc.org/etemplate.php?id=902.

21. Ma'an News Agency, 'Abbas Admits Ordering Goldstone Report Delay,' 18 October 2009, http://www.maannews.net/eng/View Details.aspx?ID=233001.

22. Akiva Eldar, 'Diskin to Abbas: Defer UN Vote on Goldstone or Face "Second Gaza,"' *Ha'aretz*, 17 January 2010, http://www. haaretz.com/hasen/spages/1143038.html.

23. United Nations, *Report of the United Nations Fact-Finding Mission on the Gaza Conflict*, Goldstone Report, 29 September 2009, http://www2.ohchr.org/english/bodies/hrcouncil/docs/12 session/A-HRC-12–48.pdf; Neil McFarquhar, 'Palestinians Halt Push on War Report,' *New York Times*, 2 October 2009, http:// www.nytimes.com/2009/10/02/world/middleeast/02mideast. html?_r=3&ref=middleeast; Amira Hass, 'Abbas Orders Probe into Goldstone Delay Request,' *Ha'aretz*, 6 October 2009, http:// www.haaretz.com/hasen/spages/1118881.html; Ma'an News Agency, 'PA Minister: Our Stance on Goldstone Report an Embarrassment,' 3 October 2009, http://www.maannews.net/eng/View-Details.aspx?ID=229447; *Ha'aretz* Service, 'Palestinian Minister Quits over PA Decision to Drop Goldstone Draft,' *Ha'aretz*, 3 October 2009, http://www.haaretz.com/hasen/spages/1118467. html; Hussam Ezzedin, 'The PLO Seeks to Investigate the Causes of Delaying a Vote on Goldstone's Report,' *Al-Ayyam*, 4 October 2009 (in Arabic), http://www.al-ayyam.ps/znews/site/template/ article.aspx?did=122953&date=10/4/2009; Ma'an News Agency, 'Abbas Orders Probe of Deferral of UN Gaza Report,' 4 October 2009, http://www.maannews.net/eng/ViewDetails.aspx?ID=229 678; Ma'an News Agency, 'Fayyad Cabinet says it Still Backs Goldstone Report,' 6 October 2009, http://www.maannews.net/ eng/ViewDetails.aspx?ID=229970; Ma'an News Agency, 'PLO Official Admits "Mistake" in Delaying Goldstone Report,' 7 October 2009, http://www.maannews.net/eng/ViewDetails.aspx?ID= 230387.

24. Ma'an News Agency, 'Abbas Takes Blame for Goldstone Delay, Commission Says,' 9 January 2010, http://www.maannews.net/ eng/ViewDetails.aspx?ID=253025.

25. Hani al-Masri, 'Mr. President: Courageous Historical Decisions are Needed,' *al-Ayyam*, 25 March 2008 (in Arabic), http://www. al-ayyam.ps/znews/site/template/Doc_View.aspx?did=80711& Date=3/25/2008.

26. http://www.pcpsr.org/survey/polls/2008/p27epressrelease.html; http://www.pcpsr.org/survey/polls/2009/p31e.html; http://www.pcpsr.org/survey/polls/2009/p32e.html; http://www.pcpsr.org/survey/polls/2009/p34epressrelease.html.

27. http://www.pcpsr.org/survey/polls/2008/p29e.html; http://www.pcpsr.org/survey/polls/2008/p30epressrelease.html; http://www.pcpsr.org/survey/polls/2009/p31e.html; http://www.pcpsr.org/survey/polls/2009/p34epressrelease.html

28. Shlomo Brom, 'Security Reform and the Political Process,' *Bitterlemons*, 11 May 2009, http://www.bitterlemons.org/previous/bl110509ed18.html#isr2.

29. Barak Ravid, 'Israel Rejects Russian Request to Give the PA Armored Vehicles,' *Ha'aretz*, 6 December 2009, http://www.haaretz.com/hasen/spages/1132925.html.

30. Yaakov Katz, 'Israel May Allow PA Counter-Terror Force,' *Jerusalem Post*, 10 July 2009, http://www.jpost.com/servlet/Satellite?cid=1246443770831&pagename=JPost%2FJPArticle%2FShowFull; Mohammed Najib, 'Security Transformation Dependent on Political Progress,' *Bitterlemons*, 11 May 2009, http://www.bitterlemons.org/previous/bl110509ed18.html#pal2; United Press International, 'Palestinian Forces to Receive Weapons,' 6 July 2009, http://www.upi.com/Top_News/2009/07/06/Palestinian-forces-to-receive-weapons/UPI-18761246880020/.

31. Karin Laub, 'US Trained Palestinian Force is Keen in Action,' Associated Press, 28 June 2009, http://www.google.com/hosted-news/ap/article/ALeqM5jrSS9anIzM-waM8ZUQzhDot5Z27AD9935UDG0.

32. Amos Harel, 'Israel–PA Relations Have Never Been So Good,' *Ha'aretz*, 4 September 2009, http://www.haaretz.com/hasen/spages/1112398.html; Amos Harel, 'The Quiet Revolution in the West Bank: More Coordination, Less Killed,' *Ha'aretz*, 4 September 2009, p. 3 (in Hebrew). On claims that Palestinian security agents who have been detaining and allegedly torturing supporters of the Islamist organization Hamas in the West Bank have been working closely with the CIA, see Ian Cobain, 'CIA Working with Palestinian Security Agents,' *The Guardian*, 17 December 2009, http://www.guardian.co.uk/world/2009/dec/17/cia-palestinian-security-agents.

33. Mati Steinberg, 'Hamas Predicts Collapse of Abbas and his Conspirators,' *Ha'aretz*, 15 December 2009, http://www.haaretz.com/hasen/spages/1134931.html.
34. Steinberg, ibid.
35. Nicholas Blincoe, 'The Dayton Force Dilemma,' *The Guardian*, 8 July 2009, http://www.guardian.co.uk/commentisfree/2009/jul/08/palestinian-dayton-force-west-bank.
36. Brom 2009; Najib 2009.
37. Avi Issacharoff and Amos Harel, 'The IDF's Preoccupation,' *Ha'aretz*, 27 November 2008, http://www.haaretz.com/hasen/spages/ 1041699.html.
38. Nathan J. Brown, 'Points for the Obama Administration in the Middle East: Avoiding Myths and Vain Hopes,' Carnegie Paper, 23 January 2009, http://carnegieendowment.org/publications/index.cfm?fa=view&id=22662&prog=zgp&proj=zme.
39. Brom 2009.
40. Amira Hass, 'Giving in to the Settlers in Beit Sahur,' *Ha'aretz*, 11 February 2010, http://www.haaretz.com/hasen/spages/1149262. html.
41. http://www.pcpsr.org/survey/polls/2009/p31e.html.
42. Khalil Nakhleh, 'Palestinians Under the Occupation,' *Counterpunch*, 24 September 2008, http://counterpunch.org/nakhleh0924 2008.html.
43. Beshara Doumani, 'Scenes from Daily Life: The View from Nablus,' *Journal of Palestine Studies*, Vol. 34 No. 1, Autumn 2004, pp. 37–50.
44. Doumani 2004.
45. Maia Carter Hallward, 'Creative Responses to Separation: Israeli and Palestinian Joint Activism in Bil'in,' *Journal of Peace Research*, Vol. 46 No. 4, 2009, pp. 541–58.
46. On Bil'in, see its websites, http://www.bilin-village.org/english/ and http://www.bilin-ffj.org/.
47. Doumani 2004.
48. Nir Hasson, Jack Khoury and Jonathan Lis, 'Islamic Movement Leader in the North Gets 9 Months for Assault,' *Ha'aretz*, 14 January 2010, http://www.haaretz.com/hasen/spages/1142513. html; Mick Dumper and Craig Larkin, 'Political Islam in Contested Jerusalem: The Emerging Role of Islamists from within

Israel,' Divided Cities/Contested States Project, Working Paper No. 12, 2009.

49. Lisa Taraki, 'Enclave Micropolice: The Paradoxical Case of Ramallah/al-Bireh,' *Journal of Palestine Studies*, Vol. 37 No. 4, Summer 2008, pp. 6–20; Menachem Klein, 'Old and New Walls in Jerusalem,' *Political Geography*, Vol. 24, January 2005, pp. 53–76; Hillel Cohen, *The Rise and Fall of Arab Jerusalem 1967–2007*, Jerusalem: the Jerusalem Institute for Israel Studies, 2007, (in Hebrew).

50. Aluf Benn, 'Let's See Him Convince Mitchell,' *Ha'aretz*, 8 June 2009, p. 82 (in Hebrew).

51. Benn, ibid.

52. Daniel C. Kurtzer and Scott B. Lasensky, *Negotiating Arab–Israeli Peace: American Leadership in the Middle East*, Washington DC: United States Institute of Peace, 2008, p. 58.

53. Ibid., pp. 28, 32, 36, 42, 70. See also Miller 2007, Chapter 9.

54. Ehud Olmert, 'How to Achieve a Lasting Peace,' *Washington Post*, 17 July 2009, http://www.washingtonpost.com/wp-dyn/content/article/2009/07/16/AR2009071603584.html.

55. Akiva Eldar, 'Ex–PM Violated Sharon–Bush Deal,' *Ha'aretz*, 20 July 2009, http://www.haaretz.com/hasen/spages/1101156.html.

56. Joe Klein, 'Q&A: Obama On His First Year In Office,' *Time*, 21 January 2010, http://www.time.com/time/politics/article/0,8599,1955 72–6,00.html.

57. Akiva Eldar, Barak Ravid and Jack Khoury, 'No Difference to US Between Outpost, East Jerusalem Construction,' *Ha'aretz*, 20 July 2009, http://www.haaretz.com/hasen/spages/1101353.html.

58. Text: Obama's Speech in Cairo, *New York Times*, 4 June 2009, http://www.nytimes.com/2009/06/04/us/politics/04obama.text.html.

59. Ethan Bronner, 'Israel Rejects US Call to Hold Off on Development,' *New York Times*, 19 July 2009, http://www.nytimes.com/2009/07/20/world/middleeast/20mideast.html?ref= middleeast; Howard Schneider, 'Netanyahu Upholds Plan to Build in East Jerusalem,' *Washington Post*, 20 July 2009, http://www.washingtonpost.com/wpdyn/content/article/2009/07/19/AR2009 071900156_pf.html.

60. Akiva Eldar, 'Despite Freeze Hundreds of Housing Units Under

Construction in Isolated Settlements,' *Ha'aretz*, 1 January 2010, http://www.haaretz.com/hasen/spages/1139226.html.

61. Amos Harel, 'Settlers Have Been Working for Months to Undermine Construction Freeze,' *Ha'aretz*, 27 November 2009, http://www.haaretz.com/hasen/spages/1131086.html.

62. Harel, ibid.

63. Eldar, 1 January 2010.

64. White House, 'Statement by White House Press Secretary Robert Gibbs on Construction in East Jerusalem,' 28 December 2009, http://www.whitehouse.gov/the-press-office/statement-white-house-press-secretary-robert-gibbs-construction-east-jerusalem.

65. Barak Ravid, 'US to Egypt: Fatah–Hamas Deal Undermines Israel–PA Talks,' *Ha'aretz*, 12 October 2009, http://www.haaretz.com/hasen/spages/1120633.html.

66. Ma'an News Agency, 'Abbas May Quit Fatah, PLO Posts,' 10 November 2009, http://www.maannews.net/eng/ViewDetails.aspx?ID=238722.

67. Ma'an News Agency, 'Erekat: PA Future in Doubt,' 12 December 2009, http://www.maannews.net/eng/ViewDetails.aspx?ID=238643.

68. Ma'an New Agency, 'PA Reaching for Diplomatic Plan B,' 12 December 2009, http://www.maannews.net/eng/ViewDetails.aspx?ID=242693.

69. Reuters, 'EU's Solana Calls for UN to Recognize Palestinian State,' 12 July 2009, http://www.reuters.com/article/featuredCrisis/idUSLC616115.

70. Glenn Kessler, 'US Pushing Netanyahu to Accept Demands for Peace Talks,' *Washington Post*, 16 March 2010, http://www.washingtonpost.com/wp-dyn/content/article/2010/03/15/AR2010031503462.html.

71. Thomas L. Friedman, 'Driving Drunk in Jerusalem,' *New York Times*, 13 March 2010, http://www.nytimes.com/2010/03/14/opinion/14friedman.html?ref=opinion. At the time of writing, April 2010, Israel did not provide its answer to the White House beyond Netanyahu's public commitment to continue building for Jews in East Jerusalem.

72. Palestinian Strategy Study Group, 'Regaining the Initiative: Palestinian Strategic Options to End Israeli Occupation,' August 2008, http://www.palestinestrategygroup.ps/.

73. Yitzhak Benhorin, 'Jordan's King: US Credibility Under Question,' *Ynet*, 7 February 2010, http://www.ynetnews.com/articles/0,7340,L-3845718,00.html.

74. The full text of the ratified Fatah Political Program, http://calevbenyefuneh.blogspot.com/2009/08/full-text-of-ratified-fatah-political.html; see also the ICG report, 'Palestine: Salvaging Fatah,' 12 November 2009, http://www.crisisgroup.org/home/index.cfm?id=6383&l=1.

75. Palestinian Strategy Study Group 2008.

76. Reuters, 'Marwan Barghouti: Peace Talks with Israel Have Failed,' *Ha'aretz*, 24 November 2009, http://www.haaretz.com/hasen/spages/1129348.html.

77. Charles Levinson, 'Abbas Says Palestinians Won't Rise Up, for Now,' *Wall Street Journal*, 22 December 2009, http://online.wsj.com/article/SB126143773752000841.html.

78. Ilene Prusher, 'Changing course, Fatah official call for Palestinian protest against Israel,' *Christian Science Monitor*, 1 April 2010, http://www.csmonitor.com/World/Middle-East/2010/0401/Changing-course-Fatah-officials-call-for-Palestinian-protests-against-Israel; Amira Hass, 'PA Ministers take to the Streets to Join anti–Israeli Popular Demonstrations,' *Ha'aretz*, 1 April 2010, http://www.haaretz.com/hasen/spages/1160339.html.

79. Avi Issacharoff, 'Weekend in the Village,' *Ha'aretz Magazine*, 8 January 2010, pp. 20–24, (in Hebrew).

80. Nir Hasson, 'Report: Israeli Cops Nab Czech Peace Activist in Ramallah Raid,' *Ha'aretz*, 22 January 2010, http://www.haaretz.com/hasen/spages/1144105.html.

81. Amira Hass, 'IDF Declared West Bank Protest Village a Closed Military Area,' *Ha'aretz*, 15 March 2010, http://www.haaretz.com/hasen/spages/1156536.html.

82. Amira Hass, 'Danger: Popular Struggle,' *Ha'aretz*, 23 December 2009, http://www.haaretz.com/hasen/spages/1137056.html.

83. Palestinian National Authority, 'Palestine: Ending the Occupation, Establishing the State, Program of the Thirteenth Government,' August 2009, http://www.americantaskforce.org/palestinian_national_authority_ending_occupation_establishing_state.

3. THE SETTLEMENT—SECURITY SYMBIOSIS

1. Baruch Kimmerling, *Immigrants, Settlers and Natives: Israel Between Plurality of Cultures and Cultural Wars*, Tel Aviv: Am Oved, 2003, (in Hebrew).
2. Gershom Gorenberg, 'A Guide to Israeli Settlements,' *Los Angeles Times*, 29 June 2009, http://www.latimes.com/news/opinion/commentary/la-oe-gorenberg28–2009jun28,0,6704423.story.
3. B'tselem, 'The Establishment and Expansion Plans of the Ma'ale Adumim Settlement,' December 2009, Joint Report with Bimkom–Planners for Planning Rights, http://www.btselem.org/english/publications/summaries/200912_maale_adummim.asp.
4. Gershom Gorenberg, *The Accidental Empire: Israel and the Birth of the Settlements, 1967–1977*, New York: Times Books, p. 358. The Foundation for Middle East Peace database shows that in 1972 there were 10,608 settlers; in 1983 they numbered 106,595; in 1985, 158,700; in 1989, 199,900; and in 1993, 281,800. See http://www.fmep.org/settlement_info/settlement-info-and-tables/stats-data/comprehensive-settlement-population-1972–2006. For the Palestinian perspective on settlement growth, see Raja Shehade, *Palestinian Walks: Notes on a Vanishing Landscape*, Profile Books, 2007.
5. Akiva Eldar, 'Gush Etzion Today is Seven Times Its Historical Size,' *Ha'aretz*, 31 July 2009, p. 7 [Hebrew].
6. B'tselem 2009.
7. Jerusalem Institute for Israel Studies data for 2006, http://www.jiis.org.il/imageBank/File/articles/FACTS-2007–heb.pdf [Hebrew only]. As of 2009, Ir Amim reports that East Jerusalem's Jewish population numbers about 190,000. Ir Amim, 'Jerusalem 2008 State of Affairs: Political Developments and Changes on the Ground,' December 2008, p. 17, http://www.ir-amim.org.il/Eng/_Uploads/dbsAttachedFiles/AnnualReport2008Eng(1).pdf.
8. Israel Central Bureau of Statistics, http://www1.cbs.gov.il/population/new_2008/table3_07.pdf.
9. Haim Levinson, 'More than 300,000 Settlers Live in the West Bank,' *Ha'aretz*, 27 July 2009, http://www.haaretz.com/hasen/spages/1103125.html.
10. International Crisis Group [ICG], 'Israel's Religious Right and the Question of Settlements, Middle East Report Number 89,'

20 July 2009, p. 2, http://www.crisisgroup.org/library/documents/middle_east___north_africa/arab_israeli_conflict/89_israels_religious_right_and_the_question_of_settlements.pdf.

11. Gorenberg 2006; Idith Zertal and Akiva Eldar, *Lords of the Land: The War for Israel's Settlements in the Occupied Territories, 1967–2007*, New York: Nation Books, 2007; Settler and settlement statistics, Foundation for Middle East Peace, http://www.fmep.org/settlement_info/.

12. Meron Benvenisti, *Son of the Cypresses: Memories, Reflections and Regrets from a Political Life*, Berkeley: University of California Press, 2007, p. 200.

13. Chaim Levinson, 'Settlements Have Cost Israel 17$ Billion Study Sais' *Ha'aretz*, 23 March 2010, http://www.haaretz.com/hasen/pages/ShArtStEng.jhtml?itemNo=1158308&contrassID=1&sub ContrassID=1&title='Settlements%20have%20cost%20 Israel%20$17%20billion,%20study%20finds'&dyn_server= 172.20.5.5.

14. ICG 2009, pp. 32–33, note 315.

15. Meirav Arlosorov, 'The Virtual Reality of Gaza,' *Ha'aretz—The Marker*, 14 January 2010, p. 20 (in Hebrew). It is reasonable to assume that the state provides similar assistance to West Bank settlers.

16. Tovah Lazaroff, 'Government Spent 22.3% More on Settlements,' *Jerusalem Post*, 22 July 2009, http://www.jpost.com/servlet/Satellite?pagename=JPost/JPArticle/ShowFull&cid=1246 443872990; Reuters, 'Study: Settlements Get More State Funding then Israeli Cities,' *Ha'aretz*, 21 July 2009, http://www.haaretz.com/hasen/spages/1101829.html.

17. Hagit Ofran, Report: The Price of Settlements in the 2009–2010 Budget Proposal, Peace Now, June 2009, http://www.peacenow.org.il/site/en/peace.asp?pi=61&fld=495&docid=3711.

18. *Ha'aretz*, 26 July 2009, p. 2 [in Hebrew].

19. ICG 2009, p. 27.

20. B'tselem, 'Land Grab: Israel's Settlement Policy in the West Bank,' Jerusalem: May 2002, p. 55, http://www.btselem.org/Download, /200205_Land_Grab_Eng.pdf. The original order in Hebrew can be found at http://www.aka.idf.il/SIP_STORAGE/FILES/0/60630. pdf.

21. Shaul Arieli, 'Without Any Tricks,' *Ha'aretz*, 3 July 2009, http://www.haaretz.com/hasen/spages/1097241.html. B'tselem May 2002, pp. 46–63.

22. Peace Now, 'The West Bank: Facts and Figures,' August 2005, http://www.peacenow.org.il/site/en/peace.asp?pi=195&docid=1430.

23. Shaul Arieli, 'Natural Growth or Immigration?!' http://www.shaularieli.com/image/users/77951/ftp/my_files/Netunim/translated.doc.

24. Foundation for Middle East Peace, 'Map: Olmert's Final Status Map,' *Settlement Report*, Vol. 18, No. 6, November–December 2008, http://www.fmep.org/reports/archive/vol.-18/no.-6/olmerts-final-status-map. On the Barrier, see below.

25. Shaul Arieli, 'A new freezing point,' *Ha'aretz*, 5 January 2010, http://www.haaretz.com/hasen/spages/1140024.html.

26. ICG 2009, p. 9.

27. Peace Now, 'Bypassing the Settlement Freeze: Semi–Annual Report,' August 2009, http://peacenow.org.il/site/en/peace.asp?pi=61&docid=4364.

28. Shaul Arieli 5 January 2010.

29. Peace Now, 'Israel is Eliminating the Green Line and Continuing to Build in Isolated Settlements: The First Half of 2008 (Since Annapolis),' Settlement Watch Team Report, August 2008, http://www.peacenow.org.il/data/SIP_STORAGE/files//5/3775.pdf.

30. ICG 2009, p. 33, note 317.

31. http://www.peacenow.org.il/data/SIP_STORAGE/files/6/2846.pdf; Uri Blau, 'We Came, Looked, Occupied,' *Ha'aretz Magazine*, December 30, 2009, pp. 24–28 [in Hebrew]. The full data base can be found at http://www.haaretz.co.il/hasite/images/printed/P300109/uriib.mht.

32. Peace Now, August 2008.

33. Peace Now, 'Top 5 Bogus Excuses for Opposing a Settlement Freeze,' *Settlements in Focus*, Vol. 5, Issue 3, 19 June 2009. http://www.peacenow.org/updates.asp?rid=0&cid=6329.

34. http://www.peacenow.org.il/data/SIP_STORAGE/files/1/3201.pdf.

35. Ben Lynfield, 'How Israel Put the Brakes on Another Palestinian Dream,' 16 January 2010, http://www.independent.co.uk/news/

world/middle-east/how-israel-put-the-brakes-on-another-palestinian-dream-1869535.html.

36. Amira Hass, 'UN: Much of West Bank Closed to Palestinian Building,' *Ha'aretz*, 16 December 2009, http://www.haaretz.com/hasen/spages/1135421.html.

37. Robert Fisk, 'In the West Bank's Stony Hills, Palestine is Slowly Dying,' *The Independent*, 30 January 2010, http://www.independent.co.uk/news/world/middle-east/in-the-west-banks-stony-hills-palestine-is-slowly-dying-1883669.html; Amira Hass, 'In the West They Say It's Rain,' *Ha'aretz*, 26 January 2010, http://www.haaretz.com/hasen/spages/1145204.html.

38. Bimkom, 'The Prohibited Zone: Israeli Planning Policy in the Palestinian Villages of Area C,' June 2008 [in Hebrew], http://www.bimkom.org/publicationView.asp?publicationId=141; Alon Cohen–Lifshitz, 'Mocking the Poor with the Economic Peace,' *Ha'aretz*, 16 April 2009 [in Hebrew].

39. OCHA–Occupied Palestinian Territory, 'The Planning Crisis in East Jerusalem: Understanding the Phenomenon of 'Illegal' Construction,' Special Report, April 2009, p. 11, http://www.ochaopt.org/documents/ocha_opt_planning_crisis_east_jerusalem_april_2009_english.pdf; Hass 2009.

40. Ir Amim 2008, pp. 20, 22, 30; East Jerusalem EU Heads of Mission Report, December 2008, first published in Rory McCarthy, Israel Annexing East Jerusalem, Says EU,' *Guardian*, 7 March 2009, http://www.guardian.co.uk/world/2009/mar/07/israel-palestine-eu-report-jerusalem. The author possesses a copy of the original document. A list of Jewish settlements in East Jerusalem and their development up to August 2009. primarily in and adjacent to the Old City, can be found in Ir Amim, 'Israeli Settlement in Palestinian Communities in East Jerusalem,' http://www.ir-amim.org.il/eng/.

41. Ir Amim 2009, p. 18.

42. Roni Sofer, 'State Officials Say US Knew About Jerusalem Building Plan,' YNET, 28 December 2009, http://www.ynetnews.com/articles/0,7340,L-3826058,00.html.

43. The Clinton proposals can be found in Klein 2003, p. 200.

44. Nir Hasson, 'Plans for Largest East Jerusalem Settlement Filed for Approval,' *Ha'aretz*, 25 August 2009, http://www.haaretz.com/hasen/spages/1109426.html.

45. Nir Hasson, 'Settlers Marketing East Jerusalem Homes for 22 Jewish Families,' *Ha'aretz*, 27 September 2009, http://www.haaretz.com/hasen/spages/1117288.html.

46. Uri Blau, 'US Group Invests Tax–Free Millions in East Jerusalem Land,' *Ha'aretz*, 17 August 2009, http://www.haaretz.com/hasen/spages/1107975.html.

47. Nir Hasson, 'Right-Wing Activists Sabotage Jerusalem Master Plan,' *Ha'aretz*, 23 July 2009, http://www.haaretz.com/hasen/spages/1102010.html.

48. Amos Harel, 'New West Bank Roads Jeopardizing Chances for Peace Accord,' *Ha'aretz*, 15 May 2009. On the impact of Israeli actions in Bethlehem area see OCHA, 'Shrinking Space Urban Contraction and Rural Fragmentation in the Bethlehem Governorate,' Special Focus, May 2009, http://www.ochaopt.org/documents/ocha_opt_bethlehem_shrinking_space_may_2009_english.pdf.

49. Uri Misgav, 'This Police Station is brought to You By a Right Wing NGO,' *Yedioth Aharonoth*, 22 January 2010, http://coteret.com/2010/01/22/yediot-expose-settler-orgs-fund-police-infrastructure-in-east-jerusalem/.

50. Ir Amim 2008, p. 28; Peace Now, 'Israeli Government Plans to Deepen Hold over Jerusalem,' May 2002, http://www.peacenow.org.il/site/en/peace.asp?pi=61&fld=620&docid=3644; on how the Silwan digs endanger Palestinian houses, on Elad's methods, and on the support it receives from Israeli courts, the Jerusalem municipality, and government agencies, see Akiva Eldar, 'WATCH: Organizer Admits City of David Endangers Arab Homes,' *Ha'aretz*, 6 October 2009, http://www.haaretz.com/hasen/spages/1118883.html.

51. Raphael Greenberg, 'A Shallow and Brutal Archeology,' *Ha'aretz*, 9 October 2009, http://www.haaretz.com/hasen/spages/1119641.html.

52. Nir Hasson, 'Will Preservation of Ancient Roman Road Destroy the Western Wall?' *Ha'aretz*, 19 October 2009, http://www.haaretz.com/hasen/spages/1121969.html.

53. Ir Amim 2008, pp. 26–27.

54. Ir Amim 2008, p. 29. On the Israeli plans, see also a May 2009 Peace Now May 2009.

55. Press Release by Mayor Barkat's foreign Affairs and media office, 'Mayor Barkat Presents 2010 Budget for Jerusalem,' 20 December 2009, http://www.esnips.com/doc/49001f7b-2c83–4181–af56–6-aa315a3e7d1/JRS-Municipality-press-release—2010–JRS-budget.

56. Yair Ettinger, 'Religious Zionist Rabbis: Ascend the Temple Mount,' *Ha'aretz*, 26 October 2009, http://www.haaretz.com/hasen/spages/1123702.html.

57. Ir Amim 2008, pp. 30–31; United Nations Office for the Coordination of Humanitarian Affairs [OCHA], Special Focus: *The Planning Crisis in East Jerusalem: Understanding the Phenomenon of 'Illegal' Construction*, April 2009, http://www.ochaopt.org/documents/ocha_opt_planning_crisis_east_jerusalem_april_2009_english.pdf.

58. Blau 17 August 2009.

59. Nir Hasson and Akiva Eldar, 'Jerusalem Mayor Bows to Pressure Vows to Shutter Beit Yonatan,' *Ha'aretz*, 4 February 2010, http://www.haaretz.com/hasen/spages/1147459.html.

60. Hasson and Eldar, 4 February 2010; Nir Hasson, 'Officials: Jewish Bid for East Jerusalem Home Likely to Fail,' *Ha'aretz*, 9 February 2010, http://www.haaretz.com/hasen/spages/1148528.html; Nir Hasson, 'Prosecutor to Jerusalem Mayor—Evict Settlers from Arab Neighborhood,' *Ha'aretz*, 29 January 2010, http://www.haaretz.com/hasen/spages/1145883.html; Akiva Eldar, 'Mayor Defies Court Order to Evacuate Jews from East Jerusalem Home,' *Ha'aretz*, 22 January 2010, http://www.haaretz.com/hasen/spages/1144441.html.

61. Dan Izenberg, Herb Keinon, Abe Selig, 'MK Ariel: PM Takes Control Over Jerusalem Demolitions,' *Jerusalem Post*, 14 December 2009, http://www.jpost.com/servlet/Satellite?cid=126044743 1785&pagename=JPost%2FJPArticle%2FShowFull.

62. Supreme Court, 7192/04 and 7800/05, 15 June 2009 [in Hebrew], http://elyon1.court.gov.il/files/04/920/071/v53/040719 20.v53.htm.

63. Menachem Klein, *Jerusalem: the Contested City*, London: C. Hurst and New York: New York University Press, 2001, pp. 274–6.

64. The Swedish draft appears in Barak Ravid, 'Ha'aretz Exclusive: EU Draft Document on Division of Jerusalem,' *Ha'aretz*, 2 Decem-

ber 2009, http://www.haaretz.com/hasen/spages/1131988.html; the EU Foreign Ministers' Statement, Ma'an News Agency, 'Full Text: EU Foreign Ministers' Statement on Middle East,' 9 December 2009, http://www.maannews.net/eng/ViewDetails.aspx?ID= 245290. In her first speech, Catherine Ashton, the European Union's high representative for foreign affairs and security policy and vice president of the European Commission, adopted most of the EU foreign ministers' positions on Israeli occupation of East Jerusalem, home demolitions, and deportation of Palestinians from their homes. Akiva Eldar, 'The New EU Foreign Policy Chief Lambasts Israeli Occupation,' *Ha'aretz*, 17 December 2009, http://www.haaretz.com/hasen/spages/1135787.html.

65. Oded Haklai, 'Religious—Nationalist Mobilization and State Penetration: Lessons From Jewish Settlers' Activism in Israel and the West Bank,' *Comparative Political Studies*, 2007, 40, pp. 713–739.

66. In January 2010 Minister of Defense Barak approved the upgrading to university status of the Ariel University Center of Samaria, located in the settlement city of Ariel. Barak's decision followed by five years a cabinet resolution calling for this change. Since the institution is located outside the area on which the Israeli legal system is in force, the country's statutory higher education accrediting and funding body, the Council for Higher Education, has no authority over it. A special Council for Higher Education in Judea and Samaria, functioning under the aegis of the military government, oversees Israeli higher education institutions in the West Bank. This body had previously authorized the school, then called the College of Judea and Samaria, to change its name to Ariel University Center, as a preliminary step to receiving the status heretofore reserved for Israel's large research institutions. The Israeli Council for Higher Education opposes the status change. Yaheli Moran Zelikovich, 'Barak Okays University Recognition of Ariel College,' Ynet, 20 January 2010, http://www.ynetnews.com/articles/0,7340,L-3837183,00.html.

67. Amos Harel, 'Settlers Are Encountering Their First Real Opponent—Obama,' *Ha'aretz*, 10 July 2009, http://www.haaretz.com/hasen/spages/1099076.html.

68. On the Sasson Report, and for a summary of it.

69. Daniel C. Kurtzer, 'Do Settlements Matter? An American Perspective,' *Israel Journal of Foreign Affairs* III:2, 2009, pp. 23–30.

70. Chaim Levinson, 'High Court: Israel Turns Blind Eye to Illegal Settlement Construction,' *Ha'aretz*, 30 October 2009, http://www.haaretz.com/hasen/spages/1124441.html.

71. Peace Now and ICG data in ICG 2009, p. 2, note 10.

72. ICG 2009, pp. 4–5.

73. Chaim Levinson, 'Hesder Yeshiva Rabbis: Torah Law is Above IDF,' *Ha'aretz*, 18 December 2009, http://www.haaretz.com/hasen/spages/1135864.html. On the context of this statement, see below.

74. Chaim Levinson, 'Who Is Leading the Settlers' Fight for the West Bank Outposts?' *Ha'aretz*, 23 August 2009, http://www.haaretz.com/hasen/spages/1108989.html.

75. ICG 2009, pp. 7–10, 26, 34 footnote 336. On their parallel system, see pages 25–27.

76. ICG 2009, p. 27, note 260. Settlers elsewhere consider him to be their chief rabbi.

77. ICG 2009, p. 27, 22. On settler attacks against Palestinians encouraged by these views, see below.

78. Chaim Levinson, 'Settlers Attack Palestinians to Avenge West Bank Outpost Demolition,' *Ha'aretz*, 27 January 2010, http://www.haaretz.com/hasen/spages/1145463.html.

79. OCHA, 'Israeli Settler Violence and the Evacuation of Outposts,' November 2009, http://www.ochaopt.org/documents/ocha_opt_settler_violence_fact_sheet_2009_11_15_english.pdf.

80. ICG 2009, p. 29, note 284.

81. Ma'an News Agency, 'West Bank Settlers Set Fire to Mosque,' 11 December 2009, http://www.maannews.net/eng/ViewDetails.aspx?ID=245954; Associated Press, 'Settlers Suspected of Vandalizing West Bank Mosque,' *Ha'aretz*, 11 December 2009, http://www.haaretz.com/hasen/spages/1134455.html.

82. OCHA 2009, p. 5.

83. ICG 2009, pp. 28–32.

84. ICG 2009, p. 30.

85. ICG 2009, p. 31, note 302.

86. Ma'an News Agency, 'Settler Authors Guideline on Killing Gentiles,' 9 November 2009, http://www.maannews.net/eng/ViewDetails.aspx?ID=238444.

87. ICG 2009, p. 31, note 310.

88. Ethan Bronner, 'Israelis Arrest West Bank Settler in Attacks,' *New York Times*, 2 November 2009, http://www.nytimes.com/2009/11/02/world/middleeast/02israel.html?_r=2&ref=middleeast.

89. ICG 2009, p. 31, note 305. See others who share this conclusion.

90. ICG 2009, p. 31, note 306.

91. ICG 2009, pp. 12–13; p. 16, note 152.

92. ICG 2009, p. 13, note 123; p. 14.

93. ICG 2009, pp. 14–15.

94. Kobi Nahshoni, 'Rabbi Ovadia Slams U.S.: We Aren't their Slaves,' Ynetnews, 26 July 2009, http://www.ynetnews.com/articles/0,7340,L-3752180,00.html.

95. Matthew Wagner, 'Amar: U.S. Settlements Policy Contravene Torah,' *Jerusalem Post*, 21 July 2009, http://www.jpost.com/servlet/Satellite?cid=1246443863443&pagename=JPost%2FJPArticle%2FShowFull.

96. Quoted in Akiva Eldar, 'Border Control/We Have No Incitement Here,' *Ha'aretz*, 12 January 2010, http://www.haaretz.com/hasen/spages/1142074.html.

97. ICG 2009, p. 15, based on Tamar Hermann's studies and polls.

98. ICG 2009, p. 29.

99. ICG 2009, p. 23, note 218; one of those incidents is described in Amira Hass, 'Palestinians Say Troops Tracking Missing Goats Searched their Home Illegally,' *Ha'aretz*, 27 January 2010, http://www.haaretz.com/hasen/spages/1145456.html.

100. ICG 2009, p. 22, note 208.

101. ICG 2009, p. 22.

102. Yagil Levy, 'The IDF Is Disintegrating,' *Ha'aretz*, 5 November 2008, http://www.haaretz.com/hasen/spages/1034322.html; ICG Report 89, p. 25.

103. Chaim Levinson, 'Settlers Fume as Army Set New Rules Curbing Authority of West Bank Security Coordinators,' *Ha'aretz*, 25 December 2009, http://www.haaretz.com/hasen/spages/1137588.html.

104. Levy 2008.

105. ICG 2009, p. 20, note 192.

106. ICG 2009, p. 33, note 325.

107. ICG 2009, pp. 20–25, 26.

108. ICG 2009, p. 23.

109. Chaim Levinson, 'The IDF Has Not Received Orders to Evacuate Outposts,' *Ha'aretz*, 28 July 2009, http://www.haaretz.com/hasen/spages/1103444.html.

110. Chaim Levinson, 'Israel Dismantled West Bank Settler Outpost,' *Ha'aretz*, 29 July 2009, http://www.haaretz.com/hasen/spages/1103702.html.

111. Amir Oren, 'IDF: One Third of Soldiers Might Refuse to Evacuate Outposts,' *Ha'aretz*, 19 August 2009, http://www.haaretz.com/hasen/spages/1108560.html.

112. Chaim Levinson, 'IDF General Israel Incapable of West Bank Pullout,' *Ha'aretz*, 7 September 2009, http://www.haaretz.com/hasen/spages/1112876.html.

113. Amos Harel, 'IDF Task Force Looks for Ways to End Soldier Insubordination,' *Ha'aretz*, 11 December 2009, http://www.haaretz.com/hasen/spages/1134303.html.

114. Chaim Levinson, 'Rabbis Unite Against Barak in IDF-Yeshiva Row,' *Ha'aretz*, 17 December 2009, http://www.haaretz.com/hasen/spages/1135825.html.

115. Chaim Levinson, 'Settlers Fume as Army Set New Rules Curbing Authority of West Bank Security Coordinators,' *Ha'aretz*, 25 December 2009, http://www.haaretz.com/hasen/spages/1137588.html.

4. THE ISRAELI CONTROL SYSTEM

1. OCHA, 'Closure Update,' 20 April to 11 September 2008, http://www.ochaopt.org/documents/ocha_opt_closure_update_2008_09_english.pdf; OCHA, 'Movement and Access Update,' May 2009, http://www.ochaopt.org/documents/ocha_opt_movement_and_access_2009_05_25_english.pdf; for B'tselem data on 2007, see B'Tselem, 'Ground to a Halt: Denial of Palestinians' Freedom of Movement in the West Bank,' August 2007, http://www.btselem.org/english/publications/summaries/200708_ground_to_a_halt.asp.

2. ACRI, 'High Court Rules: "Israeli–Only" Route to be Open to Palestinians,' 30 December 2009, http://www.acri.org.il/eng/story. aspx?id=698.

3. http://www.adalah.org/newsletter/eng/apr08/5.pdf; http://www. btselem.org/english/statistics/detainees_and_prisoners.asp.

4. Amira Hass, 'Institutionalized Voyeurism,' *Ha'aretz*, 26 November 2009, http://www.haaretz.com/hasen/spages/1130498.html.

5. OCHA 2008.

6. OCHA, 'Closure Maps,' June 2009, http://www.ochaopt.org/ documents/Closure_Maps_Book_Web.pdf.

7. Avi Issacharoff and Anshel Pfeffer, 'IDF Agrees to Expanded Activity by PA Forces in West Bank Towns,' *Ha'aretz*, 26 June 2009, http://www.haaretz.com/hasen/spages/1095794.html; Amos Harel and Avi Issacharoff, 'Israel Removes Dozens of West Bank Roadblocks,' *Ha'aretz*, 24 June 2009, http://www.haaretz.com/ hasen/spages/1095231.html.

8. BBC News, 17 July 2009, http://news.bbc.co.uk/2/hi/middle_ east/8153871.stm.

9. OCHA, 'The Humanitarian Monitor,' August 2009, http://www. ochaopt.org/documents/ocha_opt_the_humanitarian_monitor_ 2009_august_english.pdf.

10. OCHA, 'Protection of Civilians,' 30 September to 6 October 2009, http://www.ochaopt.org/documents/ocha_opt_protection_ of_civilians_weekly_report_2009_10_06_english.pdf.

11. OCHA, 'West Bank Movement and Access Update,' November 2009, http://www.ochaopt.org/documents/ocha_opt_movement_ access_2009_november_english.pdf.

12. OCHA, May 2009. On the collaboration between settlers, the IDF, and the civilian legal system to take land from Palestinians for the purpose of settlement expansion, see Akiva Eldar, 'Evacuation Law Without Compensation,' *Ha'aretz Magazine*, 5 June 2009, p. 5, (in Hebrew).

13. Amit Cohen, 'Bustling Nablus Returning to Normal after Checkpoint Changes,' *Ma'ariv*, 31 July 2009, http://www.americantask-force.org/daily_news_article/2009/07/31/1249012800_10.

14. Giorgia Giambi, 'The "Jenin Pilot" Monitoring Report,' Center for Democracy and Community Development, July 2009, http:// cd-cd.org/default.asp?mode=more&NewsID=221.

15. World Bank, 'A Palestinian State in Two Years: Institutions for Economic Revival,' Economic Monitoring Report to the Ad Hoc Liaison Committee, 22 September 2009, http://siteresources. worldbank.org/INTWESTBANKGAZA/Resources/AHLCSept09-WBreportfinal.pdf, pp. 4–5.

16. Ibid.

17. Ibid.

18. Akiva Eldar, 'A Far Cry from Prosperity,' *Ha'aretz*, 16 October 2009, http://www.haaretz.com/hasen/spages/1121526.html.

19. Israel Central Bureau of Statistics, *Statistical Abstract of Israel*, 2007, http://www1.cbs.gov.il/reader/shnaton/templ_shnaton_e. html?num_tab=st02_01&CYear=2007.

20. ACRI, *The State of Human Rights in Israel and the Occupied Territories*, 2008, http://www.acri.org.il/pdf/state2008.pdf; Report of the State Commission of Inquiry into the Clashes between Security Forces and Israeli Civilians [Or Commission], 2003, http:// www. haaretz.com/hasen/pages/ShArt.jhtml?itemNo=335594&c ontrassID=2&subContrassID=1&sbSubContrassID=0&listSrc=Y.

21. Or Kashti, 'Israel Aids its Needy Jewish Students more than Arab Counterparts,' *Ha'aretz*, 12 August 2009, http://www.haaretz. com/hasen/spages/1106955.html.

22. Jacky Khoury, 'Education Ministry Requires "Positive View" of Israel for Top Positions within Arab Community,' *Ha'aretz*, 3 December 2009, http://www.haaretz.com/hasen/spages/1132417. html.

23. Akiva Eldar, 'Shin Bet Admits Intervening in Muslim Cleric Appointments to Public Office,' *Ha'aretz*, 7 December 2008, http://www.haaretz.com/hasen/spages/1044076.html.

24. On settler rabbis urging IDF soldiers to refuse orders to evacuate settlements, see *Ha'aretz*, 2 June 2009, http://www.haaretz.com/ hasen/spages/1088739.html.

25. Akiva Eldar, 'How Israel Silenced its Gaza War Protesters,' *Ha'aretz*, 22 September 2009, http://www.haaretz.com/hasen/ spages/1116114.html; Adalah, 'News Update,' 22 September 2009, http://www.adalah.org/eng/pressreleases/pr.php?file=09_ 09_22; Adalah, 'Prohibited Protest: How the Law Enforcement Authorities Limited the Freedom of Expression of Opponents of the Military Attacks on Gaza,' undated (in Hebrew), http://www. adalah.org/features/prisoners/protestors%20report.pdf.

26. Eldar 2009; Adalah 22 September 2009.

27. Eldar 2009; Adalah 22 September 2009.

28. Jerusalem Institute for Israel Studies, *Statistical Yearbook of Jerusalem*, 2007, http://www.jiis.org.il/imageBank/File/shnaton_2007_8/shnaton%20C0106.pdf. According to Ir Amim, 270,000 Palestinians resided in the annexed area of Jerusalem in 2009, as compared to 190,000 Israelis (totaling 35 per cent of the city's population). Ir Amim 2008, pp. 13, 17.

29. Klein 2001.

30. Nir Hasson, 'Jerusalem Mayor Cuts Aid Money for Toddler Care in East Jerusalem,' *Ha'aretz*, 20 December 2009, http://www.haaretz.com/hasen/spages/1136334.html.

31. ACRI 2008; ACRI, 'The State of Human Rights in East Jerusalem: Facts and Figures,' May 2009, (in Hebrew), http://www.acri.org.il/pdf/eastjer2009.pdf.

32. Palestinian Central Bureau of Statistics, 'Population, Housing and Establishment Census 2007: Preliminary Findings,' Ramallah, 2008, http://www.pcbs.gov.ps/Portals/_pcbs/PressRelease/census2007_e.pdf;http://www.pcbs.gov.ps/desktopmodules/newsscrollEnglish/newsscrollView.aspx?ItemID=686&mID=11170; http://www.pcbs.gov.ps/Census2007Portals/_PCBS/Press/gaza_census.pdf; http://www.pcbs.gov.ps/Portals/_PCBS/Downloads/book1487.pdf.

33. OCHA, 'The Humanitarian Monitor Reports of 2008,' http://ochaonline2.un.org/Default.aspx?tabid=5227; B'tselem August 2007.

34. World Bank, 'Assessment of Restrictions on Palestinian Water Sector Development,' April 2009, http://siteresources.worldbank.org/INTWESTBANKGAZA/Resources/WaterRestrictionsReport18Apr2009.pdf.

35. B'Tselem, 'The Water Crisis: The Gap in Water Consumption Between Palestinians and Israelis,' http://www.btselem.org/english/water/consumption_gap.asp; and data http://www.btselem.org/english/water/statistics.asp.

36. Shaul Arieli and Michael Sfard, *The Wall of Folly*, Tel Aviv: Yedioth Aharonoth, 2008, pp. 365–71 [in Hebrew].

37. World Bank, 'Investing in Palestinian Economic Reform and Development,' Paris, December 2007, http://siteresources.world-

bank.org/INTWESTBANKGAZA/Resources/294264–1166
525851073/ParisconferencepaperDec17.pdf; the report of the
United Nations fact-finding mission on the Gaza conflict, headed
by Judge Richard Goldstone, found strong evidence of war crimes
and crimes against humanity, see United Nations, 29 September
2009; OCHA, 'Locked In: The Humanitarian Impact of Two
Years of Blockade on the Gaza Strip, Special Focus,' August 2009,
http://www.ochaopt.org/documents/Ocha_opt_Gaza_impact_
of_two_years_of_blockade_August_2009_english.pdf.

38. Yotam Feldman and Uri Blau, 'Gaza Bonanza,' *Ha'aretz Magazine*, 11 June 2009, http://www.haaretz.com/hasen/spages/109
2196.html.

39. Amira Hass, 'This is Gaza,' *Ha'aretz*, 27 November 2008, http://
www.haaretz.com/hasen/spages/1041345.html.

40. *Ha'aretz*, 25 February 2009; 24 March 2009; 23 April 2009; 24
May 2009 (in Hebrew); Amira Hass, 'Israel Bans Books, Music
and Clothes from Entering Gaza,' *Ha'aretz*, 17 May 2009, http://
www.haaretz.com/hasen/spages/1086045.html; Feldman and
Blau 2009.

41. OCHA, 'Protection of Civilians,' 11–17 November 2009, http://
www.ochaopt.org/documents/ocha_opt_protection_of_civil-
ians_weekly_report_2009_11_17_english.pdf.

42. Jewish Telegraphic Agency, 'Israel to Transfer Cement to Gaza,'
29 July 2009, http://jta.org/news/article/2009/07/29/1006899/
israel-to-transfer-cement-to-gaza.

43. Feldman and Blau 2009.

44. OCHA August 2009.

45. Avi Issacharoff, 'Gaza's Smuggling Tunnels Feel Impact of Israel–
Egypt Crackdown,' *Ha'aretz*, 30 July 2009, http://www.haaretz.
com/hasen/spages/1103967.html.

46. Taghreed el-Khodary, 'A View from the Ground,' *Middle East
Progress*, 28 July 2009, http://middleeastprogress.org/2009/07/a-
view-from-the-ground/.

47. OCHA August 2009.

48. Avi Issacharoff, 'Are Fatah and Hamas on Road to Reconciliation?' *Ha'aretz*, 26 June 2009, http://www.haaretz.com/hasen/
spages/1095892.html.

49. B'Tselem, 'Israel Implements New Permit Regime and Policy of
Forcible Transfer of Palestinians from the West Bank to Gaza

Strip,' Press Release, 20 September 2008, http://www.btselem. org/English/Press_Releases/20080910.asp.

50. Ma'an News Agency, 'Israel's New Regulations Make Moving from Gaza to West Bank Harder,' 17 June 2009, http://www. maannews.net/en/index.php?opr=ShowDetails&ID=38613.

51. Yiftachel 2006, pp. 136–40.

52. ACRI, 'High Court: Ka'adan Family Can Build its Home in Katzir,' 2 September 2004 (in Hebrew), http://www.acri.org.il/ Story.aspx?id=925.

53. ACRI, 'High Court to Deliberate on JNF's Discriminatory Land Policy,' 23 September 2007, http://www.acri.org.il/eng/Story. aspx?id=395.

54. Jack Khoury, 'Second Galilee Town Considering "Zionist Values" Bylaws,' *Ha'aretz*, 3 June 2009, http://www.haaretz.com/hasen/ spages/1089728.html.

55. Jack Khoury, 'Another Jewish Town Adds "Zionist Loyalty" to Bylaws,' *Ha'aretz*, 16 November 2009, http://www.haaretz.com/ hasen/spages/1128408.html.

56. Jonathan Liss, 'New Bill Makes Possible to Reject Arab Settlers in Jewish Communal Settlements,' *Ha'aretz*, 6 December 2009 (in Hebrew), http://www.haaretz.co.il/hasite/spages/1132999.html.

57. Jonathan Liss, 'Israel Rejects Bill Allocating Equal Land to Jews and Arabs,' *Ha'aretz*, 3 January 2010, http://www.haaretz.com/ hasen/spages/1139584.html.

58. ACRI, 'ACRI: Retract Decision to Extend Citizenship Law,' 5 February 2007, http://www.acri.org.il/eng/Story.aspx?id=354; on other forms of discrimination against Palestinian citizens of Israel, see http://www.acri.org.il/eng/story.aspx?id=556.

59. Jonathan Liss, 'MK Aims to Keep Palestinians Married to Israelis from Gaining Citizenship,' *Ha'aretz*, 18 December 2009, http:// www.haaretz.com/hasen/spages/1135963.html.

60. ACRI 2008.

61. Matti Friedman, 'Israel Cuts Palestinian Tragedy from Textbooks,' AP, 22 July 2009, http://www.google.com/hostednews/ ap/article/ALeqM5jLMfNbrL3eakMOLBAF6ylTtwuKFQD 99JFJKO0.

62. Nadav Shragai and Mazal Mualem, '47 MKs Back Bill to Jail Deniers of "Jewish State,"' *Ha'aretz*, 28 May 2009, http://www.

haaretz.com/hasen/spages/1088804.html; Jack Khoury, 'Israeli Arabs Warn Against Dangers of "Racist Legislation,"' *Ha'aretz*, 31 May 2009, http://www.haaretz.com/hasen/spages/1089021.html.

63. Jack Khoury, 'Education Ministry Requires "Positive View" of Israel for Top Positions within Arab Community,' *Ha'aretz*, 3 December 2009, http://www.haaretz.com/hasen/spages/1132417.html.

64. Nir Hasson, 'Most Arabs Can't Buy Most Homes in West Jerusalem,' *Ha'aretz*, 21 July 2009, http://www.haaretz.com/hasen/spages/1101682.html.

65. Nir Hasson, 'Israel Strips Thousands of Jerusalem Arabs of Residency in 2008,' *Ha'aretz*, 2 December 2009, http://www.haaretz.com/hasen/spages/1132170.html.

66. Klein 2001, pp. 266–7.

67. B'Tselem, 'Land Expropriation and Settlements: Taking Control of the Land in the West Bank,' http://www.btselem.org/english/Settlements/Land_Takeover.asp.

68. Ir Amim 2009, pp. 13, 17.

69. Klein January 2005; Kobi Michael and Amnon Ramon, *A Fence Around Jerusalem: The Construction of the Security Fence Around Jerusalem, General Background and Implications for the City and its Metropolitan Area*, Jerusalem: The Jerusalem Institute for Israel Studies, 2004, http://www.jiis.org.il/imageBank/File/publications/w-fence-eng.pdf.

70. Azoulay and Ofir 2008; Ariel Hendel, 'Controlling Space through Space: Uncertainty as a Technology of Control,' *Te'oria u-Vikoret*, No. 31, 2007, pp. 101–26, (in Hebrew).

71. Amira Hass, 'Israel Restricts Palestinian Lawyers' Access to West Bank Detainees,' *Ha'aretz*, 14 January 2010, http://www.haaretz.com/hasen/spages/1142515.html.

72. B'Tselem, '15 May '04: Investigation of the IDF Action in Rafah,' Press release, 15 May 2004, http://www.btselem.org/English/Press_Releases/20040515.asp.

73. B'Tselem's data can be found in http://www.btselem.org/Download/20090909_Cast_Lead_Fatalities_Heb.pdf, (in Hebrew); Adalah's come from 'Prohibited Protest: How the Law Enforcement Authorities Limited the Freedom of Expression of Opponents of the Military Attacks on Gaza,' undated, (in Hebrew), http://www.adalah.org/features/prisoners/protestors%20report.pdf.

74. B'Tselem, 'Operation Cast Lead, 27 Dec. '08 to 18 Jan. '09,' undated, http://www.btselem.org/english/gaza_strip/castlead_operation.asp.

5. THE CHANGING PATTERN OF THE CONFLICT

1. The Palestinian Central Bureau of Statistics' data of late 2009 on the number of Palestinians is higher. According to it, 2.5 million live in the West Bank, 1.5 million in Gaza Strip and 1.25 million in Israel. Ma'an News Agency, 'PCBS: 10.88 Million Palestinians in the World, Half in Diaspora,' 31 December 2009, http://www.maannews.net/eng/ViewDetails.aspx?ID=250948.

2. Sergio Della Pergola, 'Population Trends and Scenarios in Israel and Palestine' in A.M. Kacowicz and P. Lutomski (eds.), *Population Resettlement in International Conflicts: A Comparative Study*, New York: Lexington, 2007, pp. 295–6.

3. Ir Amim 2009, pp. 17, 32. On the failure of the Israeli policy to change in its favor the demographic balance in Jerusalem since 1967, see Klein 2001.

4. See Yoram Meital, 'The Khartoum Conference and Egyptian Policy After the 1967 War: A Reexamination,' *Middle East Journal*, Vol. 54 No. 1 (Winter 2000), pp. 64–82; Mark Tessler, *A History of the Israeli–Palestinian Conflict*, Second Edition, Bloomington and Indianapolis: Indiana University Press, 2009, pp. 407–11.

5. Khalidi 2008.

6. Palestinian Center for Policy and Survey Research, 'Press Release: Joint Israeli Palestinian Poll, December 2009,' http://www.pcpsr.org/survey/polls/2009/p34ejoint.html.

7. http://www.pcpsr.org/survey/polls/2009/p34ejoint.html.

8. See the joint Israeli–Palestinian public opinion poll of June 2008, http://www.pcpsr.org/survey/polls/2008/p28ejoint.html, and that of March 2008, http://www.pcpsr.org/survey/polls/2008/p27e1.html#peace.

9. http://www.spirit.tau.ac.il/xeddexcms008/index.asp?siteid=5&lang=2.

10. Honaida Ghanim, *Reinventing the Nation: Palestinian Intellectuals in Israel*, Jerusalem: The Hebrew University: Magnes Press, 2009 (in Hebrew).

11. For the Adalah report, see http://www.adalah.org/eng/pressre-leases/pr.php?file=09_09_22; according to *Ha'aretz*, 18 January 2009, p. 6 (in Hebrew), only 763 were arrested.

12. Liel Kayzer, Jack Khoury, Fadi Eyadat and News Agencies, 'IDF Official: Neither Israel nor the PA Wants Violence', *Ha'aretz*, 16 March 2010, http://www.haaretz.com/hasen/spages/1156775. html.

13. The National Committee of the Heads of the Arab Local Author-ities in Israel, 'The Future Vision of the Palestinian Arabs in Israel,' Nazareth 2006, http://www.adalah.org/newsletter/eng/dec06/tasawor-mostaqbali.pdf. The other two are the Democratic Constitution, published by Adalah–The Legal Center for Arab Minority Rights in Israel, Shafa'amr, 2007, http://www.adalah. org/eng/democratic_constitution-e.pdf; and the Haifa Declara-tion, published by Mada al-Carmel, Arab Center for Applied Social Research, 2008, http://www.mada-research.org/archive/haifadeceng.htm.

14. National Committee of the Heads of the Arab Local Authorities in Israel 2006, pp. 10–11.

15. Amal Helow, 'Challenging Israel to Become Democratic,' *Bitter-lemons*, 29 January 2007, http://www.bitterlemons.org/previous/bl290107ed4.html; As'ad Ghanem, 'Dismantling the Tyranny of the Majority, ibid; Ghassan Khatib, 'A Civilized and Sophisti-cated Argument,' ibid.

16. Yossi Alpher, 'A Profoundly Disturbing Document,' *Bitterlemons*, 29 January 2007, http://www.bitterlemons.org/previous/bl290107 ed4.html; Uzi Benziman, 'Azmi Bishara as an Example,' *Ha'aretz*, 11 April 2007, http://209.85.229.132/search?q=cache:b6vjIyi RoiYJ:www.haaretz.com/hasen/spages/847290.html+uzi+benzim an+on+Arab+vision+documents&cd=1&hl=iw&ct=clnk&gl=il. For a socio-political Israeli Jewish analysis of the vision docu-ments, see Sami Smooha, 'The Arab Vision of Turning Israel Within the Green Line into a Binational Democracy' in Sarah Ozacky-Lazar and Mustafa Kabh (eds.), *Between Vision and Reality: The Vision Papers of the Arabs in Israel, 2006–2007*, Jerusalem: The Citizens' Accord Forum, 2008, pp. 126–39 (in Hebrew), http://soc.haifa.ac.il/~s.smooha/download/Arab_Vision_ of_Binational_State.pdf; Eli Rekhes, 'The First Word: How Pal-estinian Arabs in Israel See Their Future,' *Jerusalem Post*, 1 Janu-

ary 2007, http://english.icci.org.il/index.php?option=com_conte
nt&task=view&id=97&Itemid=72.

17. Yoav Stern, 'Diskin: We Will Prevent Subversive Activities Even
If They Are Legal,' *Ha'aretz*, 18 May 2007 (in Hebrew); Adalah,
'AG Mazuz in Response to Adalah: We Support the Work of the
GSS Against Those Who Attempt to Change the Nature of the
State,' 22 May 2007, http://www.adalah.org/eng/pressreleases/
pr.php?file=07_05_22, and also in Stern.

18. Dan Izenberg, 'We Will Monitor Subversive Groups,' *Jerusalem
Post*, 20 May 2007, http://www.jpost.com/servlet/Satellite?cid=1
178708647907&pagename=JPArticle%2FShowFull.

19. http://www.tau.ac.il/peace.

20. Israeli Democracy Institute, 'The 2009 Israeli Democracy Index,'
p. 67, 2009, http://www.idi.org.il/sites/english/PublicationsCata-
log/Documents/Democracy_Index%2009.pdf.

21. Israel Democracy Institute 2009, p. 66.

22. A list of those few cases can be found in ICG 2009, p. 32, note
313; p. 33, note 321.

23. Gil Merom, *How Democracies Lose Small Wars: State, Society
and the Failure of France in Algeria, Israel in Lebanon and the
United States in Vietnam*, Cambridge: Cambridge University
Press, 2003, pp. 83–98; Leila Farsakh, *Palestinian Labour Migra-
tion to Israel: Labour, Land and Occupation*, London: Routledge,
2005; Maya Rosenfeld, *Confronting the Occupation: Work,
Education and Political Activism of Palestinian Families in a
Refugee Camp*, Stanford: Stanford University Press, 2004.

24. Haklai 2007.

25. ICG 2009, p. 34, note 338.

26. Ian Lustick, *Unsettled States, Disputed Lands: Britain and Ireland, France and Algeria, Israel and the West Bank/Gaza*, Ithaca:
Cornell University Press, 1993, pp. 428–9; 257–95.

27. Ibid., p. 400.

28. Ibid., p. 432.

29. sMerom 2003, pp. 83–101.

30. Lustick 1993, pp. 41–51, 385–438.

31. Hendrik Spruyt, *Ending Empire: Contested Sovereignty and Territorial Partition*, Ithaca and London: Cornell University Press,
2005.

32. Shlomo Swirski, *Is There an Israeli Business Peace Disincentive?* Adva Center Report, August 2008; see also 'Who Profits from the Israeli Occupation,' http://www.whoprofits.org/, and http://www.adva.org/UserFiles/File/IsraeliBusinessPeaceDisincentivefinal(1).pdf.

33. Uri Ben Eliezer, *The Making of Israeli Militarism*, Bloomington and Indianapolis: Indiana University Press, 1998; Eldar and Zertal, 2007; Yoram Peri, *General in the Cabinet Room: How the Military Shapes Israeli Policy*, Washington DC: United States Institute of Peace, 2006; Aharon Kleiman, 'Israeli Negotiating Culture' in Tamara Cofman Wittes (ed.), *How Israelis and Palestinians Negotiate: A Cross-Cultural Analysis of the Oslo Peace Process*, Washington D.C.: United States Institute of Peace Press, 2005, pp. 81–132.

34. Hussein Agha and Robert Malley, 'Into the Lion's Den,' *New York Review of Books*, Vol. 55 No. 7, 1 May 2008.

35. Nathan J. Brown, 'Sunset for the Two State Solution?' *Carnegie Foreign Policy Paper*, Carnegie Endowment for International Peace, May 2008.

36. Bernard Chazelle, 'Why Israel Won't Accept a Two-State Solution,' http://www.cs.princeton.edu/~chazelle/.

37. Benvenisti 2007, pp. 199–206; and see his numerous articles in *Ha'aretz*. On his twofold approach to the one-state solution, see below.

38. Tony Judt, 'Israel: the Alternative,' *New York Review of Books*, Vol. 50 No. 16, 23 October 2003.

39. Among them Virginia Tilley, *The One-State Solution: A Breakthrough for Peace in the Israeli–Palestinian Deadlock*, Ann Arbor: University of Michigan Press, 2005; Ali Abunimah, *One Country: A Bold Proposal to End the Israeli–Palestinian Impasse*, New York: Metropolitan Books, 2007; Jamil Hilal, *Where Now for Palestine? The Demise of the Two-State Solution*, London: Zed Books 2006; Jonathan Cook, *Blood and Religion: The Unmasking of the Jewish and Democratic State*, London: Pluto Press, 2006. See also Ahmad Khalidi, 'Thanks But No Thanks,' *The Guardian*, 13 December 2007; Sari Nusseibeh, 'Nusseibeh Blames the Donor States for Funding the Occupation and Offers to Give Up the Right of Return in Exchange for Getting Back Jerusalem

and the Temple Mount,' *al-Quds al-Arabi*, 29 July 2008 (in Arabic), http://sari.alquds.edu/alquds_alarabi.htm; Eldar 17 August 2008, http://www.haaretz.com/hasen/spages/1011859.html; Rory McCarthy, 'Palestinians Lose Faith in Two-State Solution: Study Group Calls for New Form of Resistance to Israeli Occupation with Goal of Single Bi–National State,' *The Guardian*, 4 September 2008, http://www.guardian.co.uk/world/2008/sep/04/israel. palestinians; Palestinian Strategy Study Group August 2008.

40. Ma'an News Agency, 'Qurei': We Will Not Allow Israel to Impose Facts on the Ground,' 7 June 2008, http://www.maan-news.net/en/index.php?opr=ShowDetails&ID=29785.

41. Ma'an News Agency, 'Erekat: Two-state Solution may have to be Abandoned,' 5 November 2009, http://www.maannews.net/eng/ViewDetails.aspx?ID=237319.

42. Leslie Susser, 'One Land: How Many States?' *Jerusalem Report*, 31 March 2008.

43. Khalidi 2007.

44. Brown 2008.

45. Meron Benvenisti, 'Moot Argument,' *Ha'aretz*, 21 August 2008, http://www.haaretz.com/hasen/spages/1013974.html.

46. Smooha 2005, pp. 241–57. Quotation from p. 242.

47. Gidi Weitz, 'Ever So Politely,' *Ha'aretz Magazine*, 23 October 2009, http://www.haaretz.com/hasen/spages/1122910.html.

48. Barak Ravid, 'Defense Establishment Paper: Golan for Syria Peace, Plan for Iran Strike,' *Ha'aretz*, 23 November 2008, p. 1.

49. Bret Stephens, 'Israel Scored a Tactical Victory, but it missed a chance to finish off Hamas,' *Wall Street Journal*, 19 January 2009, http://online.wsj.com/article/SB123241373428396239.html.

50. Benvenisti 2007, pp. 89, 93, 130–56, 199–227.

51. See public opinion polls at http://www.pcpsr.org/.

52. For models used in Europe see Council of Europe, 'White Paper on Intercultural Dialogue: Living Together as Equals in Dignity,' Strasbourg June 2008, http://www.coe.int/t/dg4/intercultural/Source/White%20Paper_final_revised_en.pdf.

BIBLIOGRAPHY

Abbas, Mahmoud, 'Israel and Palestine Can Still Achieve Peace,' *Wall Street Journal*, 19 September 2008, http://online.wsj.com/article/SB122178624406455063.html?mod=googlenews_wsj.

Abunimah, Ali, *One Country: A Bold Proposal to End the Israeli–Palestinian Impasse*, New York: Metropolitan Books, 2007.

ACRI, 'ACRI: Retract Decision to Extend Citizenship Law,' 5 February 2007, http://www.acri.org.il/eng/Story.aspx?id=354.

——— 'High Court: Ka'adan Family Can Build its Home in Katzir,' 2 September 2004, (in Hebrew), http://www.acri.org.il/Story.aspx?id=925.

——— 'High Court Rules: "Israeli–Only" Route to be Open to Palestinians,' 30 December 2009, http://www.acri.org.il/eng/story.aspx?id=698.

——— 'High Court to Deliberate on JNF's Discriminatory Land Policy,' 23 September 2007, http://www.acri.org.il/eng/Story.aspx?id=395.

——— *The State of Human Rights in East Jerusalem: Facts and Figures*, May 2009, (in Hebrew), http://www.acri.org.il/pdf/eastjer2009.pdf.

——— *The State of Human Rights in Israel and the Occupied Territories*, 2008, http://www.acri.org.il/pdf/state2008.pdf.

Adalah, 'AG Mazuz in Response to Adalah: We Support the Work of the GSS Against Those Who Attempt to Change the Nature of the State,' 22 May 2007, http://www.adalah.org/eng/pressreleases/pr.php?file=07_05_22.

——— 'News Update,' 22 September 2009, http://www.adalah.org/eng/pressreleases/pr.php?file=09_09_22.

––––– 'Prohibited Protest: How the Law Enforcement Authorities Limited the Freedom of Expression of Opponents of the Military Attacks on Gaza,' undated, (in Hebrew), http://www.adalah.org/features/prisoners/protestors%20report.pdf.

––––– 'The Democratic Constitution,' Shafa'amr, 2007, http://www.adalah.org/eng/democratic_constitution-e.pdf.

Agha, Hussein and Robert Malley, 'Into the Lion's Den,' *New York Review of Books*, Vol. 55 No. 7, 1 May 2008.

––––– 'Obama and the Middle East,' *The New York Review of Books*, Vol. 56 No. 10, 11 June 2009, http://www.nybooks.com/articles/22731.

al-Hayat, 14 December 2008, http://www.alhayat.com/arab_news/levant_news/12–2008/Article-20081213–31f94b21–c0a8–10ed-0088–d0c18c7d7244/story.html.

al-Masri, Hani, 'Mr. President: Courageous Historical Decisions are Needed,' *al-Ayyam*, 25 March 2008 (in Arabic), http://www.al-ayyam.ps/znews/site/template/Doc_View.aspx?did=80711&Date=3/25/2008.

Alpher, Yossi, 'A Profoundly Disturbing Document,' *Bitterlemons*, 29 January 2007, http://www.bitterlemons.org/previous/bl290107ed4.html.

Arieli, Shaul, 'A New Freezing Point,' *Ha'aretz*, 5 January 2010, http://www.haaretz.com/hasen/spages/1140024.html.

––––– 'Natural growth or growth bymmigration?!' http://www.shaularieli.com/image/users/77951/ftp/my_files/Netunim/translated.doc.

––––– 'Without Any Tricks,' *Ha'aretz*, 3 July 2009, http://www.haaretz.com/hasen/spages/1097241.html.

Arieli, Shaul and Michael Sfard, *The Wall of Folly*, Tel Aviv: Yedioth Aharonoth, 2008 (in Hebrew).

Arlosorov, Meirav, 'The Virtual Reality of Gaza,' *Ha'aretz—The Marker*, 14 January 2010, p. 20 (in Hebrew).

Associated Press, 'Settlers Suspected of Vandalizing West Bank Mosque,' *Ha'aretz*, 11 December 2009, http://www.haaretz.com/hasen/spages/1134455.html.

Azoulay, Ariella and Adi Ophir, *This Regime Which Is Not One: Occupation and Democracy between the Sea and the River 1967–*, Tel Aviv: Resling, 2008 (in Hebrew).

B'Tselem, '15 May 04: Investigation of the IDF Action in Rafah,' Press release, 15 May 2004, http://www.btselem.org/English/Press_ Releases/20040515.asp.

——— 'Ground to a Halt: Denial of Palestinians' Freedom of Movement in the West Bank,' August 2007, http://www.btselem.org/ english/publications/summaries/200708_ground_to_a_halt.asp.

——— 'Israel Implements New Permit Regime and Policy of Forcible Transfer of Palestinians from the West Bank to Gaza Strip,' Press Release, 10 September 2008, http://www.btselem.org/English/Press_ Releases/20080910.asp.

——— 'Land Expropriation and Settlements: Taking Control of the Land in the West Bank,' http://www.btselem.org/english/Settlements/Land_Takeover.asp.

——— 'Land Grab: Israel's Settlement Policy in the West Bank,' Jerusalem: May 2002, http://www.btselem.org/Download, /200205_ Land_Grab_Eng.pdf.

——— 'Operation Cast Lead, 27 Dec. '08–18 Jan. '09, undated, http:// www.btselem.org/english/gaza_strip/castlead_operation.asp.

——— 'The Establishment and Expansion Plans of the Ma'ale Adummim Settlement,' December 2009, Joint Report with Bimkom— Planners for Planning Rights, http://www.btselem.org/english/ publications/summaries/200912_maale_adummim.asp.

——— 'The Water Crisis: The Gap in Water Consumption Between Palestinians and Israelis,' http://www.btselem.org/english/water/ consumption_gap.asp; and data http://www.btselem.org/english/ water/statistics.asp.

Ben Eliezer, Uri, *The Making of Israeli Militarism*, Bloomington and Indianapolis: Indiana University Press, 1998.

Benhorin, Yitzhak, 'Jordan's King: US Credibility Under Question,' Ynet, 7 February 2010. http://www.ynetnews.com/articles/0,7340,L-3845718,00.html.

Benn, Aluf, '*Ha'aretz* Exclusive: Olmert's Plan for Peace,' *Ha'aretz*, 17 December 2009, http://www.haaretz.com/hasen/spages/1135699. html.

——— 'Let's See Him Convince Mitchell,' *Ha'aretz*, 8 June 2009, p. B2 (in Hebrew).

——— 'Renewing Israeli–Palestinian Talks is Obvious Way to End Impasse,' *Ha'aretz*, 15 January 2010, http://www.haaretz.com/ hasen/spages/1142741.html.

Benvenisti, Meron, 'Moot Argument,' *Ha'aretz*, 21 August 2008, http://www.haaretz.com/hasen/spages/1013974.html.

—— *Son of the Cypresses: Memories, Reflections and Regrets from a Political Life*, Berkeley: University of California Press, 2007.

Benziman, Uzi, 'Azmi Bishara as an Example,' *Ha'aretz*, 11 April 2007, http://209.85.229.132/search?q=cache:b6vjIyiRoiYJ:www.haaretz.com/hasen/spages/847290.html+uzi+benziman+on+Arab+vision+documents&cd=1&hl=iw&ct=clnk&gl=il.

Bil'in, http://www.bilin-village.org/english/, http://www.bilin-ffj.org/.

Bimkom, 'The Prohibited Zone: Israeli Planning Policy in the Palestinian Villages of Area C,' June 2008 (in Hebrew). http://www.bimkom.org/publicationView.asp?publicationId=141.

Blau, Uri, 'US Group Invests Tax–Free Millions in East Jerusalem Land,' *Ha'aretz*, 17 August 2009, http://www.haaretz.com/hasen/spages/1107975.html.

—— 'We Came, Looked, Occupied,' *Ha'aretz Magazine*, 30 December 2009, pp. 24–8 (in Hebrew).

Blincoe, Nicholas, 'The Dayton Force Dilemma,' *The Guardian*, 8 July 2009, http://www.guardian.co.uk/commentisfree/2009/jul/08/palestinian-dayton-force-west-bank.

Brom, Shlomo, 'Security Reform and the Political Process,' *Bitterlemons*, 11 May 2009, http://www.bitterlemons.org/previous/bl110509ed18.html#isr2.

Bronner, Ethan, 'Israelis Arrest West Bank Settler in Attacks,' *New York Times*, 2 November 2009, http://www.nytimes.com/2009/11/02/world/middleeast/02israel.html?_r=2&ref=middleeast.

—— 'Israel Rejects US Call to Hold Off on Development,' *New York Times*, 19 July 2009, http://www.nytimes.com/2009/07/20/world/middleeast/20mideast.html?ref=middleeast.

Brown, Nathan J., 'Points for the Obama Administration in the Middle East: Avoiding Myths and Vain Hopes,' Carnegie Paper, 23 January 2009, http://carnegieendowment.org/publications/index.cfm?fa=view&id=22662&prog=zgp&proj=zme.

—— 'Sunset for the Two State Solution?' *Carnegie Foreign Policy Paper*, Carnegie Endowment for International Peace, May 2008.

Chazelle, Bernard, 'Why Israel Won't Accept a Two-State Solution,' http://www.cs.princeton.edu/~chazelle/.

Cobain, Ian, 'CIA Working with Palestinian Security Agents,' *The Guardian*, 17 December 2009, http://www.guardian.co.uk/world/2009/dec/17/cia-palestinian-security-agents.

Cohen, Amit, 'Bustling Nablus Returning to Normal after Checkpoint Changes,' *Ma'ariv*, 31 July 2009, http://www.americantaskforce.org/daily_news_article/2009/07/31/1249012800_10.

Cohen, Hillel, *The Rise and Fall of Arab Jerusalem 1967–2007*, Jerusalem: Jerusalem Institute for Israel Studies, 2007 (in Hebrew).

Cohen-Lifshitz, Alon, 'Mocking the Poor with the Economic Peace,' *Ha'aretz*, 16 April 2009 (in Hebrew).

Cook, Jonathan, *Blood and Religion: The Unmasking of the Jewish and Democratic State*, London: Pluto Press, 2006.

Council of Europe, 'White Paper on Intercultural Dialogue: Living Together as Equals in Dignity,' Strasbourg: June 2008. http://www.coe.int/t/dg4/intercultural/Source/White%20Paper_final_revised_en.pdf.

Della Pergola, Sergio, 'Population Trends and Scenarios in Israel and Palestine' in A.M. Kacowicz and P. Lutomski (eds.), *Population Resettlement in International Conflicts: A Comparative Study*, New York: Lexington, 2007, pp. 295–6.

Doumani, Beshara, 'Scenes from Daily Life: The View from Nablus,' *Journal of Palestine Studies*, Vol. 34 No. 1, Autumn 2004, pp. 37–50.

Dumper, Mick and Craig Larkin, 'Political Islam in Contested Jerusalem: The Emerging Role of Islamists from within Israel,' Divided Cities/Contested States Project, Working Paper No. 12, 2009.

Efrat, Elisha, *The West Bank and Gaza Strip: A Geography of Occupation*, Abingdon: Routledge, 2006.

Eldar, Akiva, 'A Far Cry from Prosperity,' *Ha'aretz*, 16 October 2009, http://www.haaretz.com/hasen/spages/1121526.html.

——— 'Border Control/We Have No Incitement Here,' *Ha'aretz*, 12 January 2010, http://www.haaretz.com/hasen/spages/1142074.html.

——— 'Despite Freeze Hundreds of Housing Units Under Construction in Isolated Settlements,' *Ha'aretz*, 1 January 2010, http://www.haaretz.com/hasen/spages/1139226.html.

——— 'Diskin to Abbas: Defer UN Vote on Goldstone or Face "Second Gaza,"' *Ha'aretz*, 17 January 2010, http://www.haaretz.com/hasen/spages/1143038.html.

———— 'Evacuation Law Without Compensation,' *Ha'aretz Magazine*, 5 June 2009, p. 5 (in Hebrew).

———— 'Ex–PM Violated Sharon–Bush Deal,' *Ha'aretz*, 20 July 2009, http://www.haaretz.com/hasen/spages/1101156.html.

———— 'Gush Etzion Today is Seven Times Its Historical Size,' *Ha'aretz*, 31 July 2009, p. 7 (in Hebrew).

———— 'How Israel Silenced its Gaza War Protesters,' *Ha'aretz*, 22 September 2009, http://www.haaretz.com/hasen/spages/1116114.html.

———— 'Mayor Defies Court Order to Evacuate Jews from East Jerusalem Home,' *Ha'aretz*, 22 January 2010, http://www.haaretz.com/hasen/spages/1144441.html.

Eldar, Akiva, 'Shin Bet Admits Intervening in Muslim Cleric Appointments to Public Office,' *Ha'aretz*, 7 December 2008, http://www.haaretz.com/hasen/spages/1044076.html.

———— 'The New EU Foreign Policy Chief Lambasts Israeli Occupation,' *Ha'aretz*, 17 December 2009, http://www.haaretz.com/hasen/spages/1135787.html.

———— 'WATCH: Organizer Admits City of David Endangers Arab Homes,' *Ha'aretz*, 6 October 2009. http://www.haaretz.com/hasen/spages/1118883.html.

———— 'We are running out of time for a two-state solution,' *Ha'aretz*, 17 August 2008, http://www.haaretz.com/hasen/spages/1011859.html.

———— Barak Ravid and Jack Khoury, 'No Difference to US Between Outpost, East Jerusalem Construction,' *Ha'aretz*, 20 July 2009, http://www.haaretz.com/hasen/spages/1101353.html.

el-Khodary, Taghreed, 'A View from the Ground,' *Middle East Progress*, 28 July 2009, http://middleeastprogress.org/2009/07/a-view-from-the-ground/.

Ettinger, Yair, 'Religious Zionist Rabbis: Ascend the Temple Mount,' *Ha'aretz*, 26 October 2009, http://www.haaretz.com/hasen/spages/1123702.html.

Ezzedin, Hussam, 'The PLO Seeks to Investigate the Causes of Delaying a Vote on Goldstone's Report,' *Al-Ayyam*, 4 October 2009 (in Arabic), http://www.al-ayyam.ps/znews/site/template/article.aspx?did=122953&date=10/4/2009.

Falah, Ghazi Walid, 'The Geopolitics of Enclavisation and the Demise of the Two-State Solution to the Israeli–Palestinian Conflict,' *Third World Quarterly*, Vol. 26 No. 8, 2005, pp. 1341–72.

Farsakh, Leila, 'Independence, Cantons or Bantustans: Whither the Palestinian State?' *Middle East Journal*, Vol. 59 No. 2, Spring 2005, pp. 230–45.

––––––– *Palestinian Labour Migration to Israel: Labour, Land and Occupation*, London: Routledge, 2005.

Fatah Political Program, http://calevbenyefuneh.blogspot.com/2009/08/full-text-of-ratified-fatah-political.html.

Feldman, Yotam and Uri Blau, 'Gaza Bonanza,' *Ha'aretz Magazine*, 11 June 2009, http://www.haaretz.com/hasen/spages/1092196.html.

Final Statement of the International Donors' Conference for the Palestinian State, Paris, December 2007, http://www.diplomatie.gouv.fr/en/country-files_156/israel-palestinian-territories_290/peace-process_2155/international-donors-conference-for-the-palestinian-state-17.12.07_10439.html.

Fisk, Robert. 'In the West Bank's Stony Hills, Palestine is Slowly Dying,' *The Independent*, 30 January 2010, http://www.independent.co.uk/news/world/middle-east/in-the-west-banks-stony-hills-palestine-is-slowly-dying-1883669.html.

FMEP, 'Map: Olmert's Final Status Map,' *Settlement Report*, Vol. 18 No. 6, November–December 2008, http://www.fmep.org/reports/archive/vol.-18/no.-6/olmerts-final-status-map.

––––––– 'Report on Israeli Settlements in the Occupied Palestinian Territories, November–December 2008,' http://www.fmep.org/reports/archive/vol.-18/no.-6/olmerts-final-status-map.

Friedman, Matti, 'Israel Cuts Palestinian Tragedy from Textbooks,' AP, 22 July 2009, http://www.google.com/hostednews/ap/article/ALeqM5jLMfNbrL3eakMOLBAF6ylTtwuKFQD99JFJKO0.

Friedman, Thomas L., 'Driving Drunk in Jerusalem,' *New York Times*, 13 March 2010, http://www.nytimes.com/2010/03/14/opinion/14friedman.html?ref=opinion.

Garfinkle, Adam, *Israel and Jordan in the Shadow of War: Functional Ties and Futile Diplomacy in a Small Place*, New York: St. Martin's Press, 1992.

Ghanem, As'ad, 'Dismantling the Tyranny of the Majority,' *Bitterlemons*, 29 January 2007, http://www.bitterlemons.org/previous/bl290107ed4.html.

Ghanim, Honaida, *Reinventing the Nation: Palestinian Intellectuals in Israel*, Jerusalem: The Hebrew University, Magnes Press, 2009, (in Hebrew).

Giambi, Giorgia, 'The "Jenin Pilot" Monitoring Report,' Center for Democracy and Community Development, July 2009, http://cd-cd.org/default.asp?mode=more&NewsID=221.

Gordon, Neve, *Israel's Occupation*, Berkeley: University of California Press, 2008.

Gorenberg, Gershom, 'A Guide to Israeli Settlements,' *Los Angeles Times*, 29 June 2009, http://www.latimes.com/news/opinion/commentary/la-oe-gorenberg28–2009jun28,0,6704423.story.

———— *The Accidental Empire: Israel and the Birth of the Settlements, 1967–1977*, New York: Times Books, 2006.

Greenberg, Raphael, 'Shallow and Brutal Archaeology,' *Ha'aretz*, 9 October 2009, http://www.haaretz.com/hasen/spages/1119641.html.

Ha'aretz Service, 'Ex–US Envoy: Livni Told Palestinians to Reject Olmert Peace Offer,' *Ha'aretz*, 22 October 2009, http://www.haaretz.com/hasen/spages/1122879.html.

———— 'Palestinian Minister Quits over PA Decision to Drop Goldstone Draft,' *Ha'aretz*, 3 October 2009, http://www.haaretz.com/hasen/spages/1118467.html.

Haklai, Oded, 'Religious–Nationalist Mobilization and State Penetration: Lessons From Jewish Settlers' Activism in Israel and the West Bank,' *Comparative Political Studies*, 2007, 40, pp. 713–39.

Hallward, Maia Carter, 'Creative Responses to Separation: Israeli and Palestinian Joint Activism in Bil'in,' *Journal of Peace Research*, Vol. 46 No. 4, (2009), pp. 541–58.

Halper, Jeff, 'Dismantling the Matrix of Control,' MERIP, 11 September 2009, http://www.merip.org/mero/mero091109.html.

———— 'The 94 Percent Solution: A Matrix of Control,' MERIP 216 (Fall 2000), http://www.merip.org/mer/mer216/216_halper.html.

———— 'The Key to Peace: Dismantling the Matrix of Control,' http://www.icahd.org/eng/articles.asp?menu=6&submenu=3.

Hanafi, Sari, 'Spacio-cide and Bio-politics: The Israeli Colonial Conflict from 1947 to the Wall' in Michael Sorkin (ed.), *Against the Wall: Israel's Barrier to Peace*, New York: The New Press, 2005.

Harel, Amos, 'IDF Task Force Looks for Ways to End Soldier Insubordination,' *Ha'aretz*, 11 December 2009, http://www.haaretz.com/hasen/spages/1134303.html.

———— 'Israel–PA Relations Have Never Been So Good,' *Ha'aretz*, 4 September 2009, http://www.haaretz.com/hasen/spages/1112398.html.

———— 'New West Bank Roads Jeopardizing Chances for Peace Accord,' *Ha'aretz*, 15 May 2009.

———— 'Settlers Are Encountering Their First Real Opponent—Obama,' *Ha'aretz*, 10 July 2009, http://www.haaretz.com/hasen/spages/1099076.html.

———— 'Settlers Have Been Working for Months to Undermine Construction Freeze,' *Ha'aretz*, 27 November 2009, http://www.haaretz.com/hasen/spages/1131086.html.

———— 'The Quiet Revolution in the West Bank: More Coordination, Less Killed,' *Ha'aretz*, 4 September 2009, p. 3 (in Hebrew).

Harel, Amos and Avi Issacharoff, 'Israel Removes Dozens of West Bank Roadblocks,' *Ha'aretz*, 24 June 2009, http://www.haaretz.com/hasen/spages/1095231.html.

Hass, Amira, 'Abbas Orders Probe into Goldstone Delay Request,' *Ha'aretz*, 6 October 2009, http://www.haaretz.com/hasen/spages/1118881.html.

———— 'Danger: Popular Struggle,' *Ha'aretz*, 23 December 2009, http://www.haaretz.com/hasen/spages/1137056.html.

———— 'Giving in to the Settlers in Beit Sahur,' *Ha'aretz*, 11 February 2010, http://www.haaretz.com/hasen/spages/1149262.html.

———— 'IDF Declared West Bank Protest Village a Closed Military Area,' *Ha'aretz*, 15 March 2010, http://www.haaretz.com/hasen/spages/1156536.html

———— 'Institutionalized Voyeurism,' *Ha'aretz*, 26 November 2009, http://www.haaretz.com/hasen/spages/1130498.html.

———— 'In the West They Say It's Rain,' *Ha'aretz*, 26 January 2010, http://www.haaretz.com/hasen/spages/1145204.html.

———— 'Israel Bans Books, Music and Clothes from Entering Gaza,' *Ha'aretz*, 17 May 2009, http://www.haaretz.com/hasen/spages/1086045.html.

———— 'Israel Restricts Palestinian Lawyers' Access to West Bank Detainees,' *Ha'aretz*, 14 January 2010, http://www.haaretz.com/hasen/spages/1142515.html.

———— 'Palestinians Say Troops Tracking Missing Goats Searched their Home Illegally,' *Ha'aretz*, 27 January 2010, http://www.haaretz.com/hasen/spages/1145456.html.

—— 'PA Ministers take to the Streets to Join anti–Israeli Popular Demonstrations,' *Ha'aretz*, 1 April 2010, http://www.haaretz.com/hasen/spages/1160339.html.

—— 'This is Gaza,' *Ha'aretz*, 27 November 2008, http://www.haaretz.com/hasen/spages/1041345.html.

—— 'UN: Much of West Bank Closed to Palestinian Building,' *Ha'aretz*, 16 December 2009, http://www.haaretz.com/hasen/spages/113 5421.html.

Hasson, Nir, 'Israel Strips Thousands of Jerusalem Arabs of Residency in 2008,' *Ha'aretz*, 2 December 2009, http://www.haaretz.com/hasen/spages/1132170.html.

—— 'Jerusalem Mayor Cuts Aid Money for Toddler Care in East Jerusalem,' *Ha'aretz*, 20 December 2009, http://www.haaretz.com/hasen/spages/1136334.html.

—— 'Most Arabs Can't Buy Most Homes in West Jerusalem,' *Ha'aretz*, 21 July 2009, http://www.haaretz.com/hasen/spages/110 1682.html.

—— 'Officials: Jewish Bid for East Jerusalem Home Likely to Fail,' *Ha'aretz*, 9 February 2010, http://www.haaretz.com/hasen/spages/1148528.html.

—— 'Plans for Largest East Jerusalem Settlement Filed for Approval,' *Ha'aretz*, 25 August 2009, http://www.haaretz.com/hasen/spages/1109426.html.

—— 'Prosecutor to Jerusalem Mayor—Evict Settlers from Arab Neighborhood,' *Ha'aretz*, 29 January 2010, http://www.haaretz.com/hasen/spages/1145883.html.

—— 'Report: Israeli Cops Nab Czech Peace Activist in Ramallah Raid,' *Ha'aretz*, 22 January 2010, http://www.haaretz.com/hasen/spages/1144105.html.

—— 'Right-Wing Activists Sabotage Jerusalem Master Plan,' *Ha'aretz*, 23 July 2009, http://www.haaretz.com/hasen/spages/1102 010.html.

—— 'Settlers Marketing East Jerusalem Homes for 22 Jewish Families,' *Ha'aretz*, 27 September 2009, http://www.haaretz.com/hasen/spages/1117288.html.

—— 'Will Preservation of Ancient Roman Road Destroy the Western Wall?' *Ha'aretz*, 19 October 2009, http://www.haaretz.com/hasen/spages/1121969.html.

Hasson, Nir and Akiva Eldar, 'Jerusalem Mayor Bows to Pressure, Vows to Shutter Beit Yonatan,' *Ha'aretz*, 4 February 2010, http://www.haaretz.com/hasen/spages/1147459.html.

—— Jack Khoury and Jonathan Liss, 'Islamic Movement Leader in the North Gets 9 Months for Assault,' *Ha'aretz*, 14 January 2010, http://www.haaretz.com/hasen/spages/1142513.html.

Helow, Amal, 'Challenging Israel to Become Democratic,' *Bitterlemons*, 29 January 2007, http://www.bitterlemons.org/previous/bl290 107 ed4.html.

Hendel, Ariel, 'Controlling Space through Space: Uncertainty as a Technology of Control,' *Te'oria u-Vikoret*, No. 31, 2007, pp. 101–26, (in Hebrew).

Hilal, Jamil, *Where Now for Palestine? The Demise of the Two-State Solution*, London: Zed Books, 2006.

Human Science Research Council of South Africa, *Occupation, Colonialism, Apartheid: A Reassessment of Israel's Practices in the Occupied Palestinian Territories Under International Law*, Cape Town: May 2009, http://www.hsrc.ac.za/Media_Release-378.phtml.

ICG, 'Israel's Religious Right and the Question of Settlements, Middle East Report Number 89,' 20 July 2009, p. 2, http://www.crisisgroup.org/library/documents/middle_east___north_africa/arab_israeli_conflict/89_israels_religious_right_and_the_question_of_settlements.pdf.

—— 'Palestine: Salvaging Fatah,' 12 November 2009, http://www.crisisgroup.org/home/index.cfm?id=6383&l=1.

—— reports on the Palestinian Authority, http://www.crisisgroup.org/home/index.cfm?l=1&id=1271&sr=1.

Ir Amim, 'Jerusalem 2008 State of Affairs: Political Developments and Changes on the Ground,' December 2008, p. 17, http://www.ir-amim.org.il/Eng/_Uploads/dbsAttachedFiles/AnnualReport2008 Eng(1).pdf.

Israel Central Bureau of Statistics, *Statistical Abstract of Israel*, 2007, http://www1.cbs.gov.il/reader/shnaton/templ_shnaton_e.html?num_tab=st02_01&CYear=2007.

Israel Defense Forces, 'Order No. 58: Order on Abandoned Property (Private Property),' 23 July 1967, (in Hebrew), http://www.aka.idf.il/SIP_STORAGE/FILES/0/60630.pdf.

Israel Ministry of Foreign Affairs, 'The Declaration of the Establishment of the State of Israel May 14, 1948,' http://www.mfa.gov.il/MFA/Peace+Process/Guide+to+the+Peace+Process/Declaration+of+Establishment+of+State+of+Israel.htm.

Israeli Democracy Institute, 'The 2009 Israeli Democracy Index,' 2009, p. 67, http://www.idi.org.il/sites/english/PublicationsCatalog/Documents/Democracy_Index%2009.pdf.

Issacharoff, Avi, 'Abbas to *Ha'aretz*: Peace Possible in 6 Months if Israel Freezes All Settlements,' *Ha'aretz*, 16 December 2009, http://www.haaretz.com/hasen/spages/1135431.html.

Issacharoff, Avi, 'Are Fatah and Hamas on Road to Reconciliation?' *Ha'aretz*, 26 June 2009, http://www.haaretz.com/hasen/spages/1095892.html.

——— 'Gaza's Smuggling Tunnels Feel Impact of Israel–Egypt Crackdown,' *Ha'aretz*, 30 July 2009, http://www.haaretz.com/hasen/spages/1103967.html.

——— 'Weekend in the Village,' *Ha'aretz Magazine*, 8 January 2010, pp. 20–24, (in Hebrew).

Issacharoff, Avi, and Amos Harel, 'The IDF's Preoccupation,' *Ha'aretz*, 27 November 2008, http://www.haaretz.com/hasen/spages/1041699.html.

Issacharoff, Avi, and Anshel Pfeffer, 'IDF Agrees to Expanded Activity by PA Forces in West Bank Towns,' *Ha'aretz*, 26 June 2009, http://www.haaretz.com/hasen/spages/1095794.html.

Izenberg, Dan, 'We Will Monitor Subversive Groups,' *Jerusalem Post*, 20 May 2007, http://www.jpost.com/servlet/Satellite?cid=1178708647907&pagename=JPArticle%2FShowFull.

——— Herb Keinon and Abe Selig, 'MK Ariel: PM Takes Control Over Jerusalem Demolitions,' *Jerusalem Post*, 14 December 2009, http://www.jpost.com/servlet/Satellite?cid=1260447431785&pagename=JPost%2FJPArticle%2FShowFull.

Jerusalem Institute for Israel Studies, *Statistical Yearbook of Jerusalem*, 2007, http://www.jiis.org.il/imageBank/File/shnaton_2007_8/shnaton%20C0106.pdf.

Jerusalem Municipality, 'Mayor Barkat Presents 2010 Budget for Jerusalem,' 20 December 2009, http://www.esnips.com/doc/49001f7b-2c83-4181-af56-6aa315a3e7d1/JRS-Municipality-press-release—2010-JRS-budget.

Jewish Telegraphic Agency, 'Israel to Transfer Cement to Gaza,' 29 July 2009, http://jta.org/news/article/2009/07/29/1006899/israel-to-transfer-cement-to-gaza.

Judt, Tony, 'Israel: the Alternative,' *New York Review of Books*, Vol. 50 No. 16, 23 October 2003.

Kashti, Or, 'Israel Aids its Needy Jewish Students more than Arab Counterparts,' *Ha'aretz*, 12 August 2009, http://www.haaretz.com/hasen/spages/1106955.html.

Katz, Yaakov, 'Israel May Allow PA Counter-Terror Force,' *Jerusalem Post*, 10 July 2009, http://www.jpost.com/servlet/Satellite?cid=1246443770831&pagename=JPost%2FJPArticle%2FShowFull.

Kayzer Liel, Jack Khoury, Fadi Eyadat and News Agencies, 'IDF Official: Neither Israel nor the PA Wants Violence,' *Ha'aretz*, 16 March 2010, http://www.haaretz.com/hasen/spages/1156775.html.Kessler, Glenn, 'US Pushing Netanyahu to Accept Demands for Peace Talks,' *Washington Post*, 16 March 2010, http://www.washingtonpost.com/wp-dyn/content/article/2010/03/15/AR2010031503462.html.

Khalidi, Ahmad, 'Thanks But No Thanks,' *The Guardian*, 13 December 2007.

Khalidi, Rashid, 'Palestine: Liberation Deferred,' *The Nation*, 8 May 2008.

Khatib, Ghassan, 'A Civilized and Sophisticated Argument,' *Bitterlemons*, 29 January 2007, http://www.bitterlemons.org/previous/bl290107ed4.html.

Khoury, Jack, 'Another Jewish Town Adds "Zionist Loyalty" to Bylaws,' *Ha'aretz*, 16 November 2009, http://www.haaretz.com/hasen/spages/1128408.html.

Khoury, Jack, 'Education Ministry Requires "Positive View" of Israel for Top Positions within Arab Community,' *Ha'aretz*, 3 December 2009, http://www.haaretz.com/hasen/spages/1132417.html.

—— 'Israeli Arabs Warn Against Dangers of "Racist Legislation,"' *Ha'aretz*, 31 May 2009, http://www.haaretz.com/hasen/spages/1089021.html.

—— 'Second Galilee Town Considering "Zionist Values" Bylaws,' *Ha'aretz*, 3 June 2009, http://www.haaretz.com/hasen/spages/1089728.html.

Kimmerling, Baruch, 'Boundaries and Frontiers of the Israeli Control System' in Baruch Kimmerling (ed.), *The Israeli State and Society:*

Boundaries and Frontiers, Albany: State University of New York Press, 1989.

Kimmerling, Baruch, *Immigrants, Settlers and Natives: Israel Between Plurality of Cultures and Cultural Wars*, Tel Aviv: Am Oved, 2003, (in Hebrew).

Kimmerling, Baruch and Joel S. Migdal, *The Palestinian People: A History*, Cambridge, Massachusetts: Harvard University Press, 2003.

Kleiman, Aharon, 'Israeli Negotiating Culture' in Tamara Cofman Wittes (ed.), *How Israelis and Palestinians Negotiate: A Cross-Cultural Analysis of the Oslo Peace Process*, Washington D.C.: United States Institute of Peace Press, 2005.

Klein, Joe, 'Q&A: Obama On His First Year In Office,' *Time*, 21 January 2010, http://www.time.com/time/politics/article/0,8599,195 5072–6,00.html.

Klein, Menachem, *A Possible Peace Between Israel and Palestine: An Insider's Account of the Geneva Initiative*, New York: Columbia University Press, 2007.

—— *Jerusalem: The Contested City*, London: C. Hurst and New York: New York University Press, 2001.

—— 'Nothing New in Jerusalem: Jerusalem in the Current Final Status Talks,' *Bitterlemons* 35, 8 September 2008, http://www.bitterlemons.org/previous/bl090908ed35.html.

—— 'Old and New Walls in Jerusalem,' *Political Geography*, Vol. 24, January 2005, pp. 53–76.

—— 'One State in the Holy Land: Dream or Nightmare?' *The International Spectator*, Vol. 43 No. 4, December 2008, pp. 89–102.

—— 'Rule and Role in Jerusalem: Israel, Jordan and the PLO in a Peace-Building Process' in Marshall J. Breger and Ora Ahimeir (eds.), *Jerusalem: A City and its Future*, Syracuse: Syracuse University Press, 2002, pp. 137–74.

—— 'Settlements and Security' in Daanish Faruqi (ed.), *From Camp David to 'Cast Lead': Essays on Israel, Palestine and the Future of the Peace Process*, Lanham, Md.: Lexington Books, 2010.

—— *The Jerusalem Problem: The Struggle for Permanent Status*, Gainesville: University Press of Florida, 2003.

Kretzmer, David, *The Occupation of Justice: The Supreme Court of Israel and the Occupied Palestinian Territories*, Albany: State University of New York Press, 2002.

Kurtzer, Daniel C., 'Do Settlements Matter? An American Perspective,' *Israel Journal of Foreign Affairs* III:2, 2009, pp. 23–30.

Kurtzer, Daniel C., and Scott B. Lasensky, *Negotiating Arab–Israeli Peace: American Leadership in the Middle East*, Washington DC: United States Institute of Peace, 2008.

Laub, Karin, 'US Trained Palestinian Force is Keen in Action,' Associated Press, 28 June 2009, http://www.google.com/hostednews/ap/article/ALeqM5jrSS9anIzM-waM8ZUQzhDot5Z27AD9935 UDG0.

Laub, Karin, 'US Transfers $200 Million in Aid to Palestinians,' Associated Press, 24 July 2009, http://www.google.com/hostednews/ap/article/ALeqM5jw6c6W7D_lf3F_aBJvrojp0NKUWQD99L1JB00.

Lazaroff, Tovah, 'Government Spent 22.3% More on Settlements,' *Jerusalem Post*, 22 July 2009, http://www.jpost.com/servlet/Satellite?pagename=JPost/JPArticle/ShowFull&cid=124644 3872990.

——— 'The World Bank to Give Palestinians $33.5 M in Aid,' *Jerusalem Post*, 14 July 2009, http://www.jpost.com/servlet/Satellite?cid=1246443808810&pagename=JPost%2FJPArticle%2FShowFull.

Levinson, Chaim, 'Hesder Yeshiva Rabbis: Torah Law is above IDF,' *Ha'aretz*, 18 December 2009, http://www.haaretz.com/hasen/spages/113 5864.html.

Levinson, Chaim, 'High Court: Israel Turns Blind Eye to Illegal Settlement Construction,' *Ha'aretz*, 30 October 2009, http://www.haaretz.com/hasen/spages/1124441.html.

——— 'IDF General Israel Incapable of West Bank Pullout,' *Ha'aretz*, 7 September 2009, http://www.haaretz.com/hasen/spages/1112876.html.

——— 'Israel Dismantled West Bank Settler Outpost,' *Ha'aretz*, 29 July 2009, http://www.haaretz.com/hasen/spages/1103702.html.

——— 'More than 300,000 Settlers Live in the West Bank,' *Ha'aretz*, 27 July 2009, http://www.haaretz.com/hasen/spages/1103125.html.

——— 'Rabbis Unite Against Barak in IDF–Yeshiva Row,' *Ha'aretz*, 17 December 2009, http://www.haaretz.com/hasen/spages/1135825.html.

——— 'Settlements Have Cost Israel 17$ Billion, Study Finds,' *Ha'aretz*, 23 March 2010, http://www.haaretz.com/hasen/pages/ShArtStEng.jhtml?itemNo=1158308&contrassID=1&subContrass

ID=1&title='Settlements%20have%20cost%20Israel%20$17%20 billion,%20study%20finds'&dyn_server=172.20.5.5.

——— 'Settlers Fume as Army Set New Rules Curbing Authority of West Bank Security Coordinators,' *Ha'aretz*, 25 December 2009, http://www.haaretz.com/hasen/spages/1137588.html.

——— 'The IDF has not Received Orders to Evacuate Outposts,' *Ha'aretz*, 28 July 2009, http://www.haaretz.com/hasen/spages/ 1103444.html.

——— 'Who Is Leading the Settlers' Fight for the West Bank Outposts?' *Ha'aretz*, 23 August 2009, http://www.haaretz.com/hasen/ spages/1108989.html.

Levinson, Charles, 'Abbas Says Palestinians Won't Rise Up, for Now,' *Wall Street Journal*, 22 December 2009, http://online.wsj.com/article/SB126143773752000841.html.

Levy, Yagil, 'The IDF is Disintegrating,' *Ha'aretz*, 5 November 2008, http://www.haaretz.com/hasen/spages/1034322.html.

Liss, Jonathan, 'Israel Rejects Bill Allocating Equal Land to Jews and Arabs,' *Ha'aretz*, 3 January 2010, http://www.haaretz.com/hasen/ spages/1139584.html.

——— 'MK Aims to Keep Palestinians Married to Israelis from Gaining Citizenship,' *Ha'aretz*, 18 December 2009, http://www.haaretz. com/hasen/spages/1135963.html.

——— 'New Bill Makes Possible to Reject Arab Settlers in Jewish Communal Settlements,' *Ha'aretz*, 6 December 2009, (in Hebrew), http://www.haaretz.co.il/hasite/spages/1132999.html.

Lustick, Ian, *Unsettled States, Disputed Lands: Britain and Ireland, France and Algeria, Israel and the West Bank/Gaza*, Ithaca: Cornell University Press, 1993.

Lynfield, Ben. 'How Israel Put the Brakes on Another Palestinian Dream,' *The Independent*, 16 January 2010, http://www.independent.co.uk/news/world/middle-east/how-israel-put-the-brakes-on-another-palestinian-dream-1869535.html.

Ma'an News Agency, 'Abbas Admits Ordering Goldstone Report Delay,' 18 October 2009, http://www.maannews.net/eng/ViewDetails. aspx?ID=233001.

——— 'Abbas May Quit Fatah, PLO Posts,' 10 November 2009, http:// www.maannews.net/eng/ViewDetails.aspx?ID=238722.

——— 'Abbas Orders Probe of Deferral of UN Gaza Report,' 4 October 2009, http://www.maannew.net/eng/ViewDetails.aspx?ID= 229678.

——— 'Abbas Takes Blame for Goldstone Delay, Commission Says,' 9 January 2010, http://www.maannews.net/eng/ViewDetails.aspx? ID=253025.

——— 'Donors Pledge 400 million USD for PA Shortfall,' 27 September 2009, http://www.maannews.net/eng/ViewDetails.aspx?ID=227 388.

——— 'Erekat: PA Future in Doubt,' 12 December 2009, http://www. maannews.net/eng/ViewDetails.aspx?ID=238643.

——— 'Erekat: Two-state Solution may have to be Abandoned,' 5 November 2009, http://www.maannews.net/eng/ViewDetails.aspx? ID=237319.

Ma'an News Agency, 'EU Pledged 160 Million Euros to Palestinian Authority,' 19 January 2010, http://www.maannews.net/eng/View-Details.aspx?ID=255218.

Ma'an News Agency, 'Fayyad Cabinet says it Still Backs Goldstone Report,' 6 October 2009, http://www.maannews.net/eng/View-Details.aspx?ID=229970.

——— 'Full Text: EU Foreign Ministers' Statement on Middle East,' 9 December 2009, http://www.maannews.net/eng/ViewDetails. aspx?ID=245290.

——— 'Israel's New Regulations Make Moving from Gaza to West Bank Harder,' 17 June 2009, http://www.maannews.net/en/index. php?opr=ShowDetails&ID=38613.

——— 'PA Minister: Our Stance on Goldstone Report an Embarrassment,' 3 October 2009. http://www.maannews.net/eng/ViewDetails. aspx?ID=229447.

——— 'PA Reaching for Diplomatic Plan B,' 12 December 2009, http://www.maannews.net/eng/ViewDetails.aspx?ID=242693.

——— 'PCBS: 10.88 Million Palestinians in the World, Half in Diaspora,' 31 December 2009, http://www.maannews.net/eng/ ViewDetails.aspx?ID=250948.

——— 'PLO Official Admits "Mistake" in Delaying Goldstone Report,' 7 October 2009, http://www.maannews.net/eng/ViewDetails. aspx?ID=230387.

———— 'Qurei': We Will Not Allow Israel to Impose Facts on the Ground,' 7 June 2008, http://www.maannews.net/en/index.php?opr=ShowDetails&ID=29785.

———— 'Settler Rabbi Authors Guideline on Killing Gentiles,' 9 November 2009, http://www.maannews.net/eng/ViewDetails.aspx?ID=238 444.

———— 'West Bank Settlers Set Fire to Mosque,' 11 December 2009, http://www.maannews.net/eng/ViewDetails.aspx?ID=245954.

Mada al-Carmel, 'Haifa Declaration,' Haifa: Arab Center for Applied Social Research, 2008, http://www.mada-research.org/archive/haifadeceng.htm.

McCarthy, Rory, 'Israel Annexing East Jerusalem, Says EU,' *The Guardian*, 7 March 2009, http://www.guardian.co.uk/world/2009/mar/07/israel-palestine-eu-report-jerusalem.

———— 'Palestinians Lose Faith in Two-State Solution: Study Group Calls for New Form of Resistance to Israeli Occupation with Goal of Single Bi–National State,' *The Guardian*, 4 September 2008, http://www.guardian.co.uk/world/2008/sep/04/israel.palestinians.

McFarquhar, Neil, 'Palestinians Halt Push on War Report,' *New York Times*, 2 October 2009, http://www.nytimes.com/2009/10/02/world/middleeast/02mideast.html?_r=3&ref=middleeast.

Meital, Yoram, 'The Khartoum Conference and Egyptian Policy After the 1967 War: A Reexamination,' *Middle East Journal*, Vol. 54 No. 1, Winter 2000, pp. 64–82.

Merom, Gil, *How Democracies Lose Small Wars: State, Society and the Failure of France in Algeria, Israel in Lebanon and the United States in Vietnam*, Cambridge: Cambridge University Press, 2003.

Michael, Kobi and Amnon Ramon, *A Fence Around Jerusalem: The Construction of the Security Fence Around Jerusalem, General Background and Implications for the City and its Metropolitan Area*, Jerusalem: The Jerusalem Institute for Israel Studies, 2004, http://www.jiis.org.il/imageBank/File/publications/w-fence-eng.pdf.

Miller, Aaron David, *The Much Too Promised Land: America's Elusive Search for Arab–Israeli Peace*, New York: Bantam Dell, 2007.

Misgav, Uri, 'This Police Station is brought to you by a Right-Wing NGO,' *Yedioth Aharonoth*, 22 January 2010, http://coteret.com/2010/01/22/yediot-expose-settler-orgs-fund-police-infrastructure-in-east-jerusalem/.

Nahshoni, Kobi, 'Rabbi Ovadia Slams US: We Aren't their Slaves,' Ynet, 26 July 2009, http://www.ynetnews.com/articles/0,7340,L-3752180,00.html.

Najib, Mohammed, 'Security Transformation Dependent on Political Progress,' *Bitterlemons*, 11 May 2009, http://www.bitterlemons.org/previous/bl110509ed18.html#pal2.

Nakhleh, Khalil, 'Palestinians Under the Occupation,' *Counterpunch*, 24 September 2008, http://counterpunch.org/nakhleh09242008.html.

National Committee of the Heads of the Arab Local Authorities in Israel, 'The Future Vision of the Palestinian Arabs in Israel,' Nazareth 2006, http://www.adalah.org/newsletter/eng/dec06/tasawor-mostaqbali.pdf.

Nusseibeh, Sari, 'Nusseibeh Blames the Donor States for Funding the Occupation and Offers to Give Up the Right of Return in Exchange for Getting Back Jerusalem and the Temple Mount,' *al-Quds al-Arabi*, 29 July 2008 (in Arabic), http://sari.alquds.edu/alquds_alarabi.htm.

Obama, Barack, 'Text: Obama's Speech in Cairo,' *New York Times*, 4 June 2009, http://www.nytimes.com/2009/06/04/us/politics/04obama.text.html.

OCHA, 'Closure Maps,' June 2009, http://www.ochaopt.org/documents/Closure_Maps_Book_Web.pdf.

—— 'Closure Update,' 30 April–11 September 2008, http://www.ochaopt.org/documents/ocha_opt_closure_update_2008_09_english.pdf.

—— 'Israeli Settler Violence and the Evacuation of Outposts,' November 2009, http://www.ochaopt.org/documents/ocha_opt_settler_violence_fact_sheet_2009_11_15_english.pdf.

—— 'Locked In: The Humanitarian Impact of Two Years of Blockade on the Gaza Strip, Special Focus,' August 2009, http://www.ochaopt.org/documents/Ocha_opt_Gaza_impact_of_two_years_of_blockade_August_2009_english.pdf.

—— 'Movement and Access Update,' May 2009, http://www.ochaopt.org/documents/ocha_opt_movement_and_access_2009_05_25_english.pdf; November 2009, http://www.ochaopt.org/documents/ocha_opt_movement_access_2009_november_english.pdf.

—— 'Protection of Civilians,' 30 September–6 October 2009, http://www.ochaopt.org/documents/ocha_opt_protection_of_civilians_weekly_report_2009_10_06_english.pdf; 11–17 November 2009, http://www.ochaopt.org/documents/ocha_opt_protection_of_civilians_weekly_report_2009_11_17_english.pdf.

—— 'Shrinking Space, Urban Contraction and Rural Fragmentation in the Bethlehem Governorate,' Special Focus, May 2009, http://www.ochaopt.org/documents/ocha_opt_bethlehem_shrinking_space_may_2009_english.pdf.

—— 'The Humanitarian Monitor,' 2008, http://ochaonline2.un.org/Default.aspx?tabid=8510; August 2009, http://www.ochaopt.org/documents/ocha_opt_the_humanitarian_monitor_2009_august_english.pdf.

OCHA–Occupied Palestinian Territory, 'The Planning Crisis in East Jerusalem: Understanding the Phenomenon of "Illegal" Construction,' Special Focus, April 2009, p. 11, http://www.ochaopt.org/documents/ocha_opt_planning_crisis_east_jerusalem_april_2009_english.pdf.

Ofran, Hagit, 'Report: The Price of Settlements in the 2009–2010 Budget Proposal,' Peace Now, June 2009, http://www.peacenow.org.il/site/en/peace.asp?pi=61&fld=495&docid=3711.

Olmert, Ehud, 'How to Achieve a Lasting Peace,' *Washington Post*, 17 July 2009, http://www.washingtonpost.com/wp-dyn/content/article/2009/07/16/AR2009071603584.html.

Oren, Amir, 'IDF: One Third of Soldiers Might Refuse to Evacuate Outposts,' *Ha'aretz*, 19 August 2009, http://www.haaretz.com/hasen/spages/1108560.html.

Palestine Media Center, 'Palestinian Declaration of Independence, 15 November 1948,' http://www.palestine-pmc.com/details.asp? cat=11&id=27.

Palestinian Center for Policy and Survey Research, Palestinian Public Opinion Polls, http://www.pcpsr.org.

Palestinian Central Bureau of Statistics, 'Population, Housing and Establishment Census 2007: Preliminary Findings,' Ramallah, 2008, http://www.pcbs.gov.ps/Portals/_pcbs/PressRelease/census2007_e.pdf;http://www.pcbs.gov.ps/desktopmodules/newsscrollEnglish/newsscrollView.aspx?ItemID=686&mID=11170; http://www.pcbs.gov.ps/Census2007/Portals/_PCBS/Press/gaza_census.pdf; http://www.pcbs.gov.ps/Portals/_PCBS/Downloads/book1487.pdf.

Palestinian National Authority, 'Palestine: Ending the Occupation, Establishing the State, Program of the Thirteenth Government,' August 2009, http://www.americantaskforce.org/palestinian_national_authority_ending_occupation_establishing_state.

Palestinian Strategy Study Group, 'Regaining the Initiative: Palestinian Strategic Options to End Israeli Occupation,' August 2008, http://www.palestinestrategygroup.ps/.

Peace Now, 'Bypassing the Settlement Freeze: Semi–Annual Report,' August 2009, http://peacenow.org.il/site/en/peace.asp?pi=61&docid=4364.

——— 'Israel is Eliminating the Green Line and Continuing to Build in Isolated Settlements: The First Half of 2008 (Since Annapolis),' Settlement Watch Team Report, August 2008, http://www.peacenow.org.il/data/SIP_STORAGE/files//5/3775.pdf.

——— 'Israeli Government Plans to Deepen Hold over Jerusalem,' May 2009, http://www.peacenow.org.il/site/en/peace.asp?pi=61&fld=620&docid=3644.

——— 'The West Bank: Facts and Figures,' August 2005, http://www.peacenow.org.il/site/en/peace.asp?pi=195&docid=1430.

——— 'Top 5 Bogus Excuses for Opposing a Settlement Freeze,' *Settlements in Focus*, Vol. 5 Issue 3, 19 June 2009, http://www.peacenow.org/updates.asp?rid=0&cid=6329.

Peraino, Kevin, 'Olmert's Lament,' *Newsweek*, 13 June 2009, http://www.newsweek.com/id/201937.

Peri, Yoram, *General in the Cabinet Room: How the Military Shapes Israeli Policy*, Washington DC: United States Institute of Peace, 2006.

Peteet, Julie, 'Beyond Compare,' *Middle East Report* 253, Winter 2009, http://merip.org/mer/mer253/peteet.html.

Pressman, Jeremy, 'Visions in Collision: What Happened in Camp David and Taba,' *International Security*, Vol. 28 No. 2, Fall 2003, pp. 5–43, http://belfercenter.ksg.harvard.edu/files/pressman.pdf.

Prusher Ilene, 'Changing course, Fatah official call for Palestinian protest against Israel,' *Christian Science Monitor*, 1 April 2010, http://www.csmonitor.com/World/Middle-East/2010/0401/Changing-course-Fatah-officials-call-for-Palestinian-protests-against-Israel.

Quartet Statement, Sharm El-Sheikh, 9 November 2008, http://209.
85.229.132/search?q=cache:VYqmed9lZSMJ:www.un.org/News/
Press/docs/2008/sg2145.doc.htm+quartet+middle+east+statement+
november+2008&cd=1&hl=iw&ct=clnk&gl=il.

Rabinovich, Itamar, *The Road Not Taken*, New York: Oxford University Press, 1991.

Ravid, Barak, 'Defense Establishment Paper: Golan for Syria Peace, Plan for Iran Strike,' *Ha'aretz*, 23 November 2008, p. 1.

——— 'Ha'aretz Exclusive: EU Draft Document on Division of Jerusalem,' *Ha'aretz*, 2 December 2009, http://www.haaretz.com/hasen/spages/1131988.html.

——— 'Israel Rejects Russian Request to Give the PA Armored Vehicles,' *Ha'aretz*, 6 December 2009, http://www.haaretz.com/hasen/spages/1132925.html.

——— 'US to Egypt: Fatah–Hamas Deal Undermines Israel–PA Talks,' *Ha'aretz*, 12 October 2009, http://www.haaretz.com/hasen/spages/1120633.html.

Rekhes, Eli, 'The First Word: How Palestinian Arabs in Israel See Their Future,' *Jerusalem Post*, 1 January 2007, http://english.icci.org.il/index.php?option=com_content&task=view&id=97&Itemid=72.

Report of the State Commission of Inquiry into the Clashes between Security Forces and Israeli Civilians [Or Commission], 2003, http://www.haaretz.com/hasen/pages/ShArt.jhtml?itemNo=335594&contrassID=2&subContrassID=1&sbSubContrassID=0&listSrc=Y.

Reuters, 'EU's Solana Calls for UN to Recognize Palestinian State,' 12 July 2009, http://www.reuters.com/article/featuredCrisis/idUSLC616115.

——— 'Marwan Barghouti: Peace Talks with Israel Have Failed,' *Ha'aretz*, 24 November 2009, http://www.haaretz.com/hasen/spages/1129348.html.

——— 'Study: Settlements Get More State Funding than Israeli Cities,' *Ha'aretz*, 21 July 2009, http://www.haaretz.com/hasen/spages/1101829.html.

Robinson, Glenn E., *Building a Palestinian State: The Incomplete Revolution*, Bloomington and Indianapolis: Indiana University Press, 1997.

Rosenfeld, Maya, *Confronting the Occupation: Work, Education and Political Activism of Palestinian Families in a Refugee Camp*, Stanford: Stanford University Press, 2004.

Rouhana, Nadim, *Palestinian Citizens in an Ethnic Jewish State: Identities in Conflict*, New Haven and London: Yale University Press, 1997.

Satloff, Robert, *From Abdullah to Hussein: Jordan in Transition*, New York: Oxford University Press, 1994.

Sayigh, Yezid, 'Inducing a Failed State in Palestine,' *Survival*, 49, Autumn 2007, pp. 7–40.

Schneider, Howard, 'Netanyahu Upholds Plan to Build in East Jerusalem,' *Washington Post*, 20 July 2009, http://www.washingtonpost.com/wpdyn/content/article/2009/07/19/AR2009071900156_pf.html.

Shafir, Gershon, 'Israeli Society: A Counterview,' *Israel Studies*, Vol. 1 No. 2, Fall 1996, pp. 189–213.

—— *Land, Labor and the Origins of the Israeli–Palestinian Conflict 1882–1914*, Cambridge: Cambridge University Press, 1989.

Shehadeh, Raja, *Palestinian Walks: Notes on a Vanishing Landscape*, London: Profile Books, 2007.

Sher, Gilad, *The Israeli–Palestinian Peace Negotiations 1999–2001, Within Reach*, New York: Routledge, 2006.

Shlaim, Avi, *Collusion Across the Jordan: King Abdullah, the Zionist Movement and the Partition of Palestine*, Oxford: Clarendon Press, 1988.

—— *Lion of Jordan: The Life of King Hussein in War and Peace*, London: Allen Lane, 2007.

Shragai, Nadav and Mazal Mualem, '47 MKs Back Bill to Jail Deniers of "Jewish State,"' *Ha'aretz*, 28 May 2009, http://www.haaretz.com/hasen/spages/1088804.html.

Smooha, Sami, 'Has Indeed the Occupation of the Territories Permeated Inside? The Modest Contribution of Israeli Sociology to the Study of Occupation Issues,' *Sociologia Yisraelit* 9, 2, 2008, pp. 255–62, (in Hebrew).

—— 'The Arab Vision of Turning Israel Within the Green Line into a Binational Democracy' in Sarah Ozacky-Lazar and Mustafa Kabh (eds.), *Between Vision and Reality: The Vision Papers of the Arabs in Israel, 2006–2007*, Jerusalem: The Citizens' Accord Forum, 2008, pp. 126–39, (in Hebrew), http://soc.haifa.ac.il/~s.smooha/download/Arab_Vision_of_Binational_State.pdf.

Smooha, Sammy, 'The Model of Ethnic Democracy' in Sammy Smooha and Priit Järve (eds.), *The Fate of Ethnic Democracy in*

Post-Communist Europe, Budapest: Open Society Institute, 2005, pp. 5–60, http://soc.haifa.ac.il/~s.smooha/download/SmoohaJarve-BookEthDemoPostCommunistEurope.pdf.

Sofer, Roni, 'State Officials Say US Knew About Jerusalem Building Plan,' Ynet, 28 December 2009, http://www.ynetnews.com/articles/0,7340,L-3826058,00.html.

Spruyt, Hendrik, *Ending Empire: Contested Sovereignty and Territorial Partition*, Ithaca and London: Cornell University Press, 2005.

Steinberg, Mati, 'Hamas Predicts Collapse of Abbas and his Conspirators,' *Ha'aretz*, 15 December 2009, http://www.haaretz.com/hasen/spages/1134931.html.

Stephens, Bret, 'Israel Scored a Tactical Victory, but it missed a chance to finish off Hamas,' *Wall Street Journal*, 19 January 2009, http://online.wsj.com/article/SB123241373428396239.html.

Stern, Yoav, 'Diskin: We Will Prevent Subversive Activities Even If They Are Legal,' *Ha'aretz*, 18 May 2007, (in Hebrew).

Supreme Court, 7192/04 and 7800/05, 15 June 2009 (in Hebrew), http://elyon1.court.gov.il/files/04/920/071/v53/04071920.v53.htm.

Susser, Leslie, 'One Land: How Many States?' *Jerusalem Report*, 31 March 2008.

Swirski, Shlomo, *Is There an Israeli Business Peace Disincentive?* Adva Center, August 2008.

Swisher, Clayton, *The Truth About Camp David: The Untold Story About the Collapse of the Middle East Peace Process*, New York: Nation Books, 2004.

Taraki, Lisa, 'Enclave Micropolice: The Paradoxical Case of Ramallah/al-Bireh,' *Journal of Palestine Studies*, Vol. 37 No. 4, Summer 2008, pp. 6–20.

Tessler, Mark, *A History of the Israeli–Palestinian Conflict*, Second Edition, Bloomington and Indianapolis: Indiana University Press, 2009.

Tilley, Virginia, *The One-State Solution: A Breakthrough for Peace in the Israeli–Palestinian Deadlock*, Ann Arbor: University of Michigan Press, 2005.

United Nations, 'A Performance-Based Road Map to a Permanent Two-State Solution to the Israeli–Palestinian Conflict,' June 2002, http://www.un.org/media/main/roadmap122002.html.

————— 'International Convention on the Suppression and Punishment of the Crime of Apartheid,' New York: 30 November 1973, http://untreaty.un.org/cod/avl/ha/cspca/cspca.html.

————— *Report of the United Nations Fact-Finding Mission on the Gaza Conflict* (Goldstone Report), 29 September 2009, http://www2.ohchr.org/english/bodies/hrcouncil/docs/12session/A-HRC-12–48.pdf.

United Press International, 'Palestinian Forces to Receive Weapons,' 6 July 2009, http://www.upi.com/Top_News/2009/07/06/Palestinian-forces-to-receive-weapons/UPI-18761246880020/.

US Department of State, 'Secretary Rice, Palestinian President Abbas in Amman, Jordan,' 31 March 2008, http://www.america.gov/st/texttrans-english/2008/March/20080331190345xjsnommis0.2582666.html.

Wagner, Matthew, 'Amar: US Settlements Policy Contravenes Torah,' *Jerusalem Post*, 21 July 2009, http://www.jpost.com/servlet/Satellite?cid=1246443863443&pagename=JPost%2FJPArticle%2FShowFull.

Weitz, Gidi, 'Ever So Politely,' *Ha'aretz Magazine*, 23 October 2009, http://www.haaretz.com/hasen/spages/1122910.html.

Weizman, Eyal, *Hollow Land: Israel's Architecture of Occupation*, London: Verso, 2007.

White House, 'Statement by White House Press Secretary Robert Gibbs on Construction in East Jerusalem,' 28 December 2009, http://www.whitehouse.gov/the-press-office/statement-white-house-press-secretary-robert-gibbs-construction-east-jerusalem.

World Bank, 'A Palestinian State in Two Years: Institutions for Economic Revival,' Economic Monitoring Report to the Ad Hoc Liaison Committee, 22 September 2009, http://siteresources.worldbank.org/INTWESTBANKGAZA/Resources/AHLCSept09WBreportfinal.pdf.

————— 'Assessment of Restrictions on Palestinian Water Sector Development,' April 2009, http://siteresources.worldbank.org/INTWESTBANKGAZA/Resources/WaterRestrictionsReport18Ar2009.pdf.

————— 'Investing in Palestinian Economic Reform and Development,' Paris, December 2007, http://siteresources.worldbank.org/INTWESTBANKGAZA/Resources/294264–1166525851073/ParisconferencepaperDec17.pdf.

Yaghi, Mohammed, 'The PA Financial Crisis: Causes and Implications,' Washington Institute for Near East Policy, http://www.washingtoninstitute.org/templateC05.php?CID=3084.

Yiftachel, Oren, *Ethnocracy: Land and Identity in Israel/Palestine*, Philadelphia: University of Pennsylvania Press, 2006.

Zelikovich, Yaheli Moran, 'Barak Okays University Recognition of Ariel College,' Ynet, 20 January 2010, http://www.ynetnews.com/articles/0,7340,L-3837183,00.html.

Zertal, Idith and Akiva Eldar, *Lords of the Land: The War for Israel's Settlements in the Occupied Territories, 1967–2007*, New York: Nation Books, 2007.

INDEX